THE LONDON BLITZ
A Fireman's Tale

Burning, burning image
Of self, projected in
The years, as in a book,
Today has opened on the page
That paints your soul reflected in
The hell on which you look.

DESTRUCTION AND RESURRECTION
AUXILIARY FIREMAN STEPHEN SPENDER

THE LONDON BLITZ
A Fireman's Tale

Cyril Demarne O.B.E.

AFTER THE BATTLE

Credits

© Cyril Demarne O.B.E. 1991

ISBN: 0 900913 67 3

Printed in Great Britain
Designed by Gordon Ramsey
Assistant Editor, *After the Battle* magazine

PUBLISHERS
Battle of Britain Prints International Limited
Church House, Church Street
London E15 3JA
Telephone: 081-534 8833

PRINTERS
Plaistow Press Limited
Church House, Church Street
London E15 3JA

FRONT COVER
Fire crews at work in Eastcheap on the night of May 10th, 1941.

REAR COVER
The Firemen's Memorial by John W. Mills, which commemorates all those Fire Service personnel who died due to enemy action, unveiled by Queen Elizabeth, the Queen Mother in Old Change Court, by St Paul's Cathedral on May 4th, 1991.

FRONT ENDPAPER
Firemen still hard at it in an unidentified London street on the morning of May 11th, 1941, drawing their ammunition from the 500-gallon portable dam mounted on the lorry at centre left.

REAR ENDPAPER
Taken from the Stone Gallery of St Paul's Cathedral on February 25th, 1941 this picture shows the dismal sight of a ravaged Paternoster Square, by now cleared of most debris following the heavy raid of December 29th/30th, 1941.

FRONTISPIECE
A roaring fire; a line of hose laid out; a powerful jet knocking down the flames on the ground floor: then the water runs out! The fire claws back all the territory lost to the firemen when water was flowing. Now it advances to encompass all combustibles within reach. The firemen are provoked into using bad language to relieve their frustration, but that will not restore the water supply. Meanwhile, the fire roars on . . . October 14th, 1940.

PAGE 6
The morning after in Cheapside . . . weary yet cheerful, this bunch of firemen, just relieved by fresh crews start on their way back to their station for a shower, a change of clothing, breakfast and most blessed of all — sleep.

Author's Acknowledgements

My grateful thanks to A.F.S. and N.F.S. comrades for their stories: Betty Butler (née Barrett), who survived the Surrey Commercial Docks onslaught on September 7th, 1940. Harry Berkshire — Thameshaven, Woolwich Arsenal and the City Blitz. Eric Earl — the City Blitz and Bisson Road, E16; a good friend and comrade at West Ham with whom I shared many exciting moments during thirty years answering the bells. Rod Handslip — Albany Road, SE and the Paul public house. Dave Millar, the Chief Superintendent's driver — the City Blitz, the BBC, the Palace of Westminster, Westminster Abbey. Tom Stothard, the Ilford part-timer, who did much of his firefighting away from home — the City Blitz, Bromley, Kent, the Royal Docks, Stratford. Bill Ward for his nightmare in the Surrey Commercial Docks. To Gordon White and staff of the L.F.B. Press Office for invaluable help. To A. P. Watt Ltd on behalf of Crystal Hale and Jocelyn Herbert for permission to quote the extract from A. P. Herbert's *Independent Member*. Special thanks to Howard Bloch, Local Studies Library, Newham. To H.M. Stationery Office Photographic Library. To the London Fire Brigade Photographic Library, and to C. Fox-Smith, for the extract from his poem *All alone I went a-walking* . . .

Cyril Demarne, O.B.E.

CONTENTS

FOREWORD
G. D. CLARKSON CBE, QFSM, BA (HONS)
Chief Fire Officer and Chief Executive London Fire & Civil Defence Authority

Recognising the special significance of this, the 50th anniversary of the Blitz on the capital, I was most pleased to respond to Cyril Demarne's request for me to write the foreword for this book.

The comfortable style advanced by the author in recalling the events of this era, together with the graphic description of the scenes, depicting the resolute determination and sacrifice of those involved, is much to be admired. This book is about ordinary people in extraordinary circumstances, who through their fortitude and great courage became very far from ordinary.

London has been engulfed by fire more than once and I believe that Londoners through time have developed a special regard for Firefighters, although most people probably know little about the actions of the men and women who have contributed so much to their daily safety. *The London Blitz — A Fireman's Tale* is a chronicle of the war years, which seeks to establish in the mind of the reader, the daily horrors of the Blitz whilst recalling the everyday experiences of men and women who, despite the odds, got on with their job.

This is a true story, told by a fireman in a way that only a fireman can tell it. It is my pleasure and great privilege to be associated with the book and its author.

London, 1990

1

Toil and sweat

I HAD been fighting fires in the highly industrialised County Borough of West Ham for close on fourteen years. Fires in houses and offices; in paint and varnish works; in ships and dock warehouses; oil depots, gas works, chemical factories, timber yards. I had cut my firefighting teeth on just about everything ranking high on the list of fire hazards, for they are all there, packed cheek-by-jowl in the seven and a half square miles that comprised the borough.

I enjoyed my work as a fireman and relished active firefighting. My watch-mates at Stratford Fire Station were a fine bunch of men, full of joie-de-vivre but every button on duty when a call came in.

Discipline was firm but not harsh. We were always up to some practical joke or other and if one of us found himself on the receiving end, he was expected to work it off against one of his mates. Nobody told on the perpetrator so the whole watch was fair game for the reprisal and all pranks were taken in good part. They had to be; anyone taking umbrage would incur the wrath of the entire watch. We learned to give and take and bore no animosity; it was all part of the fun.

But clouds were forming on our horizon. Hitler's aggression was growing and some of us thought he ought to be jumped on before he became really dangerous. His territorial demands became frequent and ever more outrageous but still the Democracies did nothing to stop him. Eventually, Britain, now convinced of the inevitability of war, abandoned the ideal of Collective Security and began to re-arm.

Among the defence measures taken was the passing of the Air Raids Precautions Act of 1937 under which local authorities were required to draw up emergency fire schemes for their area for submission to the Secretary of State. Plans were laid for the recruitment of an Auxiliary Fire Service but the County Borough of West Ham was at odds with the central Government over the amount of local authority contributions to the cost of the new service. West Ham refused to carry out its obligations under the Act until better terms for depressed areas like West Ham were conceded.

There was also a row over who was to be the Air Raid Precautions Controller for the County Borough. The Council wanted to appoint the Mayor Elect but the Regional Commissioner preferred the greater experience of the Town Clerk. The situation worsened and the Commissioner threatened to take the matter out of the Council's hands. Reluctantly, the Council gave way and in March 1939, recruitment for the A.F.S. and Civil Defence began. Headquarters for the A.F.S. was set up in Abbey Road School, West Ham and I was appointed a member of an instructional team of six. The school was left vacant by the dispersal of the children as part of the preparation for their evacuation in the event of war.

The class-rooms and assembly halls were ideal for training small squads of men in the theoretical side of the work whilst the playgrounds had ample space for practical drills. Recruits were advised of the place and date of training sessions and instructors were on hand to receive the first trainees. We were looking forward to their arrival and received pretty well what we had expected, a fairly representative selection of the local male population: clerks, labourers, lorry drivers, draughtsmen, musicians, dock workers, industrial chemists, and so on.

Few had much to say during the early days, wondering what it was all about. We instructors set out to create an

These are the men attached to Stratford Fire Station, photographed in the middle 'thirties. On the outbreak of war they were dispersed throughout the Borough to form a nucleus of experienced firemen in the twenty West Ham Auxiliary fire stations. Station Officer Albert Garnham is the officer in charge; on his left is Sub-Officer Henry Goldsmith, later to become a Divisional Officer in the N.F.S. Wally Turley, who was killed on the first night of the Blitz, stands on the extreme left of the second row. Harry Webb, who accompanied him into the building, is third from right in the third row. Eric Earl, who spent 24 hectic hours in the City on December 29/30th, 1940, is fourth from right in the second row; his colleague in the water relay, Percy Smither, is on the extreme right, third row. The author sits second from left, front row.

atmosphere designed to put the men at ease and provide motivation for their new interest. There was no difficulty in instilling discipline: many of the men were ex-servicemen who appreciated the value of discipline under war conditions. After a week or two, friendships developed amid growing enthusiasm for the training. Practical work was popular and we fostered the competitive spirit among squads. Stop-watches were brought into use to time the various operations and it became common to hear a cheer go up from a corner of the training ground as someone's time was bettered. On fine evenings, the playgrounds were the scene of great activity. Hose was being run out from pumps and ladders were extended to upper floors as men learned to climb confidently, carrying fire hose aloft. The fireman's lift was being practised and a line of men carried mates on their shoulders in practice rescues.

Uniform clothing arrived piecemeal but, eventually, a full kit was issued to the early volunteers. The sight of these smartly dressed men on the streets gave a further fillip to recruitment and we were hard pressed to find accommodation for all who reported for training. Some of the more advanced auxiliaries were given the opportunity of attending one of the local fire stations for their weekly spell of duty, during which they rode to any fire call that came in. This plan achieved the dual purpose of easing accommodation problems and providing valuable fire experience.

Some of the men attached to West Ham No. 4 Station, Abbey Road, September 1939. They spent the 'phoney war' period perfecting their familiarity with fire appliances and equipment, acquiring a modicum of experience at a few 'peace time' fires. But they were novices when it came to dealing with the chaotic conditions in dockland on the opening night of the Blitz when, like Tennyson's cavalry, they rode into the jaws of Death, into the very mouth of Hell. All these men returned, next day. Eight months later they had become seasoned, veteran firefighters.

Towards the end of August, the final realisation that the clouds of war were about to burst came when my girls, seven and five, brought notes from their school teachers giving details of the evacuation plan. We were given a list of the articles they were to take with them; change of underwear, stout shoes, spare stockings, raincoat, etc., all to be packed in a small case. My wife and I talked for hours before we came to a decision. I was influenced by my knowledge of war gases and the fearful consequences if they were to be employed against the civilian population, We had no illusions about German frightfulness; we knew all about the activities of the Luftwaffe against civilians in the Spanish Civil War. So I was all for sending the kids away. I wanted my wife to accompany them but she refused to leave me.

A few days later, crocodiles of school children converged on Barking railway station. Each was prominently labelled with name, address and school; box respirators were slung across shoulders and each carried a small case, a brown paper bag or a pathetic little bundle containing their bits and pieces. Ours came along with their school mates and we walked down the stairs to the platform together.

We gave them a parting hug and kiss and saw them into the train, bound Heaven knows where. Like most of the hundreds of parents crowding the platform, we couldn't hold back a tear. Bloody, bloody Hitler.

We returned home, empty without the kids, to sit and stew, wondering if we'd done the right thing. Three days later we received a postcard; they were billeted with a family at Bradford on Avon in Wiltshire. My wife immediately made arrangements to visit them.

I had plenty to occupy my mind. We were in the midst of enrolling and training hundreds of AFS men, equipping and transporting them to their stations throughout West Ham. Schools, about to be left vacant by the evacuation of children to safer areas, had been earmarked for use as auxiliary fire stations. In the docks, accommodation in sheds and warehouses had been made available by the Port of London Authority. Most of the outer London brigades numbered their auxiliary fire stations consecutively after their regular stations. West Ham, for instance, with three regular fire stations, commissioned 20 auxiliary stations and numbered them 4 to 23.

The system in the London Fire Brigade area revolved around the regular stations. Each station had five satellites, designated U, V, W, X and Y respectively, prefixed with the number of the local station. Thus No. 28 Station Whitechapel's satellites became 28U, 28V, 28W, 28X and 28Y. This system was changed when the fire service was nationalised.

Each auxiliary fire station would have a nucleus of experienced firemen working to introduce a routine and mould the auxiliaries into efficient fire crews. None knew at that stage that we should have twelve months grace in which to prepare for the first air attack and all laboured hard and long to be ready for the coming of the bombers.

Sunday September 3rd, 1939 dawned bright and sunny. We were all busy at 9 a.m. catching up with outstanding tasks. At 11 o'clock Prime Minister Neville Chamberlain broadcast to the Nation, announcing that we now were at war with Germany. As he finished speaking the sirens sounded in anger for the first time; an air raid within minutes of the Declaration of War.

The reaction of many people was similar to that of a couple walking along Abbey Road. As the first note of the siren reached them they halted in mid stride; looked at each other for a moment then started running in the direction of West Ham Church. The girl, wearing an attractive flowery summer frock and a large hat, was not dressed for running. I don't think she knew where she was going and, as she passed, I could see that she was very distressed.

I think our ears grew to twice their normal size as we strained to catch the first note of approaching aircraft, but all we heard was the sirens sounding the all clear. It had been a false alarm, caused by a French light aircraft entering British airspace unannounced.

We returned to our work with renewed urgency.

Drill class days were over for a section of auxiliary firemen. They had been enrolled for full time duty at £3 a week and, tomorrow, they would be reporting to their new stations. Tonight, they would meet for a final drink with mates posted to other stations.

The Greyhound pub, just across the road from their training centre, Abbey Road School, had been a favourite rendezvous and now it was packed for the last time until a new batch of trainees was assembled.

The instructors, too, joined in, enjoying a pint and keeping an eye on those who might be overcome by the emotion of parting and partake of one or two more than they could carry. A nod is as good as a wink and the pals of one or two were persuaded to ferry their worse for wear mates across the road to the safety of the dormitory.

I had returned to the instructors' room just before closing time and was enjoying a snack and a chat with my colleagues.

From the street came a ragged and discordant rendering of 'Nellie Dean,' growing louder as the revellers entered the building, where the last chorus was belted out with great gusto and a hearty, if not very successful, attempt at harmony. Then, silence for a moment, followed by muttering and a knock at the door.

'Come in.'

It was a deputation of four, led by a chirpy cockney who must remain nameless.

'Good evenin,' guv.' Well, we're on our way to our new station tomorrer, and we thought we'd like to come and say goodbye and thanks for everything.'

'That's very nice of you,' I replied. 'Where are you going?'

'All us lot to No. 23 Station, Albert Dock.' He grinned, and, whipping his hand from behind his back, offered me a fine Toby jug, bearing the inscription 'Charrington's Ales' around the base.

'What's this?' I asked.

'It's a Toby jug.' The inscription bothered me; there was no doubt as to its origin: my face betrayed my thoughts.

'Wassermarrer. Doncha like it? I didn't see yer in the Grey'ound so I couldn't buy yer a drink but I pinched that jug, 'specially fer you.'

What could I say in the face of such goodwill?

'Thanks very much' I replied, a bit weakly. 'It's very nice.'

'You can always stick a bit o' tape round the bottom' he suggested, with a twinkle in his cheeky eye.

I put the jug on the bookcase with the idea of returning it to the landlord later on but I never got down to it. It disappeared after a time; someone had taken a fancy to it and it WAS a nice jug.

A.F.S. Recruits had been instructed to hold themselves in readiness to report to their nearest fire station for full time enrolment and, on September 1st, 1939, the Mobilisation Order went out. Thousands of men and women made their way to local fire stations that day, among them Margaret Foster, who reported to London Fire Brigade A13 station, Belsize Park. Auxiliary Firewoman Foster was 'signed on' and instructed to report to the factory owned by Messrs Manser, Hunt and Cotty who, among other items, made Christmas crackers. On arrival, Fw. Foster, with colleagues similarly posted, found the factory, apart from some quite large machinery and stacks of cardboard, absolutely empty. There was no black-out up at the windows, no domestic arrangements, no water, no means of making tea, nothing.

'My mother — don't ask me how — got to hear that there were no beds available so she dug out a camp bed we had and brought it, with pillows and blankets, to our temporary abode,' said Fw. Foster. 'At least, I would have a bed to sleep on. As it grew dark, we had to find our way about by the light of torches; we dare not switch the lights on as there were no black-out curtains up.

'During the evening, I was told to accompany a woman driver on a petrol delivery round. This was the first night of the black-out and she was nervous of going out alone.'

Arriving back 'home' after about two hours, Margaret decided to go to bed but, she relates, 'when I reached it, there was a very large fireman, fully dressed in firefighting gear, boots and all, laying on his back and snoring loudly. So what could I do? Here was I, a young girl just nineteen and very shy, confronted by a man in my bed. I slept on the floor!'

This most unsatisfactory state of affairs lasted only two days before fresh accommodation was found at St Dominic's School.'

All alone I went a-walking by the London Docks one day,
For to see the ship's discharging in the basins where they lay;
And the cargoes that I saw there they were every sort and kind,
Every blessed brand of merchandise a man could bring to
* mind;*
There were things in crates and boxes, there was stuff in bags
* and bales.*
There were tea chests wrapped in matting, there were Eastern
* looking frails.*

There were baulks of teak and greenheart, there were stacks of
* spruce and pine.*
There was cork and frozen carcases and casks of Spanish wine.
There was spice and rice and coconuts and rum enough was
* there.*
For to warm all London's innards up and leave a drop to
* spare.*

C. FOX-SMITH

An aerial view of the Royal Docks. A vessel noses into the lock to enter the King George Vth Dock; adjacent is the Royal Albert. Stretching away into the distance is the Queen Victoria. In this picture, every berth is occupied, upwards of half a million tons of shipping. Bottom left is the ship repair works of Messrs Harland and Wolfe. Blitzed areas still remain in 1960, when this picture was taken from an aircraft flying directly over the Woolwich Arsenal.

There was no doubt in any mind that the Royal Docks would present a major target to an enemy in time of war. In the early days of 1939, up to fifty vessels, ranging from the 35,000-ton liner, *Mauritania II*, to tramp steamers of 7,000 tons or so, occupied almost every available berth in the Queen Victoria, the Royal Albert and the King George V Docks: the 'Royal's.' Ships lay stem to stern, moored alongside eleven miles of quayage, as gangs of dockworkers loaded or unloaded cargoes. The adjoining warehouses were stacked with foodstuffs, manufactured goods and raw materials, from or bound for ports throughout the world. The ship repair yards were hives of industry and the two dry-docks were seldom vacant. So here was a prime target for a fleet of enemy bombers, a fact readily apparent to the fire officer responsible for the safety of the port.

The warehouses, built close to the dockside to facilitate the loading and unloading of vessels, presented a problem. It was foreseen that extensive fire, billowing from a warehouse, might bar the approach of land-based fire appliances. Fertile minds were applied to the problem and a novel experiment developed. Four Dennis trailer fire pumps were loaded into the hold of a dumb barge, with holes cut in the coaming to allow suction hose to be set into the dock water. This improvised fire float was capable of pumping two thousand gallons of water a minute, sufficient to provide sixteen good firefighting jets with the benefit of a practically unlimited supply of water, more reliable than the River Thames, since dock water was impounded two feet six inches above Thames High Water mark.

The crippling snag, however, was that a tug would be required to move a barge about which was too expensive and unreliable, for the tug, almost certainly, would be otherwise engaged when required. So the back-room boys, practical firemen with experience of the back pressure of a fire jet, came up with the idea of utilising the thrust to propel the barge.

A tiller was constructed and mounted on the after deck, with two branches clamped to a horizontal bar. These discharged water over the stern of the vessel with sufficient power to propel it at a steady five knots. The tiller enabled the jets to be used for steering and the firemen helmsmen steadily achieved a fair degree of control over their clumsy craft. It became apparent that regular exercise in handling the barge was essential and every opportunity was taken for a run along the dock, a popular drill with the crews.

Unfortunately, the exercises came to an abrupt halt following a call to Fire Brigade H.Q. An official of the Port of London Authority requested the cessation of fire barge mobile exercises during working hours. He complained that dock workers were leaving their jobs to line the quays and cheer the strange vision of a dumb barge, with two jets of water issuing from the stern, proceeding smartly through the dock under its own 'steam.'

Eventually, four barges, the *Fred*; *Monsoon*; *Brampton* and *Sweden* were converted to auxiliary fire floats, providing useful addition to the firefighting capacity within the docks.

The fleet did, in fact, see action in circumstances which had been envisaged. Fires in buildings were attacked from the waterside but the most valuable contribution made by the fire barges was the maintenance of water supplies to land-based pumps throughout the Blitz.

An enthusiastic welcome for the London fireboat *Massey Shaw* on her return from Dunkirk. Her epic voyage began at Ramsgate, where she was placed under the command of an officer of the Royal Navy and hoisted the White Ensign. Her shallow draught enabled her to run close in to the beaches and ferry some five hundred men to larger vessels lying off shore. She was the last of the 'little ships' to leave and on her final trip brought back 96 men to Ramsgate. Rear Admiral Sir Bertram Ramsey, KCB, Flag Officer Commanding, Dover, wrote in the *London Gazette* 'Of the civilian manned craft, one of the best performances was that of the London Fire Brigade boat *Massey Shaw*. All the volunteer crew were members of the London Fire Brigade or AFS, and they succeeded in making three round trips to the beaches in their well-found craft.'

Roy Hordley, a local man on leave from the Army, took this photograph of the Admiralty Oil Depot fire from a jetty on the **Pembroke Dock waterfront. The pall of smoke could be seen as far away as Somerset.**

Enemy raiders began their attack in force on the British Isles on August 8th, 1940, following air raids on convoys and other shipping in the Channel and Dover Harbour. The enemy targets were aerodromes and dockyards and members of the Fire Service had their first taste of what was to follow in the years ahead.

The Luftwaffe mounted a heavy attack on the Admiralty Oil Installation at Pembroke Dock on August 19th, starting fires that burned for seventeen days. Firemen, many of them experiencing their first sight of a major oil fire, were confronted with an awe inspiring spectacle. Blazing oil gushed from large tanks, ruptured by high explosive and ignited by incendiary machine gun bullets and magnesium fire bombs; a great black, greasy column of smoke rising a thousand feet into the sky.

The tanks were grouped closely within earth-walled enclosures, known in the business as bunds, and the first task was to cool those threatened by the advancing sea of flame. This called for vast quantities of water to be pumped through hose lines and deployed from whatever vantage point that offered. It was a long, hard slog fraught with great danger as fresh tanks succumbed to the shrivelling heat and collapsed,

spilling their contents to add to the inferno. Nevertheless, cooling jets were brought to bear from bund walls, from the top of surrounding tanks and from within the bund itself by intrepid firemen, braving searing heat in an attempt to keep the all-consuming tide at bay. Never had the term 'firefighting' seemed more apt. But this was merely the prelude to the battle, a holding operation. Foam-making branchpipes must be brought into operation to quell the fire within tanks and to smother that running loose on the surface. Those directing foam jets into blazing tanks often found their task rendered more difficult by the alignment of the steel roof plates, distorted by heat into cylindrical form and effectively shielding the blazing surface from the foam streams.

The mass of oil in the burning tanks became heated far above ignition temperature, resulting in a heat wave which slowly descended to the bottom, where water, always present in the base of heavy oil containers, was turned to steam. The vast expansion projected the contents of a tank high into the air like lava from a volcano. The blazing oil cascaded down, enveloping a group of firemen working in the bund, incinerating five of them.

London's first experience of the bombers came later in the month, when bombs fell in the south-eastern suburbs. Eltham and Woolwich were the first of the London boroughs to feel the weight of a German air attack and to experience casualties and fires.

A sharp attack on the City occurred on the 25th when hundreds of firemen saw at first-hand what incendiary bombs could do in the congested areas of the commercial centre of the capital. The enemy then turned his attention to the great oil installations at Thameshaven and Shellhaven at the mouth of the Thames, which were bombed and set alight on September 5th. The London Fire Region was called upon for help and West Ham pumps joined the convoy.

The excellent peace-time safety record at British oil depots and refineries made outbreaks of fire something of a rarity and there were relatively few firemen in the country with experience of a major oil fire, a dangerous and alarming enough adventure without the additional hazard of exposure to machine-gunning by enemy aircraft.

Charlie Morris, a popular, happy-go-lucky Stratford fireman, had climbed to the roof of an oil tank and stood aiming his jet to cool threatened tanks, when a Messerschmitt roared in low over the depot with machine guns blazing. Men on the ground dropped their hose and ran for cover but Charlie, marooned on high with colleagues, had nowhere to go. They would be isolated, surrounded by fire and deprived of the protection of their powerful jets if the operators abandoned their pumps.

'Oi,' yelled Charlie Morris, 'Where the 'ell are you lot goin.' What about us up 'ere?'

A few paused in their headlong rush and became aware that the Messerchmitt had vanished. Charlie's mates rallied their crews and yelled a few words of encouragement aloft. 'Alright, Charlie; keep yer 'air on. Bring you up a cupper tea in a minute.'

And the battle was resumed.

Saturday dawned bright and clear, an event noted with some apprehension by those in the vicinity of the oil installations. Enemy raiders could be expected at any moment and ears were strained to catch the first snarl of approaching aircraft, whose navigators would have no need for calculations; all they had to do was to make for the huge columns of smoke rising from their target.

The first arrivals among the reinforcing fire crews were showing signs of exhaustion. They had been toiling all night, some of them within the bund, waist deep in a filthy mixture of oil, firefighting foam and water. Relief for these men was overdue but reinforcements were arriving and the weary men needed no persuasion to hand over their branches to the fresh crews and join the convoys for the journey home. Among the first to be relieved was a crew from West Ham's No. 16 Station and they wasted no time in cruising smoothly into place in the convoy heading for East London.

The leading appliances had hardly cleared the precincts of the oil depot when a Messerschmitt swooped with machine guns blazing. The airman's aim may have been affected by the smoke, for none of the appliances or the men were hit but the attack brought a colourful response from the lads. It was their unanimous opinion that the parents of the enemy pilot had not been joined in Holy Matrimony!

Harold Marriott, a veteran of the First World War, was highly indignant.

'What the bleedin' 'ell do they think they're doin,' he yelled. 'We're firemen, not bleedin' soldiers.'

Thameshaven oil refinery, attacked on September 5th, 1940. Firemen, working from the bund wall surrounding the 2,000-ton capacity tanks, direct a jet to cool the walls of an unaffected tank endangered by its blazing neighbour. Other cooling jets are directed from the roof of tanks to contain the spread of fire. Water must not be allowed to enter a burning oil tank, for severe turbulence of the superheated oil would follow, leading to a condition known as a 'slop-over'. This would result in large quantities of blazing oil spilling from the tank, to the peril of firemen working nearby and to the adjacent tanks.

'You've got a tin 'at on, aincher?' replied Len Townrow; 'that's good enough for them.'

But Fred Dell, their officer in charge, put an end to the back-chat.

'Cut the cackle and get a move on. Let's get out of here' and the remainder of the crews seemed to have the same idea for the line of fire pumps moved smartly away from the danger zone.

The men arrived back at their station in mid-morning, fit only for bed after cleaning up and bolting a hastily prepared meal. Auxiliary firemen, by order of the Fire Service Department of the Home Office, were issued with only one suit of uniform, consequently the men had no option other than to hang out tunic and trousers on clothes lines in the hope that they would dry out before the next fire call. But they were too exhausted to worry about such matters; sleep

The efficacy of the firefighting tactics employed at Thameshaven is apparent in this picture taken on September 7th, 1940. Flames from burning oil released from the collapsed tanks in the background have been prevented from enveloping those in the foreground by cooling water jets played on the threatened areas, whilst foam jets were used to extinguish the burning oil. What the picture cannot portray is the courageous tenacity of the firefighters in standing up to the fearsome, billowing flame; the searing heat and the rattle of machine gun fire from enemy airmen in what, for many of those engaged, was their first glimpse of uncontrolled fire.

was their greatest need. Silence quickly descended over the former Gainsborough Road School, now pressed into service as West Ham Fire Brigade's No. 16 Station, as even more momentous events prepared to unfold.

2

Blood and tears

SEPTEMBER 7th was a glorious summer's day with the sun shining from a clear blue sky. The activity of the previous evening, when a few isolated bombers dropped fire and explosive bombs on Silvertown and Custom House, had kept me busy until 4 a.m. and there was time only for a few hours sleep before the daily routine began at 7 a.m.

I tried to get my head down after lunch but felt uneasy and couldn't rest; premonition, perhaps? Everyone who could be spared crept away to catch up on sleep and there was little activity at Abbey Road School, the London Fire Region's 'J' District Control that Saturday afternoon, that is until shortly before 5 p.m. when the 'Air raid warning Red' message was received and the sirens began their wailing.

I was in the school yard and heard the drone of approaching aircraft rapidly swelling to a roar. Suddenly, squadrons of bombers appeared all over the eastern sky, flying very high and escorted by hundreds of fighter aircraft, glinting in the sunshine as they weaved and turned over the

Luftwaffe pilots flying over the Thameshaven oil refinery on September 7th, 1940 were rewarded with this view of their handiwork. Below the smoke cloud, firemen heaved and sweated laying long hose lines; bringing stocks of foam compound to the branch pipes; pumping thousands of gallons of foam into blazing tanks and laying a blanket of foam over lakes of flaming oil on the floor of the bund. They floundered in the foul mix of water, foam and crude oil, occasionally galvanised into evasive action by enemy airmen with a few hundred rounds of ammo to spare, practising ground-strafing techniques. Said Fred Dell: 'I could think of better places to be on a sunny Saturday morning.'

bomber formations. Rosettes of black smoke from exploding anti-aircraft shells spread across the sky as the menacing roar of aircraft engines combined, in a devilish symphony, with the bark of anti-aircraft gunfire, the scream of falling bombs and the earth-shaking thump as they exploded.

I dived for the safety of the Control Room, where calls for assistance were already flooding in from Dagenham, Barking and East Ham. The electricity mains were damaged in the first few minutes and the Fire Control operated by the light of candles set in jam jars.

The Nazi airmen had no difficulty in identifying their targets in the clear afternoon light. The first bombs fell on the Ford Motor Works at Dagenham, closely followed by a rain of high explosives and fire bombs on the Beckton Gas Works, the largest in Europe.

Below them now lay the great Thames bight at Woolwich Reach, enclosing the three Royal Docks, their warehouses and sheds stacked with foodstuff and materials vital to the war effort. Large cargo vessels lay moored at the quayside, sitting duck targets for the bomb-aimers.

An all-too-familiar scene; an unfortunate passer-by is struck down by debris as he walks along the pavement.

Now came an avalanche of bombs raining on the East End of London from an estimated 300 bombers. Flames erupted from the great warehouses and factories lining the River Thames on both banks, from North Woolwich to Tower Bridge. In the crowded dockland streets, massive warehouses and tiny houses alike came crashing down under the impact of high explosive, burying under the debris their occupants and any luckless passer-by.

Columns of fire pumps, five hundred of them ordered to West Ham alone, sped eastwards to attend fires in ships and warehouses; sugar refineries, soap works, tar distilleries, chemical works, timber stacks, paint and varnish works, the humble little homes of the workers and hundreds of other fires that, in peace time, would have made headline news.

Two hundred and fifty acres of tall timber stacks blazed out of control in the Surrey Commercial Docks; the rum quay buildings in the West India Docks, alight from end to end, gushed blazing spirit from their doors. An army of rats ran from a Silvertown soap works; a short distance along the North Woolwich Road, molten pitch from a stricken tar distillery flooded the road, bringing to a halt all emergency vehicles. On the riverside, blazing barges threatened wharves. Some were set adrift by well-intentioned people, only to be swept by the tide downstream, broadside on, to the peril of fire boats, manoeuvring to pump water ashore to feed the land pumps.

This picture, taken from a bomber flying overhead, shows two Dornier 17s over the Royal Docks. The smoke cloud on the left obscures the vast grain silo and flour mills which handled one quarter of the country's requirements. The curving road on the left is Silvertown Way, enclosing the Royal Victoria Dock and, lower, after it becomes North Woolwich Road, the Royal Albert and King George Vth Docks. The oval West Ham Stadium is seen upper centre and, bottom left, the River Thames with large industrial buildings lining the bank.

The scene from London Bridge, September 7th, 1940 at 5 p.m. Smoke from St Katherine, London and Millwall Docks mingles with that from the burning timber stacks across the river.

It was a scene of horror and chaos as Civil Defence workers, themselves shocked and terrified by their first experience of the Blitz, dug into the debris of demolished buildings in search of casualties. Others shepherded dazed and shocked men, women and children, rendered homeless but thankful to have escaped with their lives, to rest centres in schools and church halls, where they were given temporary shelter whilst arrangements were made for their more permanent accommodation. At six o'clock the raiders had gone but the 'all clear' brought no relief to firemen, striving against odds to contain the great conflagrations that raged all around them. Others laboured to prevent smaller fires from combining to create more conflagrations. The street water mains, totally inadequate to carry the vast quantities of water needed to control fires of such magnitude, were further depleted when sections fractured under the pounding of explosive bombs. Those firemen working on dockside fires were fortunate in having an almost unlimited supply of water to draw on but watched their powerful jets bore into the mass of flames without visible effect. Some of the regulars had encountered fires of equal ferocity in peacetime but never on such an overwhelming scale. The choking fumes from burning rubber and tar; the blistering heat and blinding sparks were merely unpleasant incidentals; fear was the predominant emotion that drew branchmen together in small groups, each gaining comfort from the presence of the other.

Many feared their last hour had come but they carried on, encouraged by the example of comrades slogging away at burning buildings, their heads down to protect faces from the scorching heat and flying sparks. They yelled warnings to unwary crews as slabs of masonry and coping stones from collapsing buildings began to topple. All around them lay a maze of twisting, snaking fire hose whilst the whine of dozens of fire pumps, running at full power, added their quota to the general din. Clouds of greasy, black smoke rose high into the sky, dimming the golden sunlight but billowing flames, orange and yellow, provided a weird substitute.

At 7.30 p.m. the bombers were back, about 250 of them, to drive home the attack. Succeeding squadrons of Heinkels and Dorniers queued to deliver their cargoes on a target still blazing from the afternoon raid. East Londoners had been severely punished, none more so than those living in the Tidal Basin area. Their houses had been built in the 1850s to accommodate the thousands of workers engaged in building the Royal Victoria Dock and the large factories at Silvertown. Part of the plan was to accommodate the workpeople within a short walk of their place of employment.

With the Blitz came the inevitable overspill of bombs aimed at docks and warehouses. The closely packed streets were no match for even the smallest of the German bombs.

A pump from Burdett Road fire station getting to work. Two firemen reach for hose in the locker whilst a crew-mate connects a second line of hose to the pump delivery. The pump carries a 35ft 'Ajax' extension ladder and two hook ladders.

Great gaps were torn in the terraces leaving piles of debris where once stood neat little homes. Still, grotesque figures, sprawling in the roadway, splayed against a wall or tossed in a corner like a rag doll, lay camouflaged by mortar dust, merging with surrounding rubble. Bricks and tiles, roofing timbers and shattered glass littered the road, together with cherished items that once made a home. The ghastly outlines of a mangled human being slowly materialised as one's eyes focused on what lay around.

Many families were buried in the rubble of their homes and had to be dug out by rescue squads. Those lightly buried freed themselves and immediately began digging frantically for their nearest and dearest. Some were beyond aid and scenes of heartrending grief were witnessed as survivors uncovered the mutilated bodies of loved ones. First aid parties moved in, treating the injured and covering the dead with a blanket or whatever came to hand, leaving the body stretched out on the rubble to await collection by a mortuary van.

Hour after hour the bombs rained down, demolishing yet more buildings and starting fresh fires. Great blazing embers, carried aloft in the terrific heat upcast, spread fire over the heads of firemen. Powerful jets of water seemed to be turned to steam by the great roaring flames from timber stacks; all the effort seemed to be in vain; the task was overwhelming.

After a time, the scream of falling bombs and the thunder of explosions became just the background to the brain-numbing din but, always, one was aware of tortured eyes and a dry mouth, the scorching heat and the rumble of collapsing buildings. The fearful dread of impending doom receded as time passed and the imagination dulled. Many who felt they were engaged in a hopeless task battled on, taking heart as neighbouring crews stood their ground.

Meanwhile, Civil Defence workers led the homeless to rest centres established in halls and schools. Many had superficial cuts and abrasions and were caked in dried blood; all were smothered in plaster dust from walls and ceilings. They had lost everything they possessed but cared nothing other than that the family had been spared. All windows were shattered by blast and many reached the rest centre with tiny splinters of glass embedded in face and hands.

During the evening I received word that my close friend, Wally Turley, with two members of his crew, had been buried when a building collapsed in the West Ham Transport Department depot in Abbey Road during firefighting operations. Two fire pumps had arrived and Sub-Officers Turley and Webb ran into the burning building with their crews. A quick reconnaissance and Wally shouted 'You take the back, Harry; I'll look after this side.'

The bombs that caused this damage to the North Woolwich/Stratford railway line and the West Ham decontamination centre probably came from the same stick. This one made a crater on the track and flung lengths of rail towards the flats in Manor Road, West Ham. One rail came to rest leaning against the four-storey block; another was tossed right over the block and fell at the rear.

Webb and his men ran out of the building with the intention of tackling the fire from the rear when, to quote Harry Webb, 'The whole bloody guts of the building fell in, burying the lot.' The shocked survivors tore at the great slab of concrete but found it far beyond their ability to move. Heavy lifting gear had to be brought in to recover the bodies.

This is the West Ham decontamination centre and ambulance depot, one of the very early victims of the Blitz. The crews of two fire pumps ran into the main entrance, roughly behind the man wearing the steel helmet. Sub-Officer Webb's crew had just cleared the building when it collapsed, burying Sub-Officer Walter Turley and Auxiliary Firemen Hugh Dicken and Bill Long. Eight members of the West Ham Civil Defence Corps were also killed. When I arrived an hour or so later, the place was deserted. I ducked under debris obstructing the entrance and found myself in a fairly clear space with a sloping concrete floor. After a moment, I realised that this was what had been the first floor which had come crashing down in a solid mass, burying the firemen and the CD men. As I looked about, I saw an arm protruding from under the concrete slab and had no doubt that it was my friend. Wally Turley had a malformed finger-nail on his left hand which I recognised immediately. I looked under the concrete but could see nothing but debris. I took off his wrist-watch and walked back to the station where I reported to the Chief Officer what I had seen. 'There's no doubt it is Sub-Officer Turley,' I told him. 'Don't tell anybody' he ordered. 'You can't be sure until the body is formally identified.' Mrs Turley came to the station later that evening to enquire after her husband. Whether she had a premonition of what had happened, I am not sure, but she seemed very anxious. Bearing in mind what the Chief had said, I told her I did not know where Wally was; in the docks, or somewhere! She went away unconvinced and I felt rotten about it, but I had been ordered to say nothing. Apparently she went home and expressed her doubts about what I had told her, for, a little later, along came Wally's father. He looked me straight in the eye and demanded to be told the truth. I could no longer lie and told him his son was dead, offering him the wrist-watch. The old man broke down and I was not far from tears. He examined the watch and confirmed that it was Wally's. He asked where it had happened but I would not tell him that. 'I don't want this,' he said, handing me the wrist-watch. 'You keep it.' It was only a cheap little watch and had seen better days, but I was pleased to have it as a keep-sake.

Across the river at Rotherhithe stood Pageant's Wharf Fire Station. Opened in 1903, its main purpose was to provide fire protection for the bustling Surrey Commercial Docks, the major timber importing centre in the country. Two hundred and fifty acres of storage space were stacked with timber imported mainly from North America and the Baltic. Even before the war, many local people viewed with concern the possibility of a disastrous fire occurring among the huge timber stacks but, in peacetime, outbreaks within the dock area were not frequent. On those occasions when fire did break out, the presence of an efficient firefighting unit, stationed immediately by the Lavender Pond entrance gate, ensured a swift attendance; few outbreaks were given time to extend beyond a minor stage.

When the 'Air raid warning Red' message was received in the watchroom shortly before 5 p.m., Station Officer 'Gerry' Knight and his men moved into the station yard where they had a clear view across the river. The distant sound of sirens was taken up locally and the warning passed on across the length and breadth of the Capital in ever widening circles. Some people hurried to the shelters, others stood staring at the sky. Only a small proportion of Londoners, those living on the southern and eastern outskirts, had experienced mild bombing and had learned to run for cover when the sirens wailed.

Gerry Knight and his lads had no illusions about their situation; none had any doubt that the timber stacks would attract the bombers like bees to a honey pot. Fires started by incendiary bombs certainly would be something new but they had faced up to runaway fire before. In the docks, they would be assured of a plentiful water supply and they had come to rely on the power of their pumps. Had they not had experience of 'make up' fires before and witnessed the speed with which reinforcements could be mobilised at any given spot? So what was there to worry about? But they could not comprehend the havoc Göring's men could create in such a prime target, and in other primary targets in East London's industrial area.

The sirens were still sounding as the bombers appeared high above the eastern outskirts of the Capital. Firemen standing in the yard at Pageant's Wharf saw the opening of the attack on targets they later learned were the Ford Motor Works at Dagenham; Woolwich Arsenal and the docks and factories on the north side of the Thames at Silvertown. As they watched, a squadron of bombers detached from the main stream and headed directly for the Surrey Commercial Docks swamping the timber stacks with a deluge of incendiary bombs and a quota of high explosives. The Pageant's Wharf

pump-escape and pump turned out immediately, making for the smoke already rising over a wide area.

The crews had every confidence in their station officer. Gerry Knight was an officer of long and varied experience, long past the stage at which the sight of a large area of fire had resulted in a flurry of excitement. It had become second nature to him to regard such situations as just another job. In common with colleagues of similar rank and experience, he was able to recognise a threatening fire spread and to select the spot to position jets to stop its progress.

The standard messages employed by the brigade were part of his everyday vocabulary; he had been using them since his early days as a young fireman. But this was far beyond his experience. He and his men were surrounded by fire before he realised the danger. The enemy was using magnesium incendiaries which lodged in the most inaccessible places, and oil bombs which flashed and extended fire among the stacks aided by the accumulation of wood chips, built up over decades. Where there had been no fire, suddenly there was an inferno.

Several ships carrying deck cargoes of stacked timber were berthed in the Surrey Commercial Docks when Göring's men struck. A brisk south-westerly wind swept smoke across the river to mingle with that rising from blazing warehouses in the St Katherine, London and Millwall Docks, away into north-east London and beyond. This picture vividly portrays the task facing firemen. Any further stoking of the conflagration seemed hardly necessary, yet the bombers continued to shower the docks with incendiaries and the occasional HE bomb throughout the night.

So it was not surprising that Gerry Knight, for once, lost his cool and resorted to unofficial phraseology when framing his message from the fireground: 'Send all the bloody pumps you've got; the whole bloody world's on fire!'

Firewoman Betty Barrett, who was on duty in the watchroom at Pageant's Wharf Fire Station, couldn't believe her ears. 'There was no doubt it was the Station Officer speaking but he had never used that sort of language to me,' she said. And what should she do about transmitting the message to New Cross Fire Control? She'd been trained to pass on precisely what had been received, so she had no option but to repeat faithfully the message she had been given.

Four temporary fire stations were located in the Surrey Commercial Docks, manned mainly by auxiliary firemen. They were equipped with Dennis trailer pumps, drawn by a miscellaneous collection of taxicabs, cars and light vans. Many of the auxiliaries were experiencing their first sight of a fire; all, including the regulars, were witnessing the commencement of one of the greatest conflagrations they would ever encounter. It was not a case of being sent to attend a specific fire; they were confronted with billowing flame on all fronts.

Now was the time to put to practical use the skills they had acquired at pump drills. Lengths of suction hose were coupled up in record time and lowered into the dock water. Hose lines were run out and positioned to stop the spread of fire from stacks hopelessly ablaze, to those already smoking and ready to erupt. But as fast as they knocked down fire in one stack

and switched to another, the first stack began to steam, dried out in the radiated heat from its neighbour, and again burst into flame. Telegraph poles began to smoke then ignite from base to crown, although the nearest fire was many yards away. Then the wooden-block road surface ignited in the searing heat. Firemen working in the maze of stacks were driven back, steam rising from their sodden tunics; their faces and hands scorched and eyes smarting from the effects of acrid smoke and flying sparks. In great danger of being cut off by fire, they were forced to abandon their equipment and run for their lives, passing the fire stations containing their bikes and bits and pieces of personal belongings, now blazing as fiercely as the surrounding timber.

Now fully alert to the danger, Station Officer Knight withdrew his men from situations where they were at risk of becoming engulfed in fire, to positions on the periphery. It went against the grain to withdraw from a fire; all his training and experience was to attack at close range, but this was an entirely new situation. Never before had he to contend with incendiary bombs spreading fire all around as he worked, mindful that his major responsibility was for the safety of his men.

The first shock had been absorbed and a picture of the situation in the Surrey Docks was emerging. A start had been made on isolating fires and the work quickened as more pumps and senior officers became available.

Back in the fire station watchroom, Leading Firewoman Barry, Firewoman Barrett and Firewoman Brockman were being kept at full stretch maintaining the lines of communication between the Surrey Docks conflagrations and District Control. The watchroom was continually shaken by heavy explosions but the girls stuck to their task.

'We didn't worry about the bombs, so much, although they were bad enough,' said Betty Barrett. 'We were afraid the oil depot next door would be hit, and we kept popping out to have a look every time there was a near one.'

Assistance messages were streaming back from the fireground and fresh calls were coming in. Wardens and members of the public were pulling street fire alarms or telephoning for help as fresh waves of bombers showered incendiaries on the Rotherhithe peninsula. But the calls could only be recorded and passed to District Control with the added message 'No attendance from this station.' The station doors were open and the appliance bays empty, as they had been since the commencement of the raid. On the fireground, Auxiliary Fireman Bill Ward and his mates, ordered on from 40Y Station, New Cross, were at work on the edge of blazing timber stacks. Unknown to them, they were standing near the spot where the wooden road blocks had been set afire by radiated heat. Now, so much water had been used to douse the burning road surface that the blocks had swollen and come adrift from their foundation, 'rising and falling like the swell on the river as they floated' said Bill. 'It was a weird situation,' he added 'nothing but fire and smoke to be seen everywhere; telegraph poles bursting into flame for no apparent reason and now the bloody road starts heaving.' Order was being restored, albeit slowly, from the earlier chaos.

Three hundred pumps with over a thousand men were in action at the largest of the individual fires, surrounding it with an ever tightening ring of water jets, with similar action taking place in adjoining areas. Before the night was through, one thousand pumps were at work in the Surrey Docks. A fresh problem was the task of supplying refreshment for men who had been slaving away, scorched and soaked and blinded

by smoke and sparks for several hours. Senior officers, conferring together. saw days fraught with great danger ahead before the routine message 'All fires in the Surrey Docks now under control' could be sent.

Still the squadrons droned overhead and the bombs screamed down. Not only water mains were fractured by the pounding H.E.; gas mains, power and telephone cables were equally vulnerable. These were days before radio was widely available to the Service and fire officers, unable to telephone situation reports and calls for assistance, relied upon motor cycle dispatch riders, many of them women, or the heroic teenage messenger boys with their bicycles, to maintain communications. It was no fault of the D.R.s and messengers that Controls were receiving but a hazy picture of the fire situation in the worst bombed areas. They rode through streets converted by incendiary bombs into passages with flaming walls, picking themselves up after being blasted from their machines by a near miss. They skidded around unexploded bombs and heaps of rubble, frequently arriving at control rooms to deliver their messages covered in mud and dust, often bruised and with grazed knuckles, always eager to get back to the fireground. accepting the conditions as all part of the job.

One of the heroic band of teenage cyclist messengers who enrolled in the AFS and NFS throughout the war. When the call went out in 1939, the Service was inundated with volunteers. Minimum age for recruitment was 16, but many of those eager faces, uplifted to the enrolment officers, were clearly well below that age. The query 'How old are you, son?' brought the immediate response 'Sixteen, mister' but they were unable to produce a confirmatory birth certificate, and had to be turned away. No doubt that, as the war dragged on and they reached the legal age, they re-applied. Since they were called up for military service at eighteen, there was a regular turn-over. Those that were accepted earned the admiration and praise of all who saw them in action. As telephone lines were severed, these lads — let none dare refer to them as 'kids' — rode their bicycles through streets fringed with blazing buildings and with enemy aircraft droning menacingly overhead, carrying important messages to fireground or fire station. They vied with each other to be the first to answer the shout of 'messenger', no matter that they had just returned from a nerve-stretching ride to one of the hot spots. This picture suggests that the messenger was not carrying an official message — he is not wearing his steel helmet. It would appear that he has been caught up in a random bomb incident and finds himself confronted with a grim reminder of the dangers of his job.

People living in the streets adjoining the southern boundary of the King George V Dock found themselves sandwiched between serious dock fires and a line of great factories ablaze along the length of Factory Road, opposite. Conditions in North Woolwich were unimaginable. Demolished buildings spilled debris over the roadway, blocking the passage of fire and rescue vehicles. Terrified families scurried back and forth, seeking shelter from the awesome fires and the explosions that continually rocked the area, as delayed action bombs went off and others came from fresh flights of bombers. Some refugees found their way to a public shelter at the baths in Oriental Road, only to become the target for a random bomb. The situation in the area had become out of hand and it was decided to evacuate the whole civilian population from North Woolwich. The only road giving access in or out of the district was blocked to wheeled traffic and those poor people were forced to make a nightmare journey on foot to North Woolwich Pier, where they embarked on small craft to be rowed to safety via the River Thames.

Meanwhile, people in Rotherhithe were facing an ordeal similar to that of the beleaguered citizens of North Woolwich. As the great inferno raced on, walls of flame swept over their modest little homes bordering the dock walls. Their escape from the flames barred by the river, people living in the Rotherhithe Street/Redriff Road area were forced to run the gauntlet of smoke clouds, carrying myriads of sparks and glowing embers, in their flight towards Lower Road and Evelyn Street. Like those in North Woolwich, some found a route to safety via the river, embarking in small craft, even barges.

In the fire station at Pageant's Wharf, Leading Firewoman Myra Barry and her Blue Watch colleagues, Firewomen Barrett and Brockman, were sticking it out alone. Fire calls continued to flood in as unattended fires spread and falls of incendiaries added to the conflagration surrounding their station. Every call was entered routinely in the station log book and passed to the District Control at New Cross. The mobilising officer there assumed responsibility for finding an attendance to each incident reported.

To add to her troubles, Firewoman Brockman was experiencing discomfort with her dentures. At ordinary times, with firemen coming and going, 'Brockie' would have endured the pain but now, with only her female colleagues present, she removed them. During the night, she answered a call from District Control and Myra Barry and Betty Barrett listened to one end of the conversation. With invasion expected at any moment, they thought they were hearing confirmation of their worst fears.

'No, we can't evacuate the station,' spluttered Brockie; 'there's nowhere to go.' After a short pause while she listened: 'I can't help it if they are coming up the river, we can't evacuate the station.' The officer at the other end must have thought he was dealing with a case of gross insubordination. Brockie would have made her point abundantly clear had she added that the station was hemmed in by the river on three sides and by a solid wall of fire on the other. Such craft as were passing gave the south side a wide berth so that evacuation would have been difficult to achieve.

'What's all that about?' demanded the L.Fw.

'Oh, he said the Germans had dropped two mines in the Thames and they were coming up the river and we had to evacuate the station,' replied Brockie, unaware of the shock she had given her colleagues.

In the meantime, a grim-faced L.Fw. wearing her respirator and steel helmet, 'dressed for war' as she said later, had grabbed the broom.

'What are you going to do with that?' asked Betty Barrett.

'I dunno' replied the L.Fw., but I thought I ought to do something.'

'It's easy to laugh, now,' said Betty, relating the story. 'But it wasn't so funny, then.'

About this time, Petty Officer A.P. Herbert, M.P., Oi/c H.M. Patrol Vessel *Water Gipsy* lying at Tower Pier, received orders to pick up some wire from a P.L.A. wreck lighter in the Lower Pool and take it to North Woolwich. The wire was collected and *Water Gipsy* set course for North Woolwich. Petty Officer Herbert describes the trip in his book *Independent Member*:

'We rounded Limehouse Corner and saw an astounding picture. Half a mile of the Surrey shore, ending before the Greenland entrance of the Surrey Commercial Docks, was ablaze — warehouses, wharves, piers, dolphins, barges.

'The wind was westerly, and there was a wall of smoke and sparks across the river. Burning barges were drifting everywhere but there was not a soul in sight — the small police boat ahead of us had turned back to report — and we had been ordered to Woolwich. A wooden ship, and petrol driven, we did not like the look of it much: but we put wet towels round our faces and steamed at half speed into the torrid cloud. Inside, the scene was like a lake in Hell. We could hear the hiss and roar of the conflagration ashore, but could not see it, only the burning barges and the crimson water that reflected them. It was not as alarming as it had looked outside, the main whirl of sparks and smoke went over us. We took off our towels and felt quite happy. It was something to be the only boat in Hell. We steamed on slowly, using the compass and dodging the barges, and at last the *Water Gipsy* came out safe, but sooty, the White Ensign nearly black, the other side. After that, all the other fires we passed seemed no more than night-lights, though there were some brave ones.

'I now had a feeling that nothing could touch us — a thing I never felt in a house. At the top of Blackwall Reach a bomb fell fifty yards ahead of us. I ducked down behind the wheel, I know, but truly I felt no fear, and this astonished and delighted me. We delivered our wire at Woolwich — I hope it was some use — and came back through the smoke to Westminster. Next day, Sunday, we were sent down again to investigate this and that and report. The 'Prospect of Whitby' was still standing and two barges upside down on the foreshore below. In Blackwall Reach a barge had been blown ashore and stood leaning, end up, against a house. The Greenwich Tunnel had been hit and filled. At Blackwall we went ashore and wandered in the battered streets, marvelling at the brave, worn people.'

And so it continued throughout the night. The Heinkels and Dorniers found their targets mainly in the eastern suburbs on both sides of the river, then turned for home, some to load up for a return trip. Fire pumps were mobilised from as far distant as Birmingham and Nottingham, Brighton and Swindon, bringing crews of auxiliary firemen with a sprinkling of regular officers, to face up to the fury of the Blitz. Soon, it would be the turn of their home towns, when London firemen would return the compliment.

The first glimpse of dawn tinged the eastern sky at about 5 a.m. when the Luftwaffe decided to call it a day. The All Clear sirens signalled their departure, leaving firemen in action at nineteen conflagrations (large areas of fire involving blocks of buildings, spreading and not yet under control); nineteen serious fires, each requiring the attendance of at least thirty pumps and many, many more with up to thirty pumps in attendance.

Londoners emerged from their shelters to scenes of devastation. Many came face to face with great fires, others viewed the dismal landscape; demolished factories, warehouses and whole streets of houses, with wisps of smoke and steam rising from the homes of friends and neighbours. The first thought of many was for a cup of tea but they were to be disappointed, for there was no water, gas or electricity available. They were faced with the problems that would confront them for fifty-seven mornings in succession.

The London fireboat *Massey Shaw* in home waters.

During the first day and night of the attack, 436 men, women and children were killed and some 1,600 severely injured. It was a night that none who lived through it will ever forget.

Sunday saw no daylight raiders. The sun rose and shone on a scene of desolation, with smoke from hundreds of fires slowly diminishing under the work of firemen, now nearing exhaustion after twelve hours ceaseless toil. Frequently soaked to the skin, then dried out in the searing heat, their noses constantly assailed by odiferous liquids pumped through their hosepipes. Water from dock basins, the receptacles for all kinds of rubbish deposited by ship's crews; water from Corporation swimming pools smelling strongly of chlorine; water heavy with duckweed from stagnant pools; water from bomb craters, flooded by fractured water mains. A few were lucky enough to be supplied with water from the mains, miraculously unaffected by bomb blast.

Many of them had had no food, some, not even a drink of water. Some kind neighbours brought jugs of tea or a drink of some sort, but it just was not possible, for one reason or another, to bring refreshment to all. The All Clear brought relief only from the bombs; many fires still blazed and had to be fought and brought under control, despite all the difficulties which beset them.

A typical dockland Blitz scene. Fires on the upper floors of warehouses are attacked by firemen working from the floors of warehouses opposite. Not only did this strategy give protection from falling debris, it enabled branch-men to strike at the heart of fires out of reach from street level. The men at the head of turntable ladders working in the background occupy an unenviable position, exposed to dense smoke and searing heat. The ladder operators must keep a sharp eye aloft, ready to swing the head of the turntable away from drifts of smoke or a gush of flame. Extra lengths of hose are brought up to provide yet another jet to deal with a serious situation.

The rescue squads toiled ceaselessly throughout the night, persevering with their back-breaking task in heavily dust-laden atmospheres. They burrowed into great heaps of rubble, often in imminent danger of collapse, to reach those trapped in the debris. Often, their labours led them to the mangled remains of some unfortunate, but their reward came when they succeeded in releasing a victim, miraculously still alive after being buried for hours.

Harry Berkshire joined the A.F.S. in mid-August 1940 and was posted to the auxiliary fire station in Burrage Road, Woolwich, officially designated Station No. 42V. Because of its proximity to Woolwich Arsenal Main Gate, it was generally expected that 42V would provide the first attendance to all fire calls from the Arsenal; not a pleasant prospect at any time, much less so during an air raid. But Auxiliary Fireman Berkshire's first experience of a 'real fire,' as he put it, took him some twenty-five miles beyond the Arsenal Gates, to Thameshaven Oil Refinery near Canvey Island, on September 6th, 1940. His abiding memory of the forty-eight hours spent there is one of slogging labour, performing what he considered to be a hopeless task. Thousands of cans and drums of foam compound to be carried to the appliances pumping foam onto the blazing tanks; running out countless lengths of hose to set up foam making branchpipes in new positions around the bund walls; the reek of raw oil and ducking away from machine gun bullets, sprayed on the firefighters by enemy planes. Exhausted, hungry and with their only suit of uniform saturated with stinking oil and foam, Harry and his mates arrived back at the station on Sunday afternoon, to be greeted by their colleagues: 'You lucky sods. We've been in the Surrey Docks all night!'

That night the bombers were back. For eight hours, successive waves dropped H.E. and fire bombs on the East End and the City. The raiders concentrated on the dock areas, striking hard at West Ham, Poplar and Stepney, where major fires were added to those still blazing from the previous nights' activity.

One thousand pumps crews had been at work in the Surrey Commercial Docks overnight. The great problem for fire officers now became finding relief for their exhausted crews. There were no reserves in the London Area to fall back on; such was the weight of the initial attack that every available pump was mobilised in the effort to stem the threat to London's very existence. Hundreds of reinforcing pumps were drafted in to the Capital from the large provincial towns and cities; hundreds more would follow on in anticipation of the continuing battle with the flames.

It had been a rough night for all taking part in firefighting in the Surrey Docks. Pumps were parked side by side along the waterfront, delivering hundreds of tons of water per minute to the branch-pipes. Small groups of men huddled together, massing their jets in the most effective way to beat back advancing flame. They took what cover they could as a ruthless enemy tossed in random cargoes of H.E. and incendiaries throughout the night.

Station Officer Gerry Knight had been hard at it since the first bombs fell, organising his own men and then moving on to direct inexperienced A.F.S. crews, in some cases extricating them from potentially dangerous situations. Progress was slow, and enemy intervention frequent. Nevertheless, a planned attack on the fire situation had been evolved and the spread of fire halted. It had been a tough night for Gerry, too; snatching a bite and a drink wherever he could and a few minutes rest, to take the weight off his blistered feet. Then off again to wherever his experience was of most value.

The sirens sounding the Alert for Night Two of the Blitz found Gerry Knight in Swedish Yard. The enemy soon were overhead, eager to stoke up the great conflagration and demoralise the firefighters. It is said that you never hear the one that's got your number on it; rather difficult to prove, I'd say. So we'll never know if Gerry and Auxiliary Fireman Dick Martin, who was working near him, heard it.

They never found much of Station Officer Henry William Knight, aged 44. In those days, L.F.B. station officers were issued with thigh-length fire boots; 'Gerry' Knight's served to identify his few remains.

The firewomen of Blue Watch faced up to their second day on duty at Pageant's Wharf fire station. There was no relief for their smarting eyes and raw throats, a great cloud of acrid smoke enveloped the whole of Rotherhithe and not a room in the fire station was free of the blue, stinging haze.

During the night, a leading fireman came to the watchroom bearing the charred remains of an infant he had come across in a nearby street. Betty Barrett was busy at the telephone switchboard and just caught the drift of the conversation between the L.Fm. and Myra Barry. 'I glanced over my shoulder and saw him holding the body in his hands,' said Betty. 'I turned away quickly; I didn't want to look. I don't know what he did with it; I had other things to think of.'

With the coming of dawn and the departure of the raiders, exhausted firemen began to trickle into the watchroom. They had been sent back to their station for a meal and rest and came to the watchroom to 'book in.' The firewomen were shocked at the appearance of the men. Said Betty Barrett, 'They were smoke-grimed, their eyes red, puffed and swollen from the showers of sparks flying everywhere. They were soaking wet, covered in wood ash and smelt to high heaven. Some of them were unable to speak, just stood looking at us, then sank to the ground and fell into a deep, coma-like sleep. Those that had the strength just hauled them to the dormitories and laid them out on their beds to sleep off their fatigue.

'The strain was beginning to tell on us' said Firewoman Barrett. 'Time just stood still and we carried on mechanically doing what we had to do without thinking. Before we knew where we were the sirens were sounding for the second night and the bombs began falling again. In the early hours, a relief Station Officer arrived to take charge. Then a Sub-Officer came in and I overheard him telling the Station Officer that "Gerry Knight has had it; stopped one almost to himself."

'I was deeply shocked. He was a lovely man, so kind to us girls. He used to talk to me about his premonition as I drove him around the district. "I'm never going to come through this war alive, Barrett. I came through the last lot without a scratch but not this time." I broke my heart over the news and cried for days. He used to smoke Gold Flake and always gave us a cigarette. He knew we only earned £2 a week and I kept remembering those little kindnesses.

'The next night, at about 2 a.m., I got word that my house had been hit. The Station Officer drove me home and left me standing in the road outside what remained of the house, trying to find out what had happened to my parents. I was assured by the wardens that they were alright but they couldn't tell me where they were. Eventually, I found that they had been taken to rest centres at Dartford. Just to make things awkward, my mother was in one place and my dad in another at Darenth. I couldn't do much at that time of night so I returned to the station.

'Bombed-out personnel were entitled to a week's compassionate leave but that was no good to me; I had nowhere to go so I stayed at the station. The Station Officer told me I could have short leave whenever I wanted it so the first thing was to find my parents. I set off after breakfast and soon located them and arranged for them to be reunited. Then, I sent telegrams to my brothers in the Forces asking them to get leave to help in getting things sorted out. Then I went round to the house to see what bits and pieces I could salvage from the rubble. Finally, I registered my parents as 'bombed-out' at the local Housing Department and applied for new accommodation in the district.

'By now it was getting near black-out time and I started to walk back to the station, desperately in need of a cup of tea, when the sirens started up. I put my tin hat on and was hurrying along Bush Road towards the station when I heard a big one coming down. I lay flat in the road and put my hands up to protect my face. It went off with a tremendous explosion and I was struck with a shower of shrapnel; head, arms, back, legs, all over. I had seen wounds caused by shrapnel and imagined it would be very painful but this did not seem so bad, it was more like light punches. After a moment, surprised and thankful that I was still alive, I opened my eyes and looked around. All I could see was a mass of potatoes, onions, carrots, turnips lying all over the road. This was the 'shrapnel' that had pummelled me; it came from Painter's, the greengrocers which had received a direct hit. I felt more in need of that cup of tea than ever, so I brushed myself down and started to run home to the fire station before I became a target for something more dangerous than potatoes or onions!'

A queue forms at Jackson's fruit stall in Watney Street, Stepney, on the morning after a miserable night in the shelter. It was shopping as usual for the housewives, and business as usual for the stall-holders. The notice fixed behind the stall reflects the defiance shown by East Enders and their natural sense of humour. A few weeks earlier, Mussolini had claimed the Mediterranen as 'The Italian Lake'. But the oranges had arrived in Stepney and the Jacksons could not resist the jibe.

The Royal Arsenal at Woolwich is situated on the south bank of the River Thames, clearly signposted to approaching aircraft by the three-mile stretch of water comprising the Royal Docks lying in direct line ahead, less than half a mile across the river. Any disappointment Fireman Harry Berkshire and his mates, dallying among the blazing oil tanks at Thameshaven, may have felt in missing out on a call to the Arsenal, was soon dispelled. Enemy aircraft began nightly visits to London's premier ordnance depot and the lads from Station 42V followed, inexorably, on the heels of the raiders. Harry Berkshire recalls one particularly hairy night. Bombs were finding their targets within the Arsenal as a pump drew up at the main gate. The crew were given an encouraging shout by a couple of policemen 'Goodbye and good luck!'

Several buildings had been hit and were alight. As crews were getting their branches into position, shells in one of the magazines began to explode, sending shrapnel flying in all directions.

To Station Officer Moylan, Oi/c, 42V Station, a Royal Navy veteran, the conditions were similar to those he had experienced on the Mole at Zeebrugge during World War I, with the German garrison shooting off everything they had at the naval raiding party.

Ted Moylan kept his crew working from behind what cover they could find. Joined by other crews, they succeeded in preventing a building containing H.E. from becoming involved. The German airmen, keen to inflict a crippling blow on this major target, maintained a flow of H.E. and fire bombs on the sprawling acres.

They returned at intervals throughout the night to complement the barrage of flying metal from our own exploding artillery shells, but the combination of separated buildings and resolute firefighting, averted disaster. Out of the corner of his eye, Fireman Berkshire had a glimpse of Station Officer Cesana, from Plumstead Fire Station, a somewhat flamboyant character, standing in the midst of all the flying debris

WOOLWICH ARSENAL

London under attack in the early evening hours of Saturday, September 7th, 1940. The Woolwich Arsenal, where Station Officer Ted Moylan and the men of Station 42V battled with the flames, is indicated on the picture.

encouraging his men. Suddenly, a piece of shrapnel struck sparks from his helmet, an event apparently regarded as immaterial by 'Susie,' for he totally ignored it!

During the action, an official warned firemen that a serious explosion was imminent and all personnel should get out immediately. District Officer Frank Handley, who was the senior officer present, had a brief word with officers in charge of crews, and with the full support of their men, decided to hold their ground. What Handley and Moylan knew, but the others did not, was that they were standing over vaults containing nitroglycerine.

After a long, long night, their resolution paid off. The air raid petered out and all fires were extinguished. Undoubtedly, a major disaster had been averted, as the official who had seen his warning ignored, promptly reported to his masters. Some months later, the *London Gazette* announced the award of the O.B.E. to District Officer Handley and Station Officer Moylan. Station Officer Jim Harris, New Cross; Acting Sub-Officer Harry Kinlan and Auxiliary Fireman Ted Storer, both from Plumstead Fire Station, were awarded the George Medal.

The Official Citations told the story of the gallantry of all who played a part in saving South East London from disaster:

'They remained at their post in face of flying debris and exploding shells, thereby setting an example of courage to their comrades' . . .
'Outstanding courage in the face of great danger' . . .
'Stopping the fire at a particularly vulnerable spot saved a number of buildings and magazines' . . .
'Almost reckless courage when a fire occurred in a building containing high explosives.'

And that was the first, in Harry Berkshire's own words, 'of a number of uncomfortable visits to Woolwich Arsenal.'

The air raid wardens were local people, posted to their home districts to take full advantage of local knowledge. Their main duty was reconnaissance and the reporting of bomb damage, plus first aid to the injured and elementary firefighting. They were instructed and exercised in these operations in the days before the Blitz, but few can have had any realistic conception of the terrors induced by aerial bombardment or of the horror of being called upon to handle the mutilated bodies of friends and neighbours, screaming in agony and fear. Some wardens found the ordeal too much to endure but many carried on until specialist squads arrived.

The enemy seemed determined to obliterate the West Ham dock and industrial area, for he returned night after night to rekindle fires that had, so laboriously, been extinguished the night before and to pound the area afresh with H.E. bombs. Some of the occupants of the humble little Tidal Basin houses, unable to endure their frightful ordeal, packed a few treasured possessions into a perambulator, or whatever conveyance they could procure, and trekked off to find refuge with friends a few miles distant. Others, as night approached, sought sanctuary in the peace of Epping Forest, returning the following morning to cast apprehensive glances as they neared their homes, searching for signs of overnight damage. These moves, undoubtedly, saved lives, for Tidal Basin came under merciless attack night after night.

The few who stayed came in for another mauling. Survivors, dragged from the ruins of their homes and left with no possessions other than the clothes they wore, were taken to a rest centre established at the South Hallsville School in Agate Street. They presented a pitiable and, sometimes, sickening sight as they became aware of injuries and bleeding, overlooked in the bewilderment and shock as their homes collapsed about them. Some ranted and raved; others sat in shocked silence. Hysterical weeping and wailing came from the bereaved whilst complete families sat together in tight embrace, perhaps saying a little prayer for their deliverance.

The rest centre staff, themselves in a state of shock for they, too, were in the midst of the falling bombs, coped as best they could. This was their first experience of the horror but, unhappily, there was much more to follow and they became expert in dealing with situations they now felt to be chaotic. Tea, the universal panacea, was handed round and a start made on registering the names and addresses of those admitted to the centre. Men and women were demanding to be told what was to happen to them and were told 'Don't worry. We'll get you away.'

The harassed officials, overwhelmed by the sheer weight of the problem and the demands of the homeless to be removed to a safe area, strove to arrange accommodation and transport. The officer dealing with the people at Agate Street telephoned a transport firm and ordered coaches to rendezvous at 'The George' at 3 p.m. on Monday. It did not occur to him to give the full address 'The George, Wanstead.' Everyone in East London knew The George; it was on the destination boards of buses crossing London every day and it was a favourite pub with day trippers to the Essex countryside.

But the coach operator had another 'George' in mind and the coaches were ordered to the wrong address. By the time

South Hallsville School, Agate Street, after the rescue squads had left. Houses in the streets surrounding the school were so severely damaged that they were abandoned, and all civilians were moved from the district. Later in the war, as plans for the invasion of Europe were put in hand, troops used the area as a practice ground for street fighting.

the mistake was sorted out, it was too late for transport for that day. 'We'll fix it for you tomorrow' said the man.

That night a large bomb hit the crowded rest centre and many of the hapless refugees, together with tons of debris, collapsed into a vast crater. Rescue workers faced a harrowing task.

Joe Withrington, a hard-bitten six feet two, fourteen stone Stratford fireman, wept as he described the scene to me. It was a time for rumour and the number of casualties said to have occurred increased with each telling. People spoke of four hundred and fifty dead but the official casualty list is now seventy-six. It was, nevertheless, still a major tragedy by any standards.

It was impossible to predict where the next bomb would fall but any Tidal Basin street would be a good bet. As some enjoyed lucky escapes, so others walked into trouble.

A soldier, commencing seven days leave, arrived at his Stratford home in the middle of an air raid and made his way to the Anderson shelter in the back yard. His wife and two children were sheltering there and the family reunion took place to the accompaniment of falling bombs. Then came a lull and the wife suggested she go and make a pot of tea.

'No, I'll go' said her husband. 'You stay here with the kids.' He was in the kitchen when the Anderson shelter and its occupants were wiped out by a direct hit.

Stories of this nature could be matched by others from all parts of the Capital. Firemen turned their hands to rescue work whenever the fire situation allowed but there were few who could be spared during those early nights.

Howard's timber yard on the bank of the River Lea at Canning Town carried a large stock of choice hardwood. The yard was one of the early victims of the bombers and one of the few successes for the oil bomb incendiaries used in considerable numbers during the first attacks on London. The timber stacks were saturated with oil and swamped with magnesium bombs; so many individual fires were started that the yard was doomed from the start. It became a raging inferno and blazed all night, despite the availability of ample water from the river. It was still roaring away as dawn broke

It was estimated that only 20 percent of the incendiary bombs dropped on urban areas would find flammable targets; the remainder would fall on roads, gardens and open spaces. Not all of them fired on impact; those that did burned with an intense white glare, scattering showers of molten metal particles over an area of six to eight feet. They had considerable penetrative power and would easily pierce the average tiled roof. Teenagers quickly learned to grasp a burning incendiary by the fin and give it a sharp whack on the kerb which caused the burning part to fall off, leaving the remainder as a souvenir of the night's activity. But the advent of the explosive incendiary introduced a note of caution.

and the All Clear sounded, with twenty pumps crews at work. There was no hope of saving the timber; much had already been destroyed, but it was essential to subdue the flames before nightfall so that West Ham Control could report to the Regional Fire Control at 4 p.m. 'No fire showing a light after black-out time.'

West Ham Fire Chief, Henry Johnson, made a bold decision. He ordered all pumps except four to withdraw. the crews to return to their stations for a meal and to rest. The remaining pumps would ensure that the fire would be kept within bounds, the main body being left to burn. It was arranged that ten pumps would return at 4 p.m. to make an onslaught on the remaining fire; in two hours the object had been achieved. In normal times, such action was unthinkable. A fire of such dimensions would have made front page news but, in early September 1940, it was only one of many in the medium range. There were several much larger, and all burning at the same time. Two nights later, the Luftwaffe rekindled what remained of the timber. This time, extinction was more speedy.

Half a mile down the Victoria Dock Road lay Pinchin, Johnson's paint factory, prominent on West Ham Fire Brigade's danger list. The works covered a large area between North Woolwich Road and the river front. In addition to the extensive buildings, vast quantities of highly flammable paint and varnish-making materials were stored in the large open area surrounding the works. A fall of incendiaries had ignited barrels of resin and fire was rapidly spreading. A senior officer had sent a message calling for the attendance of ten pumps when . . . whoosh. A small high explosive bomb burst in the centre of the yard, blowing out most of the fire as one would a candle. The firemen heard it coming and took cover, all escaping without a scratch. Thanks to the bomb, only a little damping down was required. The reinforcing pumps were put to work on the factory next door.

Rarely had the moon shone with such brilliance and from such clear skies as it did during those September and October nights. The River Thames, with its wide bends and sharp loops, provided a perfect signpost for the bomber pilots. The surface of the river reflected the light of the moon like a mirror, pointing unerringly to any target the enemy cared to select, and with over seven hundred square miles to aim at, it was difficult to miss finding significant targets.

I was drinking a cup of tea in the mess room at seven-thirty when the telephone rang. It was Mrs. Turley, telling me her husband was to be interred at eight-thirty that morning. I was dirty and unshaven and hastened to clean up, rounding up a

A stock of valuable newsprint goes up in smoke and the steel roof girders show signs of giving way under the heat. Replacements will have to be brought in by ships of the Merchant Navy, through the U-Boat hunter packs. Many of us experienced a feeling of dismay when essential materials were destroyed. It counted, in our minds, as a victory for the Luftwaffe.

few colleagues on the way. Together, we hurried to the cemetery where we formed up at the gates, just in time to meet the cortége. There was delay in starting the service. The priest called me aside and explained that the grave had been dug overnight but a nearby bomb explosion had filled it in. Work was proceeding and he hoped to continue without too much delay. We spent an uncomfortable ten minutes or so with the grieving relatives before the priest came to commence the service.

The onslaught on the Capital continued for fifty-seven consecutive nights, after which London was given a night's respite, for which we had to thank bad weather on the Continent. Bombing was resumed the following night until the city had suffered nightly attack for nearly three months.

The climax came on Saturday, September 15th with massive attacks on the south-eastern counties. The enemy found the defences active and alert. Spitfires and Hurricanes tore into the massed bombers with such effect that they withdrew, marking the virtual end of daylight raiding.

Night bombing, however, continued unabated, but the objectives were no longer the docks, the factories, power stations and gas works, etc. Now they set out to achieve the greatest destruction by explosion and fire. But the people showed their fibre in the midst of all these trials. They had been severely shaken by the intensity of the bombardment but quickly learned to adjust to what, clearly, was to be a long siege. They had been promised only blood, toil, tears and sweat and these they had to endure, but they gained some comfort from what the R.A.F. boys were doing to Göring's arrogant Luftwaffe, now playing second fiddle and being forced to acknowledge it.

OFFICIAL NOTICE

THE FOLLOWING INFORMATION HAS BEEN RECEIVED FROM THE MINISTRY OF HOME SECURITY :-

AIR RAID CASUALTIES IN THE WHOLE OF THE METROPOLITAN POLICE DISTRICT BETWEEN 6.30 p.m. SEPTEMBER 11th AND 6.30 p.m. SEPTEMBER 12th, were :-

KILLED 356. INJURED AND TAKEN TO HOSPITAL 377.

6.30 p.m. SEPTEMBER 12th AND 6.30 p.m. SEPTEMBER 13th

KILLED 129 INJURED AND TAKEN TO HOSPITAL 185.

6.30 p.m. SEPTEMBER 13th AND 6.30 p.m. SEPTEMBER 14th

KILLED 265. INJURED AND TAKEN TO HOSPITAL 137.

THIS STATEMENT, IT IS DESIRED, SHOULD BE POSTED AT THE TOWN HALL AND OTHER CONVENIENT CENTRES AS SOON AS POSSIBLE, BUT MUST NOT BE PUBLISHED IN THE PRESS.

MAYOR AND A.R.P. CONTROLLER.

Town Hall.
16th September, 1940.

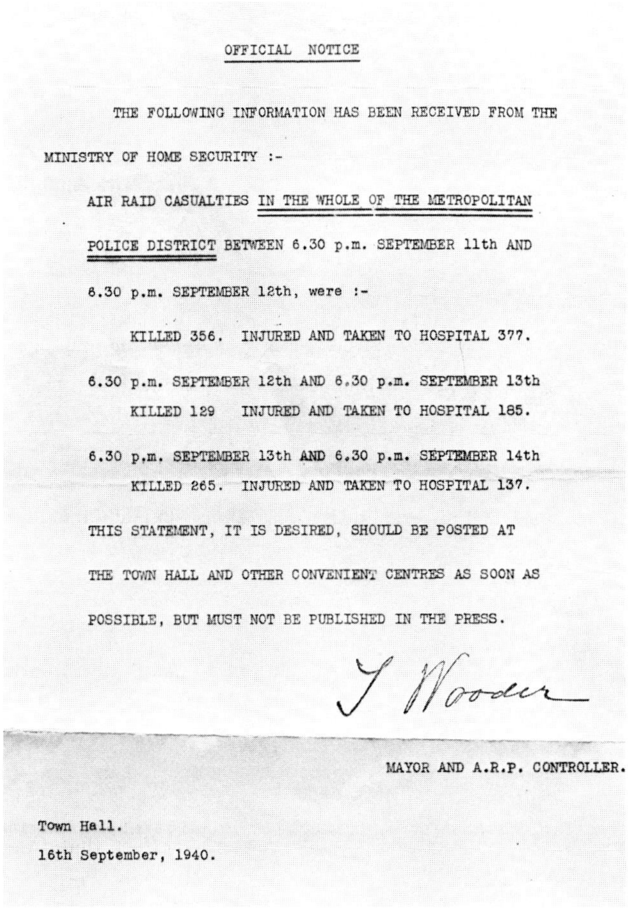

This casualty list was posted outside West Ham Town Hall.

With the abandonment of daylight raiding, the Luftwaffe set its pattern for the destruction of London by instalments. As darkness fell, the leading Nazi squadrons swamped the congested dockland factories and installations with H.E. and fire bombs, then turned for home to refuel and bomb up for the return trip, other formations probing the riverside areas for important targets.

Down on the riverfront at Silvertown, Fred Dell and his lads from No. 16 Station were enjoying a smoke. They had been battling with a difficult and dirty fire in a cattle-cake mill for several hours and had earned their stand-easy. They gazed across the river to the boroughs of Greenwich and Deptford, standing under a crimson canopy, with patches of pink marking the location of the larger fires. Fountains of brilliant light stabbed the sky as parachute mines and large H.E. bombs blasted great gusts of flame, dust and debris high into the sky. The dull, booming thunder of explosions came rolling across the river.

'Those poor sods over there are taking a real bashing,' remarked Fred to Auxiliary Fireman George Cumberland. They had survived their own 'real bashing' earlier in the evening and could anticipate a return visit from the bombers before the night was through. But, for the moment, they had sympathy to spare for the folk south of the river.

In the docks, several ships had been hit and set on fire. West Ham Fire Chief, Henry Johnson, was touring the dock area when he came upon a solitary fire crew at work on a 7,000-ton cargo steamer, its superstructure well alight. The men were playing long shots from the quayside, aiming their jets at the fire twenty feet above their heads with, of course, little effect. The Chief went storming up to the leading fireman in charge.

'What the hell do you think you're doing,' he roared. 'That's no way to tackle a ship fire. Haven't you been on a ship job before?'

'I've never SEEN a ship before' replied the man.

'Where do you come from?'

'Rugby.'

'Oh, well,' replied the Chief. 'I suppose I'd better find some of my roughnecks.' But his roughnecks were rather thin on the ground at that time and he had to collect a crew working on a nearby warehouse. Eventually, the fire was extinguished by firemen working at close quarters and the lads returned to Rugby after a novel lesson. But the experience gained was unlikely to be of much use to them back home.

3 'Getting used to it'

THE first few days of the Blitz left me with a feeling of consternation at the heavy loss of life and the appalling damage to buildings and installations. Massive factories, engaged in producing goods and materials of vital importance to the war effort, were reduced to piles of bricks and mortar or blackened shells. Great bomb craters pitted the streets, blocking the highway and revealing cast iron gas and water mains lying shattered side by side. Power cables were ripped from their conduits and multi-coloured telephone cables, hundreds of pairs of them, lay torn and twisted in a jumble of loose ends. I wondered how long we could continue to absorb the damage that was being inflicted nightly; it seemed that London was being reduced to a heap of rubble. But the repair men demonstrated what they had been doing during the 'Phoney War' period and emerged to achieve the daily miracles that restored shattered services.

Telephones began to ring in an incredibly short time. 'This is the Post Office engineer testing. What is your number, please?' and we were back in business. Electric power was restored then water, tasting strongly of chlorine but water, none the less, came flowing from the taps. The gas men took a little longer but their task, perhaps, was more difficult than their sister services. London Passenger Transport Board crews were out with their mobile towers repairing broken trolley-bus wires in time for the first services. The morning milk reappeared on doorsteps and bread continued to be baked and distributed despite all the difficulties.

Queen Mary's Hospital, Stratford, was an early victim of the bombing, suffering a direct hit in the first minutes of the raid. Despite casualties, the medical and nursing staff, supported by ancillary services, treated the constant stream of injured civilians brought in from surrounding streets. The people were simply magnificent in their skill and devotion to duty and their collective performance contributed a powerful boost to public morale. The enemy had knocked us wobbly with his opening attack but the repair squads and ordinary service workers responded with a resilience that lifted the general population to its feet. With nightly visits from the Luftwaffe, it was inevitable that some services, so skilfully and laboriously restored during the day, were again disrupted that night. The repair gangs had a word for it, in fact several words, but back they came to put things right all over again. And the Germans gave up before they did.

This bomb crater in The Strand, near the Gaiety Theatre, reveals shattered service pipes.

It became a matter of pride to West Ham firemen to make sure that their Control was able to report to Regional Fire Control at 4 p.m. each day 'No fire showing a light after black-out time in this district' no matter how arduous the night's action had been. And it was no less a matter of pride to all the Public Utilities repair squads and the factory workers and the food distributors and all who made their motto 'Business as Usual' a message of defiance to the enemy and of encouragement to neighbours to carry on.

Our diet in the fire station during those early days of the Blitz, when food supplies were temporarily suspended and we were deprived of gas and electricity for cooking, consisted mainly of corned beef sandwiches washed down with endless cups of tea. My stomach had been turned by gruesome sights and I had little appetite for food. The stink of the paraffin oil stoves over which we boiled our water was a further disincentive to eating. But as I became accustomed to this new mode of existence, my appetite returned and I even managed to swallow some dried egg, reconstituted with a little milk and water and fried in a pan over a paraffin oil burner . . . Ugh. I cast hungry eyes at the butcher's shop at the corner of Plaistow Road. I had made an occasional purchase there in the days before rationing and knew the manager to be a brusque, unsmiling man, the sort one did not bother to crack a joke with. It was Friday, September 13th, hardly a day propitious for asking favours but I was hungry and craved a cooked meal centred around a substantial steak. I marched into the shop, walked up to the manager and came straight to the point.

'I haven't had a decent meal for a week and I have no meat coupons.'

'Got any money?' he asked.

'Oh, I've got money,' I replied.

'What d'ye want, then?'

'Can you let me have a bit of steak?' He made no reply but gave his knife a few rubs on the steel and selected a choice piece of meat. It seemed a moment to push my luck.

'There are five of us,' I ventured, hopefully. He cut two enormous steaks and put them on the scale.

'Two and a half pounds. That do you?'

'Fine,' I replied.

'Come and see me again,' he said, as he gave me my change. 'Can't promise steak every time but I'll find you something.'

I thanked him and hurried across the road with my prize. In the mess room we soon had the steaks sizzling alongside a pot of potatoes, dug from the school allotment. We could not have enjoyed our meal more if we'd been dining at the Ritz. Talk was of lamb chops and tomatoes for lunch, next day.

Blitz firefighting brought a new dimension to firemen. Fires behave much the same however started, but the conditions under which they had to be fought introduced fresh hazards, as Station Officer Earl and his men found, early in the Blitz, when turning out to a fall of incendiaries in Bisson Road, a street of small houses in Stratford. As the fire station doors swung open there was a tremendous explosion about a hundred yards along Stratford High Street and the Times Furniture showrooms collapsed in a heap of debris following a direct hit. Glass came crashing from all windows in the vicinity and a vast cloud of dust billowed along the street, accompanied by a volley of bricks, masonry and other lethal missiles. The drivers paused a moment, then nosed their appliances through the thinning dust, picking up speed as they emerged into the clearer atmosphere. It took only a few minutes to reach Bisson Road. Incendiary bombs lay burning on the road and pavements and several small fires were

The Times Furniture Store stood on the bombed corner site in Stratford High Street, wrecked and set on fire by a high explosive bomb. The shored-up building next door was West Ham's Civil Defence Headquarters, which had to be evacuated when smoke from the burning store entered the Control Room in the basement.

This is the burnt out Control Room at the West Ham Civil Defence Headquarters in Stratford High Street. The reinforcing steel girders have done their job, but fire from the Times Furnishing Company's premises next door could not be prevented from spreading. The Assistant Controller, Bill Gillman, described how smoke percolated into the Control Room, growing steadily thicker until it was no longer possible to continue. Said Bill, 'I said to the women Control Room staff, "All right, girls, time to leave," but none of them moved, although they were suffering from the effects of smoke, coughing and spluttering and wiping their eyes. "Did you hear what I said?" repeated the Controller, "It's time to go." "But we've still got calls coming in," said one, and I had to pull the switchboard plugs before they would leave their seats and run along to the secondary control at the Borough Theatre, a couple of hundred yards along the street!'

beginning to take hold on roofs. Flames could be seen flickering in upper floor rooms as firemen put their shoulders to doors to gain entry. Hose reels were run out to deal with the more threatening of the fires whilst other crew members made good use of stirrup pumps and buckets of water provided at front doors for just such an occasion. Most of the residents were in their backyard Anderson shelters, blissfully unaware of the threat to their homes. What their reaction was on emerging after the raid, to find evidence of fire damage to a bedroom or the roof, plus a busted front door, is not on record.

The crews carried out a final check before leaving and noticed a light moving in an upper floor window. Station Officer Earl beat a rat-a-tat on the door knocker and an old lady appeared. 'Need any help?' he enquired. 'No, it's all right,' she replied. 'I've put it out.' 'Better let me have a look,' said Earl as he ran upstairs, accompanied by a fireman with the hose reel.

An incendiary bomb had struck the window sill and rebounded into the room, starting a small fire. But there was nothing for the firemen to do, for she had scooped up the bomb in a shovel and dumped it in a bucket of water. Then she set about the burning bedclothes and put them out, too.

'That's a nice job, ma,' said Eric Earl. 'But you should have been in the shelter, y'know; they're still about' — a reference to the drone of enemy aircraft overhead.

'Not me,' she replied emphatically. 'I ain't goin' down no shelter for 'Itler nor anybody else. 'Sides, if I'd been down there my 'ouse would've burnt down!'

The Station Officer couldn't find an answer to that, so he said good night and made his way back to Stratford Fire Station for further orders.

'We had been ordered to West Ham Fire Control but only got as far as Stratford Broadway when we were collared by an officer who told us to get to work on a row of shops, well alight, in Stratford High Street.' Leading Fireman Tom Stothard was relating his experiences on one of the most momentous nights during his fire service career.

'I decided to use a branch holder and was giving it all my attention when I became aware of something strange. All the din of the Blitz was going on; the sound of bombs exploding not very far away, the roar and crackle of the fire, the guns banging, the pumps revving at full speed but my unease had nothing to do with any of that. The sight in my left eye is not good and I had this weird feeling that something was wrong on that side. Turning my head I think my heart turned over for there stood a blooming great railway cart horse, his head almost resting on my shoulder. I suppose his stable had been hit and he'd been shooed out, wandering down to the High Street. Like most of us on a night like this, I expect he was glad of a bit of company; probably picked me out as a nice, friendly looking bloke. What do we do about this? The first thing was a gentle rub on his nose with the back of my hand. There were some men across the road watching the fire so I took the horse by the head harness and led him over. "Look after this for me," I said to one of the men and walked away before he could argue.

'A bit later I was checking around the back of the fire when I stumbled over a body lying on the pavement. It turned out to be a fireman but I couldn't find out what had happened to him. Queen Mary's Hospital was just around the corner in West Ham Lane so I picked him up with a fireman's lift and carried him there. The passage leading to the Casualty Ward was crammed with people waiting to be treated, many with splinters of glass sticking out of their faces. Others were lying on the floor, covered in blood. There was no room for my man so I took him into the ward and handed him over to a nurse. As I put him down, she said to me: "You'd better do something about your trousers."

"What's the matter with them," I asked, looking down.

"You've got no behind in them," she replied. I was quite unaware and have no idea where I ripped them but I wonder I did not feel the draught.

'I walked back to the job, clutching the flapping piece of cloth that once had been the seat of my pants, and just as I reached my pump I saw a most amazing sight. A bomb hit Gould's flour mills at Bow Bridge setting off a great, swirling ball of fire which rose high into the sky. It was a dust explosion, a well-known hazard connected with flour mills and similar places where combustible powders accumulate. And I never heard the bang!

'About this time it came on to drizzle. A canteen van arrived and I thought I had earned a cup of tea. So I joined the queue and had almost reached the counter when a fireman came running up, out of breath and very agitated.

'"Can anybody come and help me? I think our pump operator's dead." A couple of us ran along the road and there was a fireman slumped in the back of his towing vehicle, a taxi cab. Apparently, he had made himself snug inside, out of the rain, but the pump, still running, had filled his shelter with carbon monoxide. There was not much we could do so I told two of his mates to carry him round to Queen Mary's. I never heard what happened to him; I think he was dead.

The raid seemed to have quietened down and we had finished off our job. My part time crew and myself had our jobs to go to in a few hours time so I got them together and we set out for home.'

On Sunday, December 8th, 1940, the personnel attached to West Ham Fire Brigade No. 16 Station, Gainsborough Road, assembled for morning parade. The roll was called; the off-going watch was dismissed and duties for the day were read out. Drivers checked petrol and oil and the equipment on their appliances.

Routine duties were suspended on Sundays except for operational requirements and the men settled down to a leisurely day, reading the newspapers, playing cards or just sitting around chatting. Fred Dell, their officer-in-charge, had been encouraging those who would be on duty over the Christmas holiday to plan a modest programme of entertainment and several bright ideas had emerged. 'Of course, it all depends on Jerry,' remarked Fred. 'If HE decides he wants to spend Christmas at home, that'll suit us down to the ground.'

No. 16 Station had enjoyed a reasonably quiet week, with only two nights of minor enemy activity, a well-earned respite after the hectic operations of the past three months. They had endured rather more than their fair share of action, receiving their baptism of fire at the Thameshaven oil depot, two days before the commencement of the London Blitz. Returning to London, their regular nightly tryst with demon fire ranged between the Royal Docks and the string of industrial complexes stretching along the riverside from North Woolwich to the River Lea. They had been frozen and fried night after night; choked with a mixture of chemical fumes and the vile products of various combustibles. They had known fear and had narrow escapes from bomb bursts and falling masonry but, in spite of all, had managed to laugh and joke together. Adversity had bound them into a tightly knit community.

Although thankful for their present inactivity, they were not deluded into thinking it would last. Jerry would come back, literally with a bang. Experience had taught them that one of their major problems would be lack of sleep so, when Fred Dell called them together during the early evening, his words needed no explanation.

'Better get your heads down early tonight, lads. Get a bit o' shut eye while you can.' There was no dissent and they drifted towards the dormitory. At 8 p.m. the former cookery annexe at Gainsborough Road School was silent. Auxiliary Fireman Len Townrow was the only man awake; he was on duty in the watchroom.

At about twenty minutes to ten the telephone from Stratford Fire Control rang: air raid message 'Yellow.' This was the early warning that enemy aircraft were approaching the coast and Len Townrow made the appropriate entry in the station log book. Five minutes later came the second stage: air raid message 'Purple' indicating that raiders had reached the coast. This was followed at once by 'air raid warning Red,' notification that the bombers were heading for London. The distant wail of the sirens was taken up locally, swelling the melancholy moaning that never failed to leave me feeling sick, mentally and physically.

This cheerful group was photographed in September 1939, soon after the station was established. Only the two regular firemen seated in the centre had experience of uncontrolled fire at that time; the others were pitched in at the deep end a year later when the Luftwaffe attacked the oil depots at Thameshaven and Shellhaven and set them on fire. Then followed the massive raids on the Royal Docks and surrounding industrial areas when these chaps were engaged in Blitz firefighting for 57 consecutive nights. Then came the tragic night when five of the men in this picture were killed. Fred Dell, who was in charge (seated, third from right), Fireman Harold Marriott (on Dell's left), Fireman Alf Cumberland (third from left, centre row), Fireman Ted Badland (left, front row), and Fireman Albert Eyre (next to Badland). Fireman Len Townrow (centre, back row) was the sole survivor. Fred Dell was wearing a jacket similar to this one on the fatal night. Next morning, a member of No. 16 Station's complement, who had been off duty the previous night, was searching the debris and came across a cloth 'patch' pocket, ripped from a fireman's undress jacket, the flap still fastened by the small brass button. Inside were Fred's papers, including his driving licence, half perforated by a small piece of shrapnel the size of a split pea.

The faint drone of approaching aircraft penetrated the watchroom and Len Townrow decided that it was time to warn his sleeping comrades, but, before he could do so, there came the shrill whistle of a falling H.E. bomb, followed by an explosion that brought down the watchroom and buried him in the debris. He lost consciousness momentarily, but

remembers becoming aware that he must go to the aid of his mates. He staggered towards the cookery annexe, now illuminated by the flare of a burning gas main. The dormitory was wrecked and he heard groaning coming from under the debris. Len was a plumber and gas fitter in civvy street and his instinct was to find the valve and shut off the gas but, as his mind cleared, he realised he must summon help. Miraculously, the telephone was still working and he spoke to Fire Control. 'No. 16 Station's had a direct hit. Help required.' He remembers a calm female voice replying 'Stand by' before he passed out.

Auxiliary Fireman Len Townrow recovered consciousness in Queen Mary's Hospital, Stratford, his multiple injuries splinted and bandaged. It was two days later, after he had been transferred to St Margaret's Hospital, Epping, that he

Seven of the ten men killed on the night of December 8th, 1940 were buried at the East London Cemetery, three were interred privately. Here the funeral procession is seen entering the cemetery, with each flag-draped coffin carried on a West Ham fire pump. The first figure painted on the side panel of each pump is the fire station number: 'J6' was the London Fire Region cipher allotted to West Ham.

learned that the bomb had claimed the life of ten of his comrades, including the officer-in-charge, Fred Dell.

Len Townrow recovered from his injuries after six months but was judged medically unfit for service as a fireman and he was discharged from the Auxiliary Fire Service in June 1941.

Seven victims of that fatal bomb were accorded a public funeral; three were interred privately. The Vicar of St

Matthias' Church, Canning Town, the Rev. W. D. Tarling, conducted the funeral service which was attended by relatives of the deceased and the Mayor and Town Clerk of West Ham together with several hundred firemen colleagues and representatives of the Police and Civil Defence Corps.

The Vicar, in a simple and touching address, spoke of his visits to No. 16 Station. He had known all the men and had come to admire them for their devotion to duty. 'We have come not to mourn, but to honour them,' he concluded.

The Rev. Tarling was regarded with affection by people living in this heavily bombed area. He was always to be found wherever there was action; his days and nights were spent in helping the distressed in every way possible. His services were particularly sought in form-filling and in arranging transport and accommodation for those who had been bombed out. Following his usual practice, The Rev. Tarling was on his way to a bomb incident near his church in Hermit Road when he sadly suffered the same fate as befell his friends at No. 16 Station, just a few weeks after he had conducted their funeral service.

'I was standing by the gate and heard this strange noise, like washing on a clothes line flapping in the wind.' Sub-Officer Jimmy James was recounting the story of his amazing escape from death one dark night during the Blitz. 'Couldn't see a thing; I'd never heard a sound like it before and hadn't a clue what it was. Then there was a thump, over by the Greyhound.'

The 'strange noise' came from a parachute carrying a ton of high explosive which landed a matter of yards from the entrance to the auxiliary fire station opposite the Greyhound pub in Abbey Road, Stratford, where Jimmy James was standing. He moved forward to investigate and was feeling for his hand lamp when the mine exploded. Behind him, the school wall came crashing down. A few yards ahead, the pub was blasted into a great heap of rubble and there was Jimmy, laying in the road between heaps of masonry piled on either side. He staggered to his feet dazed, half-blinded by the flash and deafened by the explosion but otherwise unhurt. It is incredible that he was not blown to small pieces, with no trace of his body ever found. Had he remained standing by the gate, he would have met the blast that shattered the wall. Had he taken a couple of paces more, it most certainly would have been the end for Sub-Officer James.

This story will not surprise those who lived in bombed areas and witnessed the strange manifestations of blast. The sight of the wall of a terrace house, severed by blast from its neighbour as though by a stroke from a giant meat cleaver, was a common experience. One marvelled at the direction of the blast, powerful enough to demolish a substantial building, yet left a clock and small ornaments standing on a narrow mantelshelf and a picture hanging squarely from its hook, open to the gaze of passers-by in the street.

In my own home, glass in a casement window was shattered by blast from a bomb at the rear of the house, yet no glass was broken in the lean-to greenhouse which entirely surrounded it. By the same blast, water in a bowl of roses standing on a table by the window had been scooped from the bowl and lay in a pool on the polished table top, leaving the flowers undisturbed and standing supported by a pin-holder, exactly as they had been arranged!

'Blimey, I was lucky,' murmured Jimmy James. 'I'll never get killed after that.'

And he wasn't, but he never had a closer shave.

Mr and Mrs Ray of Finsbury Park, North London, with two policemen and a neighbour examine an unexploded landmine which landed in their back garden.

As autumn nights lengthened with the approach of winter, the enemy strategy underwent a change. Attacks by large raiding forces of two hundred or more aircraft were replaced by smaller formations which maintained bombing throughout the entire hours of darkness. The aim was to compel people to endure the discomfort of shelter life and deprive them of sleep. The outcome, it was anticipated, would be the breakdown of morale and loss of output in the factories.

The pattern soon emerged. Sirens heralded the approach of the bombers as darkness fell and the attack would commence at about 5 p.m. with a brisk burst of action followed by a lull. Then, another flurry from a fresh wave of raiders, followed by spasmodic bombing with H.E. and fire bombs throughout the night until daybreak at about seven-thirty. Some workers found themselves travelling home in an air raid, with all the frustration and dangers of interrupted bus and train journeys, and having to leave for work next morning with the raid still in progress.

Whilst these tactics placed great strain on the general public, the task of the Fire Service was considerably eased. Ample forces were available to cover the relatively few simultaneous incidents, and although fire crews were continually in action, the pace of the raid was slower and water supplies adequate for the task.

Research by Royal Air Force Bomber Command led to an enquiry addressed to the Fire Staff.

'In the light of your experience during enemy air attacks, what change of tactics by the Luftwaffe would cause you most concern?'

There was no hesitation about the reply.

'The concentration of a heavy attack into a very short space of time would swamp fire service resources, with the result that many fires would burn unhindered because they could not be attended and water supplies would be overrun.'

The point was taken. When the first 1,000 bomber raid was mounted by the R.A.F. on Cologne in May 1942, fifteen hundred tons of H.E. and fire bombs were dropped on the city in the space of ninety minutes, and the local fire service, indeed, was overwhelmed.

When R.A.F. reconnaissance aircraft reached the Dutch coast on their way to photograph the damage, navigators simply took as their guide the great column of smoke rising to a height of 15,000 feet above the stricken city.

The interior of St Paul's Cathedral, with debris piled on the High Altar following the raid of October 10th, 1940. Throughout the war, St Paul's was protected by a devoted band of 'Friends' who attended regularly, patrolling the roof and vulnerable areas during raids to guard against fire bombs. It is recorded that some 800 fire bombs struck the dome and roof of St Paul's, only one of which caused anxiety. This partly penetrated the dome and burned out of reach of the fire watchers and their stirrup pump jets. Presently the burning part broke away and the major portion of the bomb slid down the curve of the dome, coming to rest on the floor of the Stone Gallery.

When 'Moaning Minnie' began her wail shortly before 5 p.m. the signs were that we were in for one of those long drawn out nights. The threat of invasion had receded a little but, with every alert, anxious eyes scanned the skies on the look out for parachutists. Mr Churchill had warned the British people to be constantly on guard and to 'take one with you' if the attack came.

A few rounds of anti-aircraft fire were loosed off as the engine beat of a single aircraft, apparently circling the Stratford area, came woom-wooming from above.

'Wot's 'e lookin' for?' queried an auxiliary fireman of his companion, as they gazed vaguely into the sky. Whatever it was, a single bomb fell smack in the centre of Stratford gas works. Bomb splinters penetrated a gasholder and plumes of flame shed a flickering glare, lighting up surrounding gasholders and retort houses.

Station Officer Ernie Rayment and his crew of auxiliary firemen lost no time in dousing the flames by slapping poultices of sticky clay on the punctured plates, for the bomber could be heard still circling overhead. If his first shot had scored a lucky hit, they did not fancy being caught in the target area if the flames enabled the pilot to recognise a gas works!

I was sitting in the J District Control Room at Abbey Road School, chatting with my colleague, Tommy Homes, when a firewoman handed me a message slip. 'From Dagenham Control,' I read. 'Parachute troops landing on Dagenham Marshes.' The firewoman was calm but her eyes were wide as she searched my face. I endorsed the slip 'to R.F.C.' and the girl passed it to a colleague who immediately telephoned it to Regional Fire Control. The three firewomen sitting at the switchboard exchanged glances, but carried on quietly with their work. I knew that R.F.C. would pass the message to Home Office Fire Control; from there it would be flashed to the Cabinet War Room.

I also knew confirmation would be called for so I telephoned the Dagenham Mobilising Officer. Yes, the message had come from Messrs Peto and Gold's observation post; several parachutes had been seen descending on the marshes. Back came Regional Control and I passed on the confirmation, with details.

I walked over to a corner of the room and picked up the pickaxe handle which had been issued to repel boarders, and took Homes aside.

'I'm going to have one of the bastards, Tom. You stand over there to distract his attention; I'll stand behind the door and clobber him as he comes in.'

'Right,' said Tom and we waited for the sound of the approaching enemy. I was working out my plan of attack. No point in striking at his head; he'd be wearing a helmet. Better go for his collar bone; it might give me a chance of a second whack before he could use his gun.

Only later did it occur to me that I was completely barmy to imagine that I could see off an armed paratrooper with my measly club.

A new experience for firemen was the problem of dealing with 3-feet-long jets of flame issuing from the plates of gasholders punctured by bomb splinters. Gas company staff provided buckets of sticky clay, and firemen learned the technique of slapping a poultice of clay over the puncture. The job became complicated when clusters of burning gas jets spread 30 feet or so up the side of the gasholder, making it necessary to work from a ladder. Sometimes a spade was used to apply the clay in an awkward situation (as the senior officer is doing in the photo below), but the most common method was to slap on a handful. Men became adept at snuffing out a jet without getting burnt by its neighbour. The picture above shows a crew preparing to apply a poultice.

It all sounds so ridiculously melodramatic now, but it was painfully real at the time. We had been expecting to see enemy paratroops advancing along our streets since the early days of the Blitz, following the pattern of the German strategy that had been so successful against our Allies. We had seen them fall, one by one, before the might of German arms. Now the Dagenham report seemed to indicate that our turn had come.

I have thought about this many times since. My action, I think, reflected the gut reaction of many citizens at the time; witness Leading Firewoman Barry's reaction at Pageant's Wharf Fire Station on the opening night of the Blitz.

About ten minutes later, there was another message from Dagenham. The Mobilising Officer had resorted to fire brigade jargon in framing his report.

'False alarm given with good intent. Alarm caused by bomber's crew baling out.'

I blew out my cheeks and Tom blew his nose. The girls at the switchboard turned and gave us a weak grin as I walked over and dropped my pickaxe handle in its corner.

It was not until after the war that I learned of Mr Churchill's reaction to the report. He was not impressed, I was told, preferring to wait for confirmation from the Royal Observer Corps.

Paul Nash, one of the fireman artists who painted such vivid scenes of burning London, captioned one of his paintings 'The Fire Monster.' It was a strikingly apt title, for I always envisaged a large building ablaze as a living, roaring, leaping monster, eagerly advancing on fire crews as they struggled to subdue him, ever threatening to consume them with flame or engulf them with his debris, in a final, vicious thrust — and he seemed to have all the luck that was going!

Frequently, when hard-won progress was being made in checking the spread of fire in some strategically important zone, the hose would suddenly go limp and the water cease to flow. Debris from a collapsing building, somewhere in the rear, had buried hoselines. Men, clambering over rubble, laboured to restore the supply, but, by the time water was flowing again, the progress made in halting the spread had been lost. And the Thames always seemed to be at a low ebb at the time of the big raids, making it difficult to pump sufficient water from the river for firefighting. Borehole pumps, submerged from Thames bridges, were installed to provide water at all states of the tide. This supply was fed into six inch steel pipelines, laid in the streets to form a network to be tapped for firefighting at strategic points.

It was foreseen that sections might be fractured by bomb blast so, to minimise damage, divisional valves were fitted to isolate sections of the system should this happen. But this foresight was often frustrated when a valve was shattered, depriving firemen of their ammunition over a wide area. The repair squads worked hard to restore the flow, but vital time had been lost. Had water been readily available, many a fire would have been stifled at birth, instead of growing rapidly into a major outbreak.

After a period of nightly attacks, we had become accustomed to this new mode of existence and organised our lives accordingly. We had converted the front room on the ground floor of our house in Littlemoor Road, Ilford, into our shelter. I had made wooden shutters to cover the windows, which gave some protection and, additionally, helped with the black-out. Then we took delivery of one of the new Morrison steel shelters which I erected in the room. I was most impressed with the efficiency of these shelters, having seen a number of 'Morrisons' dug out from under the debris of totally collapsed houses and the families they protected released unharmed.

Littlemoor Road, like most, had its organised street fire parties, one of which was composed entirely of women. Each house had a pail of water standing by the doorstep with a stirrup pump, supplied by the Ministry of Home Security, at intervals.

My hours of duty in the hectic days before Christmas 1940 were 48 on with 24 off and although my children were still evacuated in Wiltshire, I returned home on my leave days to check on damage to the house and arrange for repairs when necessary.

I remember going home after the first week of bombing to find most of the windows shattered and a roll of bituminised paper standing in the doorway, presumably left there by the Council Works Department. My first job was to cut pieces to fit over the window frames and tack them up, where they remained, with occasional replacement, until the end of the war.

The front door had been blasted open and a sliver of timber, about eighteen inches long with the door latch attached, lay on top of the privet hedge. I tacked this back lightly and it became a repeat job each time we had a near miss. The sliver always landed in precisely the same place.

I had a particularly good crop of tomatoes ripening in the garden. When I went to pick a few I found them streaked heavily with smoke dust and pieces of charred paper, one a

The Morrison Shelter was a very robust and efficient form of protection. These children would stand a very good chance of being released without injury, even from under the debris from a demolished house. One of the steel mesh panels was left open to allow entry, but it was essential to re-fasten it when the shelterers were inside. The Morrison Shelter shown below was, in fact, recovered from under the debris from two houses.

bill head inscribed 'John Knight, Silvertown,' were lying in the border. John Knight's factory, in North Woolwich Road, Silvertown, is approximately six miles distant as the crow flies. As dusk approached, the daily job of drawing the black-out curtains was attended to and the bath, kettle and sundry saucepans, etc., filled with water for firefighting and domestic use in case the mains were fractured.

Inevitably, the sirens sounded at about 6 p.m. and the drone of bombers was heard. There was little activity in the Ilford area in the early hours of the raid and I took a walk along the road with the idea of having a word with the fire parties. But there was no one in sight in the whole street; probably they were eating their evening meal or listening to the radio, while they had the chance. The sky to the west was glowing with fire indicating that my mates at Stratford Fire Station were busy at their nightly task.

I had hardly settled down in my armchair when there came the swish of a shower of incendiary bombs. I grabbed my tin hat and rushed to the door. The street was ablaze with fire bombs along its length, spitting and spluttering and throwing out showers of dazzling white sparks while the entire population of the street, men, women and children, were out having a go. Bags of sand were dumped on bombs lying on pavements or the road. Enough buckets of water and stirrup pumps were available to deal with a dock warehouse fire, backed up by intrepid amateur fire crews.

I spotted a fire in an upper room of the house immediately opposite, occupied by an aged couple. I was concerned for their safety and rushed across the road; the door was unfastened and I entered. There sat the old couple in their chairs, entirely unaware that their bedroom was blazing.

'You've got a bit of trouble upstairs; we're going up to see to it for you,' I told the old man.

I was followed closely by the women's fire party, led by my next door neighbour, armed with a stirrup pump and bucket of water. She was followed by members of her party, carrying more pumps and buckets, all eager to go into action.

I led the way upstairs and showed the party how to use the bedroom door as cover, in case the bomb was explosive. 'Open the door only a few inches and put your hand round it, squirting the spray up towards the ceiling.'

Those women were absolutely first class; no excitement, no talking, except when they had something positive to say. 'Another bucket of water up here.' 'Give us a hand with the pump; I'm getting tired.'

Soon, it was all over and we crowded into the room where they had another lesson in dealing with smouldering embers. We had been lucky. Only one other house was set afire, and that towards the other end of the street.

I looked at their faces, flushed with exertion and showing justifiable satisfaction in a job well done. My impression was that they were rather disappointed that the action had come to an end. They were certainly ready to respond in similar fashion if Jerry left another visiting card.

The volunteer street fire parties stood ready with stirrup pumps and water buckets to protect their homes from the fire bombs. Their great advantage lay in being readily available to tackle an incendiary bomb fire before it grew to unmanageable proportions. The amateur firemen and women became very good at their job, easing the strain on the Fire Service, leaving the latter free to concentrate on major outbreaks.

My wife and I were becoming increasingly uneasy about our children. Alice had made several visits to Bradford-on-Avon to see them, each time finding it harder to return home leaving them in Wiltshire. Not that they were badly treated; on the contrary Mrs James and her family cared for them very well but the children were homesick and continually asked to be brought home. During a visit in the week before Christmas 1940 my wife spoke to a billeting officer and raised a question we were both concerned about and had been discussing at length.

'What will happen to our children if my husband and I are both killed and our home destroyed?'

'I don't rightly know,' he replied. 'I suppose they would be sent to an orphanage.'

Alice rang me as soon as she could and imparted this information. It was the nudge we required to prod us into action; the children were on their way home with their mother next morning.

We had seen the effect of bombing over the past three months and did not need to be told that London was no place for small children. On the other hand, the threat of invasion seemed to be receding. The kids missed us and how we missed them! And there seemed to be an understanding about the use of war gases; each side averred it would not be the first to use gas as a weapon.

So we were together for Christmas like many other local families whose children had been evacuated. Some came ostensibly, 'just for Christmas' but, like ours, remained at home for the duration.

There were problems, schooling for instance but these were overcome by co-operation between all concerned. We faced a common enemy and if there was a problem we faced up to it together and found a solution. We were not going to allow Hitler to disrupt our lives entirely.

We had imagined that our kids were too young to be affected by what was happening in London. But there were many older children who fed them lurid tales of London's ordeal. Later. we heard from them how they had feared for our safety. So, all in all, the advantages of being together as a family outweighed the dangers of living in a target area. Throughout the bitter winter of 1940-41, classes were held in our homes: each day a different house. Coal was in short supply, allowing each household a fire in one room only, the one set aside as classroom.

The teachers co-operated, trudging through foot-deep snow to visit each house in turn, and it was heart-warming, at least to parents shivering in an adjoining room, to listen to half a dozen youngsters repeating their lessons.

4   City Ablaze

CHRISTMAS 1940 passed quietly but, on December 29th, a large raiding force appeared over London at about 6 p.m. and showered the City — the Square Mile — with fire bombs and high explosive. All fire stations in the area were swamped with calls and reinforcements were mobilised from the whole of the London Fire Region.

Fires were joining up around St Paul's Cathedral and further serious fires were raging in Gresham Street, St Martin's le Grand, Moorgate and Queen Victoria Street. A fire involving the great warehouses in the Minories was out of hand, due to shortage of water, and the famous London Guildhall and the Wren Church of St Lawrence Jewry, nearby, were well alight. The Thames tide was at an abnormally low ebb when the raid began, making pumping from the river difficult. Fire boats pulled as close to the banks as possible, their crews wading ashore through thick mud, dragging hose lines to supply the land pumps with water. Many street water mains, as usual, had been fractured and with the great demands being made on those still carrying water, supplies were inadequate to control the great fires that were consuming the heart of London.

The area around St Paul's Cathedral was among the worst affected and the Prime Minister, appreciating what the Cathedral meant to the Nation, sent out an instruction that St Paul's, at all costs, was to be saved.

The great jumble of multi-storey buildings bounded by Ludgate Hill, Warwick Lane, Newgate Street and Paternoster Square, separated in some places by narrow alleys, received a deluge of fire bombs. Over three hundred incendiaries a minute were being showered on the City and the area around St Paul's rapidly became an inferno, with

The burnt-out interior of London's ancient Guildhall, reported to have been set afire by sparks and brands from nearby St Lawrence Jewry Church.

St Paul's Cathedral stands bathed in the glare from blazing buildings fringing the churchyard, December 29/30th, 1940.

flames bridging the streets. Debris cascaded into the narrow turnings as high explosive bombs ripped buildings apart, exposing the flammable contents to surrounding fire and the non-stop flood of incendiaries. Roads became choked with debris and it is doubtful if firemen, even with unlimited water supplies, could have made much impression on this particular area of fire.

But water was far from unlimited; it was in very short supply. Water relay crews heaved and sweated as they coupled up sections of fire hose and ran their fifty-foot lengths along the City streets from the river at Blackfriars Bridge, spurred to superhuman effort by the sight of the dome of St Paul's outlined against a background of flame, standing stark amid a myriad of swirling sparks and glowing embers.

The flow of precious water gushed all too slowly into the portable emergency dam that had been set up in St Paul's Churchyard at the top of Cheapside. Pump operators waited impatiently for sufficient depth of water to collect before commencing to pump vital fire streams, whilst members of the relay team stood having a breather before returning to Blackfriars to do it all over again.

The situation called for skilful placing of the few jets that stood between St Paul's and disaster, and it was only after long hours of slogging effort that the fiery advance on St Paul's was halted as the flames approached the Cathedral threshold.

The situation in the narrow streets around Paternoster Row, centre of London's book publishing trade, developed into a nightmare for firemen. It was the closest the Capital came to a firestorm, a phenomenon experienced in Hamburg and Tokyo in the great Allied air raids on those cities later in the war.

Picture a fire pump arriving at the job. The officer indicates the area of operation. 'We'll try to stop it there, lads.' The pump is set into a street fire hydrant and the operator crosses his fingers and prays that the mains will hold out, at least until the inevitable water relay arrives. The crew run out a line of hose along the street and two firemen work their way towards the target, clambering over heaps of debris and slithering on fragments of plate glass from shattered windows. As they proceed they splash their jet about dousing smaller fires as they advance shoulder to shoulder, arms linked to share the

This is Wallbrook, seen from the Mansion House. Reading the picture, the hose line appears to have been laid over debris, only to be buried by a later fall. It is not difficult to envisage the effect on firemen working further along the street when buildings behind collapsed, burying their hose and blocking an escape route. Situations like this were by no means unusual, and many firefighters, literally, were compelled to run for their lives after such a loss of water.

strain of the kicking branch. Their heads are bowed to protect faces from blistering heat and the stinging sparks, searing embers and hot ash swirling about the street, driven by the fierce winds that always accompany a conflagration. A crew mate lends a hand, easing the cumbersome line of hose over heaps of debris, avoiding snags and kinks.

The thump of falling incendiaries impels them to hunch their shoulders in the hope of reducing the target area of their

The wind carries heat and smoke towards these turntable ladders working in St Paul's Churchyard, December 30th, 1940. Men, normally at the head of the ladders, have been withdrawn as a safety measure. The monitors (nozzles) are throwing jets into the heart of the fire as the operators traverse their ladders to cover the area involved. This is the fire which came the closest to the Cathedral.

The 3,000-gallon Sportapool dam set up in St Paul's Churchyard was supplied with water pumped through hose lines from the river at Blackfriars Bridge, a distance of about half-a-mile. The entire output of British hose manufacturers was insufficient to satisfy the needs of the wartime fire service, and thousands of 50-foot lengths of rubber-lined hose were purchased from the United States. In pumping water over distances, loss of pressure due to friction in the hose is overcome by setting pumps into the line at 700-foot intervals. In a relay over half-a-mile, four pumps and approximately fifty lengths of hose would be required to provide one line, carrying about 200 gallons per minute. The American hose was of good quality, but heavy and bulky compared with ours. The couplings, too, were heavier, so that laying hose lines over distances was a time-consuming and very laborious job, particularly if American hose was being used. The pumps in the picture provided pressure for the jets that drove back fire threatening St Paul's.

bodies, for the eyewitness account of the screaming fireman in Pennington Street, Shadwell, with an incendiary bomb embedded in his back, is vivid in their minds. Despite the heat, they chance a quick squint aloft, on the lookout for collapsing walls or falling coping stones. They know that their officer will keep an eye open for such hazards, but he now has several crews to watch over and a large area to supervise. What was it they taught us in the drill class? One hand for yourself and one for the ship. Keep your eyes peeled.

They cry out with pain as glowing embers, driven by the mini cyclone, fly under the brim of their steel helmet and lodge on an ear, the neck or in an eye. But most stick it out, unless badly injured, for they know that the fire will engulf them if they let up and there are few reserves available if they quit. Many were the deeds of heroism performed that night. Brave deeds witnessed were reported and, subsequently, rewarded, but there were many that escaped notice in the widespread horror and destruction. It was a battle for the City and for personal survival.

Sidney Henry Burrow was a motor mechanic living in north-west London. As early as 1938 he was convinced that war with Germany was inevitable and he decided to take up some form of National Service. The London Fire Brigade had opened its drive to secure recruits for the Auxiliary Fire Service and 'Henry' Burrow was attracted by the posters calling for volunteers displayed outside his local fire station in West End Lane, Hampstead. That night, visiting his wife and newly-born son in hospital, he told his wife of his intention to join the A.F.S. So, next day, Henry visited the fire station and became one of the first volunteers to enrol in the newly-formed service.

After a few weeks he joined other recruits at West End Lane where they were instructed in the basic skills of the fireman's craft. As the men became efficient they were given rota periods standing by at the fire station, riding to any fire call that came in during their spell of duty. In this manner their interest was maintained and valuable fire experience gained but, like A.F.S. colleagues and regulars alike, they could have no idea of what lay in store for them when the Luftwaffe pulled out all the stops.

A few days before the official declaration of war, Auxiliary Fireman Burrow was enrolled for full-time service and posted to the Tower Garage at the junction of Finchley Road and Hendon Way, now designated A.F.S. Station 20U. The 'Phoney War' days were humdrum, enlivened occasionally by splashes of excitement at the larger peace-time fires and special service calls. Much of the time was taken up in perfecting their techniques.

The lads from 20U made their debut in the big league two days before the enemy launched the full weight of his attack on London. Their pump was ordered to the Thameshaven oil refinery on September 5th and the convoy had reached the Southend bypass actually being within sight of the smoke rising from the blazing tanks when it was strafed by an enemy aircraft.

The church spire of St Mary-le-Bow in Cheapside stands amid the shells of burnt-out buildings. The combination of high density, heavily stocked buildings, narrow streets, a heavy concentration of fire bombs and shortage of water offered firemen scant opportunity of controling a conflagration of this magnitude. But they persevered, suffered, and eventually succeeded in halting its progress. Picture taken from the dome of St Paul's Cathedral, March 1st, 1941.

'We baled out quick smart,' said Henry Burrow, 'and dived under the first cover we could find.' The enemy pilot also wasted no time and pulled away before he was spotted by a Spitfire. It was not until the 20U lads emerged that they found they had sheltered under a petrol tanker!

Back to London after the refinery fire had been brought under control, the crews from Tower Garage began their nightly involvement with Hitler's Blitz; the long nights of exposure to high explosive destruction from the air; to fires, the like of which they could never have imagined; to being soaked to the skin, then dried in the heat of the fires and soaked again in the early hours of the morning; to remain in that shivering condition until the time came to hand over to a relief crew. The sense of accomplishment came when they had been able to repulse fire and stop the spread to vulnerable areas, despite interruptions to their attack by water shortage. They experienced pride in the achievements of their comrades in the face of great personal danger, and a close-knit community spirit developed among the personnel at 20U Station.

Most of them had enjoyed a couple of days at home over the Christmas holiday, but the unofficial truce ended abruptly on the evening of December 29th. Shortly after the sirens had ceased their wail, 20U's pump was ordered to Redcross Street Fire Station in the City. Auxiliary Fireman Burrow, now 'Skipper' to his mates, watched the glow of fire rapidly expanding to encompass the entire horizon as they sped through Kentish Town. As they approached Redcross Street they found their way barred by piled debris in some streets whilst in others flames roared out of control. At the Fire Control, they were ordered to Jewin Street and instructed to prevent fire from crossing the street towards St Paul's. They found water in the mains and soon had two good jets working; it seemed that they would be able to achieve their object without too much difficulty but water pressure dropped and their jets became ineffective. The fire roared back and the men began to think of withdrawing. They shackled up their pump to the towing vehicle and were moving past the fires they were unable to control when buildings ahead came crashing down, barring their progress.

A typical auxiliary fire station group in the summer of 1940. They carry respirators in view of the possibilty of war gases being used. This picture was taken at the rear of 20U Station, Tower Garage. Second from left, standing behind the girls, is 'Skipper' Burrow. The men wearing peakless caps are regular LFB men, the others AFS men and women. Note the teenage messenger boys in the front row. Often scared out of their wits by the violence of the bombardment, I never heard of one refusing duty. They were more likely to try to jump the queue of those waiting to 'get on their bikes'.

Now seriously alarmed, they abandoned the appliance and set off on foot in the opposite direction. As they walked, the gutters suddenly began to blaze as burning oil flowed from a stricken building and soon the whole roadway was alight. Faces were scorched, hands were burned and their rubber boots caught fire. It was every man for himself and they ran around seeking a means of escape, slithering in the oil and incurring fresh burns in the process.

Henry Burrow, with his face scorched and hands badly burned, became confused, lost his sense of direction and his ability to think clearly. Suddenly, as he later related to his wife from his hospital bed, amid all the turmoil and din, flame

Jewin Street, just across the road from Redcross Street Fire Station, after the City Blitz. It was here that the men from 20U Station, surrounded by fire, found their road to safety barred by heaps of debris.

This picture speaks volumes. At the end of the lines of hose are courageous men who, in the face of great danger from falling debris, have battled their way to a position from which they are able to strike at the heart of the fire. Foremost in their minds would be the fear that the water supply might fail, leaving them defenceless against advancing flame. They take advantage of the protection against crumbling walls and flying brands offered by the small porches, and watch their powerful jets bore into the leaping, roaring wall of flame, apparently without effect. They begin to fear that the forces massed against them are too powerful to be overcome without assistance. The heat they face may be judged by the steaming road, and by the window frames above their heads, just beginning to ignite in the heat radiated from across the way. But that wonderful feeling of jubilation would follow the first signs that the fire was giving way and that they were about to triumph against all the odds.

and smoke, he had a vision of their small son beckoning from the doorway of a blazing building. He ran over and discovered stairs leading to the basement which he descended, finding relief from his immediate peril. He was unable to recall his movements after that but, eventually, he was discovered wandering in a street by a party of soldiers.

Next morning, firemen's wives went along to the station in accordance with the custom they had established, to help with the preparation of meals and to collect their men's saturated and grimy underwear for washing. However, none of the crews had returned and it was realised that it had been a really dreadful night. After two days there was still no news of Henry Burrow but members of his crew were discovered in various hospitals. They spoke of 'Skipper's' disregard for his own safety, returning to encourage his wavering comrades, dragging them to their feet and urging them to keep going, when all they wanted to do was to give up the struggle. They expressed their doubts that he could have survived.

That night came the dreaded knock at the door of the Burrow home. A policeman, very distressed at being the bearer of bad news, informed Mrs Burrow that her husband had been posted missing.

The soldiers who had found Henry Burrow realised that he was badly injured and secured an ambulance to take him to hospital. Eventually, he was identified and reported to be in St Bartholomew's. His wife visited him there and learned of his vision of the little boy and of his miraculous escape. Auxiliary Fireman Burrow spent several months in hospital for the treatment of his severely burned hands. Mrs Burrow told of being present on an occasion when his hands were being dressed: 'There was no flesh on them; just bones.' But Henry was a fighter and refused to accept that he would never drive a car again or hold things, as he had been told. He persevered with exercises and kept his hands moist with oil.

After a long struggle he proved the doctors wrong. Classed 'Unfit for active firefighting,' he was given employment as a mechanic in the fire service workshops in Pound Lane, Willesden. Back to the job he knew so well, he turned the work to advantage, exercising his hands in the most natural way, and regained much of his former dexterity.

There was talk of a decoration but, like so many acts of heroism during the Blitz, nothing came of it. After the war, Henry took his small son on a visit to the City area where he and his mates had endured their agony. Although he was unable to identify the streets amid the desert of rubble he told the little lad how he had appeared as a vision which had guided his dad and brought him to safety.

As men fought the fires, the enemy made the most of a well-lit target. Incendiary and high explosive bombs fell without pause; the heat was intense, igniting buildings across wide streets. Fire crews early on the scene found water available in the mains and their jets were quickly at work, checking the fire-spread faster than they dared hope. But pressure began to drop, as more and more pumps were set in and the jets lost their punch. The issue was decided when vital trunk mains carrying water to the City hydrants were shattered by a bomb.

It was a situation akin to an infantry battalion running out of ammunition in the midst of an enemy attack. There was only one course of action; retreat. Firemen watched helplessly as flames clawed out unhindered to embrace adjoining buildings.

The atmosphere was stifling. A shrivelling blast carried sparks and glowing embers to every corner of the street, sweeping them high into the air. Firemen, deprived of the protection of their jets, found breathing difficult and were forced back to positions where the air temperature permitted them to fill their lungs freely without searing the air passages.

St Giles Church, Cripplegate, enveloped in flames, threatened Redcross Street Fire Station from across the street. The whole of Jewin Street, adjoining the church and the buildings beyond, reaching back to Aldersgate Street, were doomed. Nothing could be done to save them, for great heaps of debris blocked access to the stricken area, even if sufficient water had been available to enable firemen to force entry between office blocks, blazing on each side of the street.

Up at the sharp end! Crews huddle around the branch in the early morning light after a night of back-breaking toil, fraught with great danger to life and limb. Sirens have sounded the 'Raiders passed' signal, but much remains to be done before the welcome order 'Home, lads' can be given. Fire blazes at the top of the alley, out of reach of the jet, but their officer judges it unsafe to allow a crew to approach over the debris. Meanwhile, he keeps a wary eye aloft for signs of crumbling walls. This picture was taken on May 11th, 1941 in Poppins Court, only a few yards from the spot where eight of their comrades had been killed when a building collapsed at the rear of the *Daily Express* office on December 29/30th, 1940.

Incendiary victim — St Giles, Cripplegate, December 29th, 1940.

Part-time Leading Fireman Stothard had spent Sunday on duty at the auxiliary fire station in Goodmayes Lane, Ilford. Tom Stothard was one of the early volunteers who had enroled in the A.F.S. in 1938. He had acquired considerable fire experience in the two years before the Blitz commenced and had multiplied that experience tenfold during the past three months. Tonight, he was in charge of No. 1 Trailer Pump with its crew of full-time auxiliary firemen. Like the others on this bitterly cold night, Tom was hoping that the lull in enemy activity would continue over the New Year holiday, but it was not to be.

Shortly after the sirens had sounded, the telephone from H.Q. rang: 'Order your No. 1 Trailer Pump to Whitechapel Fire Control.' Already the western sky was reflecting the fires in the City area as the Ilford pump and its crew sped along deserted streets, shrapnel from the anti-aircraft shells rattling on roads lit by clusters of incendiaries, burning with a brilliant white glare on road and pavement and spasmodically throwing out showers of sparks.

The leading fireman reported at Whitechapel and was given comprehensive instructions.

'Do you know Crutched Friars?'

'Yes.'

'Well, there's plenty of fire along there. Make for Crutched Friars and anything you pick up, it's yours!'

Passing Fenchurch Street Station, a large burning brand fell from the sky and landed with a thump on the roof of their towing vehicle; a hint, if they needed one, to find what cover they could. The railway viaduct from Fenchurch Street provided light shelter and they parked beneath its flimsy umbrella. As the officer at Whitechapel had said, there was plenty of fire and the Ilford men selected a warehouse building with fire showing in the basement and on the top floor, indicating that a shower of incendiaries had lodged in the roof whilst others had fallen down the lift shaft or stairs into the basement. Each floor had a loophole, an opening through which goods were lowered to street level by a wall crane, situated above the top loophole.

A ladder was pitched to the top floor and a branch taken up whilst other members of the crew tackled the basement fire. As they worked, the men were addressed by a voice from the opposite pavement.

'Look out for that crane, it's moving.'

Looking around, the leading fireman saw a man dressed in an ordinary lounge suit, without a hat, which struck him as rather strange on this bitter night. Then he noticed that the man was wearing a dog-collar and concluded that he was a priest from a local church.

'I'll stand here and watch that crane and call out when it moves.'

'And that's just what he did for about half an hour,' said Tom, 'putting the wind up us properly. It seemed quite secure to me but it was unnerving to hear his warning, time after time.'

'Then came a burst of machine gun fire from above and that was the last we saw of him.

'We finished off our warehouse fire and were then ordered to take a branch up into the roof void of Trinity House on Tower Hill, where a fresh fall of incendiaries had started more fires.

'We had a rough time there, narrowly escaping being cut off before a London Fire Brigade officer pulled us out. Even so, we had to run the gauntlet through a gush of fire crossing the staircase after a cluster of fire bombs came down behind us. It was then in the early hours. I was soaking wet and shivering and had to go to my job at the Department of Works in Westminster later that morning. So I asked an L.F.B. officer if I could be released. He agreed so I handed over my crew and set off for Horseferry Road on foot, clambering over fire hose that seemed to line every street in the City.

'I kept a change of clothes in my locker for just such an occasion and, after changing and a cup of tea in my office, I began to feel that life still had something to offer.'

Chief Superintendent Charles McDuell, Senior Superintendent of the London Fire Brigade, was recalled from short leave as the scale of the City raid became clear. Following a report on the situation from Brigade Control, the Chief Superintendent set out for Redcross Street Fire Station, in the heart of the City fire zone.

Appliances were flooding in from all corners of the London Fire Region; reinforcements from the large provincial cities were on the road. Outer London pumps were queueing in Redcross Street and the first job for Dave Millar, Mr McDuell's driver and general factotum, was to pilot their drivers through unfamiliar streets to their appointed fires, a regular assignment for Dave who had achieved a fair standard of physical fitness in the process; a ride to the fire, followed by a sprint back to the station to pick up the next, and so on.

Returning from one mission, Dave Millar found himself in Whitecross Street, where he had an alarming experience. Firemen working on fires on both sides of the road found themselves in a familiar situation; the water supply was failing. Jets lost power and fires began to take control in an alarming manner. Paintwork on fire appliances began to smoulder and tyres burst into flame. Rubber-lined hose and wooden ladders followed suit and, suddenly, retreat from Whitecross Street was blocked by a wall of fire at both ends trapping the firefighters in a rectangle of uncontrolled fire.

It was a desperate situation but, by great good fortune, someone in the party knew of a grating in the road leading to a tunnel. They descended and made their way beneath the fires into the safety of Farringdon Road market subway.

Woolwich Arsenal was enjoying a quiet night. The mobilising officer at New Cross Fire Control decided that the lads at 42V needed a change of scenery; they must be getting sick and tired of Woolwich Arsenal. So he ordered the pump from Burrage Road to report to the Guildhall quite early in the raid.

The No. 1 pump, with Station Officer Moylan, Leading Fireman Storey and Auxiliary Firemen Berkshire and Seely set off through the chilly streets, bound for the station officer's old stamping ground.

Fires in Whitecross Street took control when the water supply failed. Firemen were forced to abandon appliances and run for their lives. This picture shows burnt-out equipment a day or two after debris had been cleared from the roadway.

Arriving at Guildhall, they found the whole area ablaze and packed with fire pumps.

'Nothing for us, here,' remarked Ted Moylan. 'Drive along towards Chiswell Street and see what we can pick up.' There, they were attracted by banging on a large wooden door, with cries coming from the inside 'get us out of here.' The men from Woolwich soon had the door open and some twenty women and children ran out. Apparently, it was a shelter that had become threatened by fire at the other end.

There was no water in the street hydrants so Station Officer Moylan and his crew cast about, seeking water from any source to tackle the fires that surrounded them.

They found a large emergency supply in Whitbread's Brewery, which Moylan immediately announced he was taking over.

'This water belongs to Whitbread's Brewery,' said a man who turned out to be the officer in charge of Whitbread's private fire brigade. 'You mustn't touch it.'

'You try and stop me,' replied the station officer, instructing his crew to set in to the dam.

'I'll have your name and address,' replied the man. 'I intend to prosecute you.'

Station Officer Moylan was not dismayed. He knew that a fire officer was authorised to take possession of any water supply for the purpose of firefighting.

Whitbread's firemen were at work on internal fires when the London Fire Brigade pump set in beside them, taking its branches into the surrounding streets to drive back threatening fire.

Just a few of Winston Churchill's 'Heroes (and Heroines) with grimy faces'. The firewoman driver of an officer's staff car sits waiting for hospital treatment in company with firefighters straight from blitzed streets. Their faces reflect the shock and strain of the night's experiences but, after treatment and several cups of tea, normal good humour will return and they will be swapping stories and laughing over comic incidents.

But Whitbread's did not lose by the partial confiscation of their water, for, when morning dawned, Whitbread's was one of the few buildings standing more or less intact in Chiswell Street. The management's pre-Blitz decision to brick up the brewery windows contributed to its safety, but its salvation was due to the doughty work of firemen within and without the buildings.

Meanwhile, Harry Berkshire found himself clutching a high pressure jet, propped against a wall for support. He was standing under the cover of an archway but when his station officer came along he yelled 'Get the hell out of there!'

'I can't move,' Fireman Berkshire yelled back.

'Help him out, Storey!' ordered Moylan and the pair of them struggled clear a moment before the arch came crashing down.

'As the night wore on, we all began to suffer with our eyes,' said Harry Berkshire. 'Sparks were not floating about, they were being driven by the strong wind.'

Leading Fireman Storey came along the street, shading his eyes.

'Seen the guv'nor?' he asked.

'Not for some time,' replied Harry Berkshire.

'P'raps we'd better have a look for him,' replied the leading fireman; 'you never know.'

By the time water became available to tackle the fires in Fore Street Avenue, the barrage of bricks and masonry made entry impossible. The view is from Moor Lane.

They found him in Moorgate, leaning on a street rubbish bin, his hands covering his face.

'You alright, sir.'

'That you, Storey?'

'Yessir.'

'I can't see. My eyes are bunged up with sparks.'

'We've all got a dose of that, sir. I think we should go along to the hospital.'

'So we all went along to Moorfields Eye Hospital,' said Harry Berkshire. 'They put drops in our eyes and told us to return home and report to our local hospital on arrival.'

Despite his disability, Ted Moylan was able to direct the driver through the maze of City streets. Many of them on the direct route were impassable, due to fire or debris, but Ted's knowledge of the district enabled him to find alternatives. Arriving back at Woolwich in the early morning, the crew were taken to St Nicholas Hospital.

Station Officer Moylan and Fireman Seeley were detained; Leading Fireman Storey and Fireman Berkshire were placed on the sick list for fourteen days.

Dave Millar, fresh from his subterranean adventure, was making the best of his way back to Redcross Street Fire Station along Golden Lane when he was collared by an L.F.B. station officer. 'Whitbread's stables been hit. Give them a hand to get the horses out.'

'Sorry, I can't,' replied Dave 'I'm on a message for Chief Superintendent McDuell.'

'I don't care who you're on a message for. Lend a hand with those horses.'

'It was clear he wasn't going to take no for an answer,' said Dave, 'so I turned to and obeyed orders.'

The stables had been hit by incendiaries and smoke had drifted into the horse boxes, setting the famous heavy draught horses, used in happier days to draw the Lord Mayor's Coach, rearing and plunging and neighing in terror.

Leading Fireman Millar, in company with sundry others, clambered into the hay loft and beat the horses with folded sacks, driving them out into the yard where they were calmed by stablemen and led away.

Dave Millar then trotted off to join his master at Redcross Street, composing his excuse for his long absence as he went.

West Ham, for a change, had been by-passed, but the local firemen did not expect to be given a night off. The pattern of operations was the familiar one, only the venue was changed.

The Luftwaffe's radio navigational beams were not intersected over the Royal Docks, where they had been aimed for nearly three months, but over the City, five miles to the west.

Station Officer Eric Earl, officer in charge of Stratford Fire Station, had been standing by, fully rigged, since the moment the Red alert had been received. It was his experience that there would be but a short pause between the wail of the sirens and the scream of falling bombs. But tonight there was an uneasy wait before the alarm bells shrilled and a firewoman came running with the attendance slip.

'C'mon, me lads,' shouted Eric to his crew. 'We're ordered to Whitechapel Fire Control.'

The pump was quickly on its way along Stratford High Street toward the fires that were lighting up the western sky. An anti-aircraft battery in Victoria Park opened up at the invisible enemy as the pump reached Bow Church, the shells bursting directly overhead. The crew firmed their helmets and the driver crouched a little lower over his wheel as the shrapnel came whanging down, rattling on roofs and pavements and striking sparks from granite kerbs.

The Mile End Road loomed ahead, illuminated in patches by fires on both sides of the road and by incendiaries burning harmlessly on the surface. A warning jangle on the bell as they overtook a Civil Defence Rescue Squad on their errand of mercy to dig some unfortunate family from the ruins of its home. At Whitechapel Control they were ordered on to Leadenhall Street to deal with fires burning on the upper floors of office buildings.

All West Ham appliances were equipped with hose reels, supplied initially with water from an inbuilt sixty gallon tank. It is surprising what can be done with such a relatively small quantity of water in the hands of an experienced crew and Station Officer Earl and his men extinguished several fires, forcing entrance doors and racing up flights of stairs as they progressed along Leadenhall Street. There was no water in the street mains but the crew replenished the tank from emergency dams in the district.

Around 8 p.m. they were busy filling the tank from the emergency dam in the forecourt of Adelaide House, a large office block on the northern approach to London Bridge. A number of trailer pumps were at work and one glance told the station officer that water was being taken out faster than it was being put in by pumps lifting water from the river at Freshwater Quay, where the Thames had been dredged to allow coastal steamers to berth at all states of the tide. This was one of the few positions from which pumps could be set into the river that night.

Earl ran down the stairs leading to Fish Street Hill to see what he could do to improve the position. He spotted two trailer pumps and directed their crews to the quay. The suctions were connected and lowered into the murky stream whilst other members of the crews laid hose to be hoisted over the London Bridge balustrade. The new supply came gushing into the dam and the surface began to rise.

A motor cycle screeched to a halt and a London Fire Brigade superintendent stepped from the pillion seat.

'Pump and crew from Stratford, sir, Station Officer Earl in charge.'

'My name's Dann,' replied the super. 'Where are you pumping to?'

'Anywhere there's a fire, sir.'

'Good man. Tell you what I want you to do. We've got a serious situation in Moorgate and a shortage of water. Get a relay working along King William Street and I'll organise it from there. I'll keep in touch.'

'Very good, sir,' replied Earl as the super mounted his motor cycle and roared off.

At that moment another West Ham pump arrived, Station Officer Percy Smither in charge.

'Just the bloke I'm looking for,' said Earl. 'We've got to get a relay working to Moorgate, Perce. You lay a twin line along King William Street, over there, and I'll supply you from this dam.'

'Right,' replied Smither, and the officers ran off to detail their crews. Four more pumps would be required to complete the relay to Moorgate; Superintendent Dann would be supervising the work, spacing the pumps the regulation seven hundred feet apart. Earl and Smither soon had the relay under way and good progress was made despite rough going created by the debris-strewn streets.

With the centre of London in danger of becoming one huge conflagration; with two thousand pumps and some nine thousand firemen at work, the firefighters were dumbfounded, but delighted, to hear the All Clear sound before midnight. They could not believe that the Nazi's would fail to make the most of such a well-lit target but bad weather over the Channel coast had forced an early end to the night's activity.

The All Clear brought relief from the bombardment but no easing of the urgency of the situation. Fires were still spreading and much more water would be required to surround the conflagration area. None of the firefighters could relax.

'Keep it going,' yelled Superintendent Dann from his motor cycle. 'We're well past the Bank.'

And so the work continued throughout the night. More pumps on the streets supplying more lines of hose; more pumps at the riverside feeding the dam until twelve lines of hose carried water to the Moorgate conflagration from this single source. And a small boost to the fireman's morale; the tide was coming in, allowing more pumps to gain access to water from the riverside. But not all the water from the Adelaide House dam was being pumped to Moorgate; several trailer pumps were supplying water to smaller outbreaks in Gracechurch Street, Eastcheap and Lower Thames Street, where tenacious crews laboured to prevent isolated fires from merging to reach major proportions.

Dawn was breaking as a canteen van arrived at Adelaide House and never was a cup of tea and a biscuit more gratefully accepted by grimy, weary and smoke-dried firemen, now becoming painfully aware of their inflamed eyes and of the burns, cuts and abrasions accumulated during the night's action. Some sat on the curbside, emptying water from their fireboots and nursing blistered feet, chafed and raw after hours of clambering over piles of debris.

Firewoman Young (pouring tea) and Firewoman Vera Lynfield serving refreshments to firemen at the centre of operations. Not only did they venture out nightly during the London Blitz; they accompanied convoys from the London Region to Manchester, Birmingham and Portsmouth when those cities were under attack. Under orders to return to London after Manchester's Christmas 1940 ordeal, one of the canteen vans was delayed while the bodies of two Islington firemen, killed during firefighting operations, were laid in the van to be brought home. Vera Lynfield's British Empire Medal was well earned!

The usual Monday morning trek of commuters over London Bridge began. The laconic B.B.C. broadcast, of course, gave no hint of the target or of the damage done. Listeners to the early morning news heard the now familiar bulletin: 'Enemy aircraft attacked towns in the south of England during the night. Fires were started and casualties have been reported.'

The crowds of City workers emerging from London Bridge railway station saw evidence of the night's activity in the station precincts and the buildings around Guy's Hospital, but they were unprepared for the sight that met their eyes as they crossed the bridge. Many were moved to tears as they gazed at the scene of destruction, with its background of flame and smoke rising, it seemed, from the entire City. They picked their way through streets littered with debris and jagged fragments of plate glass; squeezed past bomb craters and stepped over a tangle of fire hose, only to find a pile of smoking rubble instead of the office building they expected to

. . . **They stepped over a tangle of fire hose . . .**

occupy. Others were unable to approach their workplace, for firemen were still heavily engaged in subduing the flames. But those that could set to work clearing broken glass and tidying furniture, tossed about by bomb blast, before attending to the day's correspondence, amazingly delivered by the G.P.O. Some of the workers were so affected by the plight of the firemen that they took sandwiches from their cases and offered them to the exhausted men in the only practical gesture of support they could make.

Considering the weight of the attack, the number of buildings demolished and the rapid spread of fire stoked by the thousands of incendiaries dropped by the enemy during the five hours duration of the raid, it is not surprising that casualties were heavy. One hundred and sixty civilians were killed, five hundred severely injured. Sixteen firemen died and two hundred and fifty were detained in hospital; many others with minor injuries were allowed home after hospital treatment.

The West Ham firemen came limping home exhausted, hungry, cold and wet but in good heart, just twenty-four hours after setting out. Their London and provincial comrades had answered West Ham's calls for assistance almost nightly for the past three months; now, they had been able to repay a little of the debt.

They had come safely through that dreadful night and were relieved to learn that the casualty figures were not as high as they had feared.

This is Newgate Street, looking towards Cheapside. It is a familiar scene the morning after an air-raid. Collapsed buildings, heaps of smoking debris, small groups of firemen damping down smouldering material, and lines of snaking fire hose strewn all over the roadway. 'How much longer can we keep going at this rate?' asks a fireman of his mate. But buildings are made safe; debris is cleared from streets; shattered service mains are repaired; bomb craters are filled in; the milk comes; the post goes; there is food in the shops and the Union Jack flies over bombed buildings. Our turn will come!

The burned out wreckage of a fire pump lies engulfed in a bomb crater in Queen Street Place, Southwark Bridge, on December 30th, 1940. A fire crew, flouting regulations by failing to wear steel helmets, damp down smouldering debris. They risk disciplinary action but are more likely to receive a 'tongue lashing' from their officer in charge, that is, if he catches them! I was guilty of a similar 'crime' when photographed wearing my cap at a 'special service' incident. It was my misfortune that Commander Firebrace, Chief of the Fire Staff, was shown the picture. I received a 'please explain' note from HQ!

With the situation in the City coming under control, many reinforcing appliances sent in from the outer regions were released and ordered to return to their home stations. The Thames flood tide provided ample water for the many fires still needing the attention of firemen and enabled empty emergency dams to be filled, ready for the possible return of the Nazi airmen at dusk.

Chief Superintendent McDuell decided to take a look around the City fire area to assess the situation for himself. After walking in the vicinity of Redcross Street Fire Station he instructed Leading Fireman Millar to drive him to Moorgate, where they left the car and inspected the area on foot. Strangely, the main body of fire had not crossed east of Moorgate.

'Take a look around Finsbury Square, Millar,' said the Super, 'while I check on the situation in Whitecross Street.'

Finsbury Square seemed to have escaped any damage and was as deserted as might be expected in the early hours of a dark, wintry Monday morning.

Trotting around the southern side of the Square, Millar saw a man standing on the entrance steps of an office block. He was the caretaker.

A 5,000-gallon steel dam forms the focal point for pumps working in the Ludgate Circus area of the City. The tank is topped up with water pumped through hose lines from the River Thames at Blackfriars Bridge and delivered by goose-neck fittings hooked over the rim. These men have been at work since 6 p.m. the previous evening.

'Seen any fires around here?' enquired Millar.

'No,' replied the man. 'We've had nothing round here; it seems to have been behind us and over there,' pointing to Chiswell Street.

After a few more words he said:

'Well, I must be off; I've got my breakfast on.'

'What've you got?' enquired Dave.

'Bacon and eggs.'

'Have you got enough for me?' asked Dave.

'I think I could find a rasher and an egg for you,' he replied.

'I've got my guv'nor round the corner,' said Dave. 'We've been up all night on this fire and could do with a snack.'

'Bring him round,' said the caretaker.

Leading Fireman Millar found the Superintendent in Chiswell Street.

'Could you go a bacon and egg breakfast, sir?'

'Have you got one?'

'Follow me, sir,' replied Dave.

'And that,' said Leading Fireman Millar, 'was one of the best breakfasts I ever enjoyed. There were times during the night when I doubted I would live to see the dawn, but here I was, eating bacon and eggs and drinking tea with the Chief Superintendent, provided by a man I'd never met until half an hour ago, as though it was the most natural thing to do.'

Fire Force Commander C. P. McDuell, OBE, on the left, takes charge of a major fire. Senior Company Officer 'Jimmy' Syrett operates the 'walkie-talkie' and Company Officer Obie Walker (wearing headphones) transmits messages to HQ Control. Leading Fireman Dave Millar is just visible on the right as he sits at the wheel of the FFC's staff car.

5   **Spring Offensive**

LUFTWAFFE attacks during the early months of 1941 were spasmodic, probably due to very bad flying weather over the coastal regions of northern France and the Low Countries from whence they operated.

But with the approach of better weather, the enemy stepped up his attacks on London and the big provincial cities, mounting a spectacularly heavy raid to mark the opening of the Spring Offensive on March 19th — 'The Wednesday' as it came to be known in East London.

From time to time information was received from official sources of the target for the bombers, and on the afternoon of the 19th, at about 4 p.m., came word that the target that night included the Royal Docks.

There were five auxiliary fire stations within the Group, with manpower totalling one hundred and twenty. Here was a problem. To be warned of the intended target was one thing; to consider whether it would, in fact be bombed, another. Should all appliances and men be withdrawn or should they be left to take their chance?

West Ham covers such a relatively small area that it was argued that if the men were withdrawn, they could be accommodated only in schools, and even near misses of dock targets could result in hits on the augmented stations. So it was decided to take no action, other than to direct the officers to arrange for their men to go to the shelters immediately the warning came.

At about 8 p.m. the sirens wailed and the sound of anti-aircraft gunfire was heard. Then the bombers were overhead, the scream of falling bombs mingling with the thump of gunfire. The skies were lit by clusters of parachute flares, dropped by the raiders to illuminate their target with a cold,

hard light that always left me feeling naked and isolated; a sole, prominent target for hundreds of eager marksmen. I had more than a twinge of sympathy with the ostrich; it was my instinct, too, to put my head under cover at such times.

The ack-ack guns opened up at the flares and a number of hits were scored but those that escaped the shells continued to shed their eerie, menacing light on the target area.

There was no gradual build-up to the full weight of the attack. It seemed that all the bombers over West Ham responded to a signal to drop their cargoes simultaneously and the skies were soon aglow with the glare of fires.

German aircraft were readily identifiable to us on the ground by the irregular beat of their unsynchronised engines, and we heard many, many bombers overhead that night.

Air Marshal Sir Phillip Joubert, whose radio talks brought us such comfort during the dark days, always asserted that German and British aircraft were indistinguishable from the sound of their engines alone. With all deference to the great man, I had to differ with him in this respect, unless it happened that BRITISH aircraft were showering incendiaries and high explosive on us, as we strove to put out the fires or recover our dead and wounded. We had no doubt that the deep sounding throb of engines, the woom-woom coming from above, was the precursor to the scream of falling bombs and we could not believe that the R.A.F. would treat us this way!

Among the reinforcements arriving at West Ham Fire Control that evening was a contingent from Beckenham, Kent. This small brigade had been singularly unfortunate throughout the Blitz, suffering casualties proportionally far higher than any other in the Region. Tonight was to be no

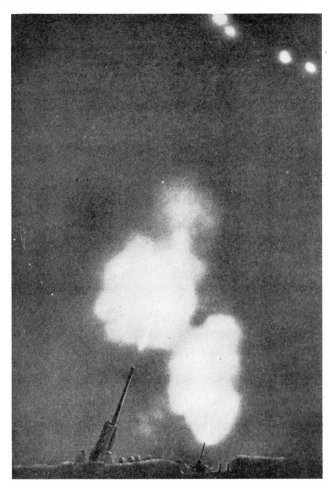

The scene in Eric Road, Forest Gate, after one of the twelve parachute mines to fall on West Ham on the night of March 19/20th, 1941 had exploded.

A parachute mine, similar to the one pictured here, was responsible for the damage in Eric Road, Forest Gate. This one has been rendered harmless by Royal Naval personnel. It came as a shock, in the midst of all the noise of an air raid, to witness a parachute mine, outlined in the glare of the burning city, silently drifting with the wind and sinking slowly to earth. The larger bombs created comparable damage, but the mine was more terrifying. A bomb could be heard whistling down, but it was only a few seconds before the explosion marked the end of that particular threat. Not so the mine. It hung there for some minutes in sight of all in the vicinity, dragging out its menace as it approached the target. We came to know only too well what would happen when it touched down, and I thank God I never saw one coming my way.

On dark nights the enemy created an artificial moonlight to help locate targets. Clusters of magnesium flares on parachutes drifted slowly to earth, shedding a pale light, like diffused moonlight, over the terrain. With all Thameside a target area, the anti-aircraft gunners blazed away, anxious to knock out the illumination before the bomb-aimers identified a target, with some success. To us on the ground, it was an eerie and menacing situation. Any large patch of water, like the river or docks, reflected the light, and we came to expect a few HEs as the bombers spotted a target, or let a few go on spec.

exception, for a Beckenham pump, one of a convoy en route to a fire at Silvertown, was obliterated in a land-mine explosion in Plaistow Road, with the loss of its entire crew. Their names — Leading Fireman Stan Short, and Firemen Charles Drew, Denis Fitzgerald, Fred Moore and Les Palmer — were subsequently added to the Beckenham Fire Service Roll of Honour.

The bombers dropped a large number of parachute mines that night, twelve of them on the County Borough of West Ham. Many casualties were suffered by civilians and Civil Defence personnel, among them Auxiliary Fireman Roy Huggett of West Ham, killed with his comrades from South London in the Plaistow Road.

Yet the Royal Docks escaped practically unscathed. An auxiliary fire station was hit but the crews were out and no one was hurt. Those responsible for the decision to stand fast breathed a sigh of relief when the All Clear sounded. The signs had been ominous in the early moments of the raid!

The heavy attack on March 19th caused widespread damage and heavy casualties. Some two thousand fires were attended by the fire service in the London Region, but this was not the total number of fires started by the enemy; hundreds more were tackled by street fire parties with their Home Office stirrup pumps and buckets. These bands of volunteers, by their prompt action, were able to extinguish many fires in their early stages without the need to call the fire service.

Part of my job at the beginning of the Blitz was to organise street fire parties into zones in which mutual aid was provided. Meetings of householders were held in pubs and church halls and I met with some resistance when I suggested that a street fire party should go to the assistance of its neighbour following a fall of incendiaries. A few flatly refused to leave their own street, even if it were undamaged, but most saw the wisdom of the plan and gave full co-operation.

A simple cyclostyled form was issued to party leaders who were asked to complete the form giving date, approximate time, name and address of the occupier and his business i.e. private house; baker's shop, etc.

Over three thousand completed forms were returned to West Ham Fire Brigade H.Q. during the eight months period of the Blitz. There can be no doubt that these, and many other fires, successfully extinguished but not recorded by the street parties, considerably lightened the burden on fire brigades, leaving them free to concentrate on the more serious outbreaks.

Strange fire engines made their appearance on East End streets; tenders constructed of soap boxes with old perambulator wheels, carrying stirrup pumps, sand bags and buckets of water.

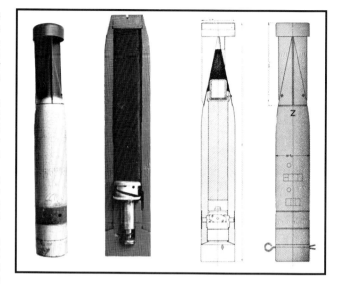

These are the German 1kg magnesium thermite fire bombs which laid waste so many of our cities. On the left is the standard bomb, used in the early days of the Blitz. Later, the Luftwaffe took to mixing in a few explosive incendiaries, shown right. There was no way of telling if the bomb was explosive or not. The object, of course, was to keep fire-bomb fighters at a distance so that the fire could take hold.

The lads of the village could hardly wait for a fall of incendiaries and fourteen-year-olds would boast, next morning, of the number of fires they had put out and produce their trophies, assorted pieces of shrapnel and partly-burned fire bombs, acquired during the night.

The explosive incendiary bombs caused many casualties among the amateur firemen who were peppered with small pieces of shrapnel. The bombs were most dangerous when nearly burned out for the explosive was located under the fin. Some drew back but there were many undeterred by the new threat.

A man in Canning Town saw two magnesium bombs drop in his backyard, one near his chicken house, the other on a concrete path. His main concern was for his hens and he tackled that first. He then turned to the other one and was about to pump water on it when it went off, blowing off a large part of his foot.

Although we had been under heavy fire for six months and had learned pretty well what to expect, I never fully overcame my fear of meeting a messy and untimely end. I had, however, become more philosophical and realised the undeniable truth of an old saying of my mother's: 'What can't be cured must be endured.'

These youngsters made use of shattered lamp-standards to play roundabouts by day. But there were more exciting things to do after dark. They serviced their soap-box fire engines, filled the water buckets and waited impatiently for the sirens to wail.

In the early days of the Blitz we were all fearful of the unknown. We had read newspaper accounts of the air raids on Guernica, Warsaw and Rotterdam but now realised that only experience could bring home all the horrors of aerial bombardment.

When I first heard the wail of sirens in anger, something happened in my stomach. I became aware of a burning sensation which was most unpleasant. But, after a few 'alerts,' the condition wore off as I found something positive to do. I realised that the A.F.S. lads who formed my crews were looking to me for guidance. I was motivated to put on a face that belied my true feelings and the pose helped, to some degree, to remove from my mind the worst fears of personal disaster.

During the heavier attacks when the din was almost overwhelming, the overriding fear was one of being dismembered or buried under a cascade of debris from a collapsing building. As showers of incendiaries came hissing down, I tried to turn away the fearful memory of that fireman in Pennington Street, Shadwell, with an incendiary bomb embedded in his back; a vision that persisted in coming vividly to mind and I never did succeed in putting it behind me. The best I could do as a diversion was to concentrate on the job in hand.

During less noisy times, the menacing throb of the bombers' engines, cruising invisibly overhead as their pilots sought targets, posed constant threat. When, eventually, the bombs were released, their screaming descent compelled us to lie flat on our faces, hopefully clear of debris from buildings the explosion would send flying all over the area. Every one of us was convinced that the bomb bearing down had his or her number on it; that it was about to score a direct hit that would scatter the bloody fragments of our bodies to the four winds.

But it was all a matter of luck and I continued to be lucky. There were occasions when, lying in the roadway as a bomb screamed down, I died a thousand deaths before it exploded half a mile away!

Just as a drowning man is said to witness a procession of important events in his lifetime in the moments before he succumbs, so similar thoughts entered our minds as we lay in the gutter, listening to the thin whistle of the bomb, seemingly falling from the stratosphere, gathering volume and depth of tone as it approached its target. After a succession of similar incidents, the hope was born that the luck might continue.

But, behind it all, was the fear that it might not.

On the night of April 16/17th, 1941 the Luftwaffe launched what was to develop into the heaviest air raid of the war on England. Shortly before 9 p.m. the first of nearly 700 bombers dropped their cargoes of destruction on the target area, defined as the banks of the River Thames from Woolwich to Tower Bridge.

As the raid intensified, the raiders widened their scope to embrace much of the City and West End and the south London boroughs of Southwark, Bermondsey and Deptford. Districts as far west as Willesden and south to Bromley in Kent, saw sharp action.

Leicester Square on the night of April 16/17th, 1941. Firemen had been here six weeks earlier when the Café de Paris, packed with guests enjoying a night out, was hit by a bomb which exploded in the ballroom, killing 34 and injuring 80. There was no joy for the firefighters on *this* night out.

Whit Sunday visitors to St Paul's Cathedral view the damage caused on the night of April 16/17th, 1940, when a bomb penetrated the roof and crashed through into the crypt. This was the second direct hit by an HE bomb on the Cathedral.

The attack commenced just before 9 p.m. and continued until 5 a.m., during which time 150,000 incendiaries and 800 tons of high explosives were dropped on London's massive sprawl. Enormous damage was done to buildings and the flood of incendiaries resulted in some 2,250 fires being started.

Very few of the London boroughs escaped damage and many notable buildings were hit. St Paul's was struck by a 250 kilo bomb which entered through the roof and came to rest in the crypt. Buildings in Oxford Street and its environs were severely damaged by blast and fire. The large block occupied by the Thomas Wallis department store, opposite Gamage's in Holborn, was burnt out and had partly fallen down. Leicester Square resembled a World War I battlefield. The Admiralty in Whitehall and the Law Courts in the Strand were among many other casualties.

The massive weight of high explosive dropped resulted in the highest total of casualties yet sustained in a single night of bombing. Nearly 1,200 people died and thousands of others were severely injured. Unlucky hits on a number of public shelters contributed to the heavy toll.

Down at the auxiliary fire station in Suffolk Road, Ilford, Tom Stothard and his men listened to the fleets of bombers cruising overhead. This, obviously, was something big. They stood ready in their firefighting gear, waiting for the summons that would start them on their journey to the scene of action; wondering what the night had in store for them.

The shrill note of the telephone from Ilford Fire Control broke the tension of waiting; it brought an unusual instruction.

'Order your No. 1 Trailer Pump to North Woolwich Pier to join a convoy for Bromley, Kent.'

The Ilford streets were strangely free from the usual din associated with an air raid, but the sky to the west, north and south glowed with all the familiar hues. Their journey through the dockland area, too, was unusually quiet and free from the activity they had come to expect in that locality.

The pumps comprising the remainder of the convoy were waiting by the pier; an officer marshalled them aboard a ferry

The King and Queen visit Caledon Road, East Ham, on April 19th, 1941. Frequently, more people than appear in this picture were killed by enemy bombs in single incidents during the Blitz.

As can be seen on the far right of this picture, the spontaneous response of battered people to Hitler's terror was inevitably immediate. Out came the Flag!

that had been held for their use and they moved off on the Kentish side on the final leg of their journey to Bromley.

'The local fire control quickly found us a job,' said Tom, 'just around the corner from the fire station where several houses in a terrace were well alight. Fortunately, there was water in the hydrants and we did good work going from one to the other. The occupier of one of the houses came up to me in a state of some distress and asked if we would recover valuables and personal papers contained in a box under the floorboards in the kitchen. We were able to oblige.

'We had been at work for several hours and had become soaked and very cold. Somebody told us that there was a canteen van in the next street so we knocked off and went along for a cup of tea. I thought it looked a bit strange; the canteen van was there alright but there was no queue waiting to be served: firemen, C.D. workers, policemen and Uncle Tom Cobley. As we reached the canteen we saw that it was one provided by the W.V.S. Inside were five old ladies in their W.V.S. uniform, not one of them, I swear, under eighty years of age.

'"I'm so terribly sorry," said one dear old soul, "we've nothing left. It's been a busy night and all the tea, coffee and sandwiches are gone. All I've got left is some boiled rice but no milk or sugar to go with it."

The Ilford lads, thankful for small mercies, gratefully accepted what was going. 'I thought it was grand,' said Leading Fireman Stothard. 'It was hot and filled that great, grumbling void in my stomach most agreeably. Those old ladies were determined to do their bit and had worked very hard, I'm sure, while their stocks lasted,' he continued, 'but they shouldn't have been out on a night like that; though I wouldn't have cared to have told them so.'

The Parish Church of St Peter and Paul, Bromley, demolished on the night that Tom Stothard and his lads feasted on plain rice.

The Chelsea and Westminster areas were undergoing severe punishment. Early in the raid, two firemen had been killed and a number of their comrades badly injured when their auxiliary station had been blasted by a near miss which brought down a block of flats next door.

A large high explosive bomb, accompanied by a shower of fire bombs, scored a hit on a furniture repository in Sutherland Street, Pimlico, starting several fires. Another H.E. in Hugh Street opened up a crater in the road, fracturing the water main. The crater began to fill and several trailer pumps were set in to this emergency water supply, unwittingly provided by the Luftwaffe.

The glare from numerous fires in the locality enabled the enemy to pick out the lines of Victoria Rail Terminus. A parachute mine was soon on its way to add to the chaos, creating havoc among the fire appliances and ambulances brought into the area to deal with the results of the earlier bomb.

Uncontrolled fire in Pimlico, April 16th, 1941. With insufficient water to bring it quickly under control, all available jets are used to hold it in check until water relays arrive and extinguishment can begin.

Fire crews at work on the furniture depository in Sutherland Street, Pimlico, at the rear of Victoria Station.

Further falls of fire bombs achieved their purpose in the Brompton Road area. Two fire crews were at work on a fire in Chelsea Square when a large H.E. struck, bringing down the building and burying eight firemen in the debris. The officer in charge, with commendable presence of mind, made 'pumps ten,' mainly for rescue purposes. Some of the fresh crews were deployed for firefighting whilst the remainder began a search for their buried comrades. By their efforts, the bodies of three of their comrades were recovered together with the remaining five men, all severely injured.

The blast had severely shaken the old Brompton Fire Station opposite, showering the firewomen in the control room with fragments of glass and covering everything with a heavy layer of dust. The incident was regarded as a temporary interruption only and the work of the control room continued as usual after a short pause.

Superintendent George Bennison was on his way back to Westminster Fire Station from the Brompton job when he saw a solitary trailer pump at work on the blazing Christ Church in Broadway. He sent a message calling for six pumps

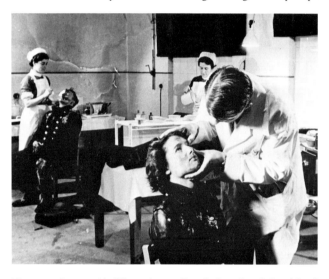

The casualty ward in Westminster Hospital on the night of April 16/17th, 1941. A firewoman driver is treated for eye injuries whilst other fire casualties are bandaged and splinted. Dedicated doctors and nurses accepted what the ambulances delivered and continued to work whilst there were patients to be treated.

and a turntable ladder. Resuming his journey to Westminster Fire Station, he was informed of a large fire in Petty France. On his way there, he noticed that some of the pumps and the T.L. [turntable ladder] he had ordered for Christ Church had arrived and were preparing to get to work. The fire was illuminating the whole area and the turntable ladder, which had come from Hammersmith, was being extended to subdue the flames rising from the eastern end of the church.

Seeing that work was proceeding, Superintendent Bennison continued his journey to Petty France, where he found a brisk fire on the tenth floor of an office building.

In the meantime, crews from Manchester Square Fire Station were laying out hose and already had two more branches at work on the church, supplementing the monitor jet from the T.L. Then came a H.E. which demolished one of the pumps and damaged others. This was followed instantly by an oil bomb which fell at the base of the T.L. and set several pumps alight. The explosion had caused the upper extension of the turntable ladders to break away, dropping on to the roof of the church. The man at the head of the ladder was knocked unconscious and, in the confusion of the moment, he was overlooked. After a few minutes he regained consciousness; unhooked himself and proceeded to walk down the ladder. In a state of shock, he stepped off the broken end of the ladder and fell fifteen feet to the ground. Senior Fireman Albert Gentry from Hammersmith Fire Station was killed instantly. Two of his mates from Hammersmith, Alex Collins and Doug Baldwin, together with Bill Herbert from Manchester Square, died later in hospital from their injuries.

On his return to Westminster Fire Station, George Bennison was informed of a fifty-pump fire at Selfridges in Oxford Street. On arrival there, he found the two upper floors well alight and firefighting operations hampered by a shortage of water. Instructions had been given to bring into use the special fire main, laid from the Serpentine in Hyde Park to Marble Arch, and to run hose relays from there to supply dams set up in Oxford Street. Sound work by fire crews, supported by an ample water supply, enabled the fire to be brought under control by 9 a.m.

Superintendent Bennison returned to his H.Q. at Manchester Square Fire Station for a quick bath and a bite to eat. But not to sleep; there was still much to be done. A tour of all the fires in the West End to ensure things were going to plan; that crews were being relieved for meals and fresh crews were being utilised for turning over. Finally, to bed at lunchtime in readiness for the next performance!

A radial branch holder at work on the John Lewis building in Oxford Street. The 1½ inch nozzle will deliver 600 gallons of water a minute with a throw of 100 feet. A crew member stands on the base plate to lend stability to the branch whilst the forward strut bites into the road surface. The back pressure from such a delivery is formidable; too dangerous to allow men to hold. A similar branch took charge whilst in use at a fire in West Ham. It thrashed about like a live thing at the end of the hose line, scattering the crew. Auxiliary Fireman A. B. Advani, an Indian who had come to West Ham before the war to gain fire experience was struck by the forward strut which penetrated his thigh. No attempt was made to remove it and he was taken to hospital with the strut still embedded in his leg. He returned to India after recovery and, eventually, became Chief Fire Officer, New Delhi.

In May 1946 I was transferred to A Division, No. 34 Area Fire Force with Headquarters at Manchester Square Fire Station. My duties frequently took me along Victoria Street, past a white-painted building standing on the corner of Broadway. The walls of many buildings in that part of London were painted white — a bit dingy, perhaps, after six years of wartime austerity but still recognisable as white. But what made this particular wall noteworthy, however, was the sharp imprint of a large wheel and tyre, about ten feet from the ground. The wheel had come from the fire pump destroyed by the H.E. that had taken the lives of the four firefighters working on Christ Church. Normally, I did not dwell on wartime memories but I regarded that imprint as an eloquent epitaph.

Broadcasting House, the home of the BBC, was among the buildings severely damaged on the night of April 16/17th, 1941. A parachute mine exploded almost directly outside the main entrance doors in Langham Place, killing and injuring several people in the street. A number of fires were started in Broadcasting House and adjoining buildings and several members of the BBC staff were trapped.

Inside Broadcasting House, the gramophone records library on an upper floor was demolished, spilling an estimated 50 tons of records into the cavity below and burying people working in their offices.

Firemen from Manchester Square had acquired considerable experience in rescuing people trapped under debris but this was something different. As fast as they tunnelled into the heap to reach those buried, fresh discs came sliding down to fill the gap and it became a frustratingly slow and tiresome job to make progress. Rescuers were able to speak to those trapped, encouraging them to hold on; eventually, all were released without serious injury.

Carrying out a search of the damaged area, Superintendent V. W. Botten and Leading Fireman Millar heard a voice coming up to them from floor level:

'Mind how you go. You'll be treading on my head.'

There, in the light of their hand torches, appeared a man's head and shoulders supported under the arms by floor joists, with the rest of his body and legs dangling into the room below. The floor boards had been carried away by falling debris and he had dropped between the joists, unable to lift himself free without assistance.

Surprisingly, in view of the damage caused, no member of the BBC staff was killed, although some 50 persons received injury.

This was the second time that Broadcasting House had received serious damage. In December 1940, the nine o'clock news broadcast was about to commence when a heavy bomb scored a direct hit. Many listeners, including myself, heard the explosion faintly without realising what it was. Some time later I heard the news reader, Bruce Belfrage, tell of the incident.

'I was so deep down that I hardly heard it. A few tiny fragments of plaster came from the ceiling but that was all.'

But BBC personnel suffered severely on that occasion, with several dead among other casualties. It was the British Broadcasting Corporation's proud boast that broadcasts to listeners at home, to Europe and the World continued without interruption throughout the war.

During raids, my constant worry was for my wife and children. Duty took fire crews far from home stations and rumours and scraps of information were exchanged when we met at fires:

'Bad land mine at Forest Gate.' . . . 'Block of flats down at Poplar.' . . . 'Pump's crew from Beckenham has had it in Plaistow Road.'

I had a friend in the Control Room at Ilford and occasionally gave him a ring to check on activity in my home area. One night he told me that an unexploded land mine had dropped nearby and that people in my street had been ordered out and taken to a rest centre.

It was a bad night and I seemed to bear a charmed life. Bombs dropped in places I had just left and others fell in areas I was bound for just before my arrival; I was straddled time and again. Soon after midnight I began to lose my fear and, what's more, ceased to worry about my wife and children. There was nothing I could do to help them and it came to me that this was to be my last night on earth, I was bound to stop one sooner or later. I could not continue to dodge the bombs or, rather, the bombs to dodge me, it was simply a matter of time.

A strange feeling of peace and tranquillity came to me in the midst of all the turmoil with fire, death and destruction all around yet I was able to carry on in a mentally serene state I had never felt before in an air raid. I wondered, without emotion, how the end would come. Even the din became subdued although the glare of fire and the brilliant flash of explosions continued to register. But, slowly, the intensity of the bombing diminished and the sky began to lighten. It was about five-thirty and as the light strengthened, I began to realise that I might, after all, live to fight another day. As the all clear sounded, the barrage balloons began to rise; the night fighters had been active.

I managed to get a few hours leave during the morning and hurried home to see my family. Due to an error in the location of the land mine, they had spent the night in a rest centre, a flimsy church hall, closer to the mine than they would have been at home. However, they were unharmed and returned thankfully to find the house relatively undamaged. Most of the windows, long since, had been shattered; a few more caused us little concern.

The children had been asleep in the Morrison shelter when the warden's knock came.

'Come on, you've got to get out, quick. There's a land mine in South Park Road.'

Alice assisted them to dress, gathering up coats and the case containing a few extra items of clothing together with our personal papers, kept in a tin box in the cooker for safety during air raids. Then, off to the rest centre, with shrapnel bouncing along the pavement, wondering if the house would be standing in the morning. If it were not, the small case would contain all our worldly possessions.

But we all lived to count our blessings. There were many far less fortunate than we.

London's most devastating raid occurred on the night of May 10/11th when a full moon coincided with the River Thames at an unusually low tide. Firemen knew they were in for a bad night with the odds stacked against them, as hundreds of bombers maintained a shuttle service across the Channel, some of them making three trips from their bases in northern France to target London.

West Ham received its usual greeting from the Luftwaffe early in the raid when several medium-sized fires developed in the dock area. A more serious outbreak was started in the Temple Mills sidings, then one of the largest railway marshalling complexes in the country; but this was a comparatively quiet night for West Ham firemen.

There were minor falls of incendiaries in various parts of the borough and these were pounced upon by the local lads and lassies, if not with glee, then certainly with the speed and efficiency born of long practice.

It was a matter of pride for them to deal with a simple fall of fire bombs without calling the Service:

'Leave the boys to deal with the big fires, mate.'

The raiders were able to choose their targets by the brilliant light of the moon shining from a cloudless sky, and later by the glare of fires stretching across London from Dagenham to

Hammersmith. Street water mains were flowing only in the early stages; demand soon overran the supply as fresh fires were started, the flow becoming further depleted with the inevitable fracturing of trunk mains.

Frustrated firemen, who had laboured to bring jets to bear on blazing buildings, watched helplessly as fire streams faltered and died. Their comrades, meanwhile, sought emergency sources of water not already crowded out by pumps with suction hose set in.

Fireboats lay fifty yards from the Thames banks, running their hose lines ashore over mud flats from what looked like a village stream, so low was the tide. But there were far more pumps seeking water than the fire boats could hope to supply; water officers directed crews to public swimming pools, canals and ponds. Some opportunist pump operators set their appliances into flooded bomb craters, even sewers, in an effort to make use of every drop of water available.

May 10th, 1941. Firemen in Charterhouse Street, Holborn, replace a burst length of hose. The man at the right is tying an overhand knot to indicate that the length is damaged. The street is festooned with sagging and broken trolley-bus wires, yet another hazard for the firefighters. Pumps were issued with a piece of equipment known as a 'shorting bar' to be hooked over a pair of trolley bus wires to create a short circuit, thus cutting off the current. I recall an incident in Stratford Broadway when conditions precluded the use of a shorting-bar. Firemen achieved the desired effect by using a ceiling hook, a long pole with a head rather like a boat-hook, carried on regular appliances. They used it to wrap a trailing trolley-bus wire around a lamp post! A nice piece of improvisation.

Fires blaze along the length of Queen Victoria Street on the night of May 10/11th, 1941. With water supplies strictly limited, firemen had no option but to abandon buildings hopelessly ablaze in order to concentrate on halting the spread of fire or working on a building they had a chance of saving. The building ablaze on the far right was the International Headquarters of the Salvation Army.

The scene from the stone gallery of St Paul's Cathedral on May 11th, 1941. Ludgate Hill, on the left, runs down to Ludgate Circus, obscured by smoke. Pumps are hard at work relaying water to fires burning in the region of Pilgrim Street and in Warwick Lane and Old Bailey. The burned out area on the right of the picture demonstrates how close the earlier conflagration of December 29th/30th, 1940 came to causing the fiery demise of St Paul's.

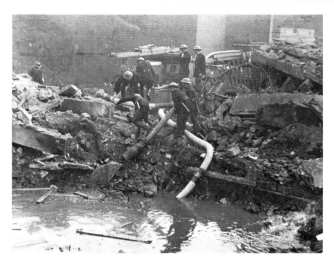

Pump crews take advantage of a flooded crater. They connect up 8 foot lengths of suction hose, fit a basket strainer over the copper strainer, to keep out stones and other objects, harmful to the centrifugal pump, then lower the strainer below the surface. They cannot tell how long it will last, that depends on what use is made of it, but it will provide some crews with the opportunity of dousing a fire before it becomes out of control. Muddy or clear; it will still conquer fire, and it's better than nothing.

Hose lines were laid from the water source to the fireground, the men clambering over debris and running themselves into the ground, driven by the urge to provide water to fight the fires ahead, growing ever larger and more menacing in the absence of extinguishing operations. To many it seemed a hopeless task, as they strove to lay hose lines with failing strength, their nerves stretched by the unending scream of falling bombs and the ever-present fear of being hit or overwhelmed in an avalanche of masonry.

But there was always someone or something to rally flagging spirits.

'Come on, lads. Don't let them bastards get you down,' shouted a fireman, lucky enough to be making good use of a powerful jet. Lorries carrying a mile of hose raised a cheer as they laid twin lines of hose at twenty miles an hour on roads clear of debris, preparing for water relays from the Thames bridges.

The L.C.C. school in Westmoreland Road, Walworth, had been converted into a training school for auxiliary firemen and also housed an operational station. Like many of their colleagues in the target areas, crews from Westmoreland Road had endured a nightmare existence during the past eight months. They had not been called upon to travel long distances to their battleground; the enemy had delivered the action to their doorstep, an impartial foe who distributed his favours indiscriminately on rows of terrace houses and factories and warehouses alike. Some of their experiences were implanted clearly and indelibly on their minds, like their introduction to Blitz firefighting amid the acres of burning timber in the Surrey Commercial Dock, when all London seemed to be on fire.

They recalled the old lady they stumbled upon, sitting in her chair in the middle of the road, surrounded by the rubble of her home. She lived in a flat built over an arch and came through the floor in her chair when her home was blasted by the stick of bombs that devastated the rest of the houses in Villa Street. Shocked and bruised, but by no means speechless, the indomitable old lady, proclaiming to the world at large her belief in the illegitimacy of the entire German nation, was carried, still in her chair, and placed aboard an ambulance.

The memory of the oil bomb on Woolworths in the Old Kent Road remained vivid, not so much for the fire as for the vile, poisonous smoke that had everybody retching and

The burned out Woolworth's store in the Old Kent Road, where fumes from the oil bomb combined with other combustibles to produce the vile smoke that so upset Sub-Officer Handslip and his crews from Westmoreland Road.

vomiting. The rest remained a confused memory of noise and stench, of horror and fear, of searing heat and numbing cold, with saturated clothing clinging to shivering bodies. Of hunger and thirst and utter weariness, all circulating against a background of swirling flame and smoke.

Tonight, as midnight approached with 'nothing doing,' their hopes were that they were in for a quiet night, but they were out of luck.

The first bombs followed swiftly on the last note of the sirens, but they fell on the north bank of the Thames.

'Looks like they're copping it in the Royals, again,' remarked Bill Seabrook to Sub-Officer Handslip. They gazed skywards, speculating on the chances of being ordered to Silvertown, if things got worse. Then the raid suddenly flared up with a wave of bombers plastering the south London riverside boroughs.

The men at Westmoreland Road scrambled into their fire gear as the swish of clusters of fire bombs and the stomach-churning scream of H.E.s signalled the end of their brief respite. A stick of high explosives fell in the direction of Albany Road, sending debris rattling into the yard of the fire station.

'That's us' shouted Rod Handslip, as the crews ran to their appliances. 'Inform Control we've gone on to Albany Road with our heavy unit and two trailer pumps.'

Over in Albany Road, flames from the blazing mineral water factory of R. White's cast a lurid glare over a scene of havoc. The atmosphere was thick with dust, still rising from demolished buildings; the first wisps of smoke and licking flame were issuing from heaps of debris. Screams for help came from people trapped in the rubble of their homes, as wardens and neighbours rushed to their aid.

Handslip summed up the situation in a glance as he jumped from the heavy unit. 'Get to work on R. White's,' he shouted to the leading fireman in charge of one of the trailer pumps and 'Make pumps ten for Albany Road' to a fireman, who set off for Westmoreland Road to pass the message to New Cross Fire Control.

The heavy unit crew concentrated on the scattered fires in debris, as lines of hose sprouted all over the street. Sub-Officer Handslip was reconnoitring the area when he was halted in his stride by a tremendous explosion and a blast which drove the air from his lungs.

Suddenly, he felt sick. Thoughts he tried to suppress came flooding into his mind.

'That's a land mine; it's caught the lads; they'll all be blown to bits; what shall I do; must get help. No, I've just made pumps ten; they'll be here soon.'

His sense of duty drove him forward, tense and fearful of what he might find. His ears were still ringing with the sound of the explosion but the whine of a fire pump, strangely comforting, reached him as he stumbled into Albany Road. His gaze swept the whole of the devastated area within the glare from the mineral water factory, searching for every spot of activity, noting every movement. Two firemen in the foreground, digging in the debris of a demolished house; another, nearby, directing a jet of water on to a small fire with others performing similar tasks up and down the street. His fears faded and he thanked God for preserving his mates.

Activity in Thames Street, Deptford, centres around a 3,000 gallon capacity 'Sportapool' dam, similar to those purchased by parents to provide garden pools for their children. Large numbers were issued by the Home Office to fire brigades throughout the country. They were readily available and easily transportable — just dump one where required and fill it with water! The canvas pool was fitted with a kapok-filled lip which floated, lifting the sides as it filled. Here, the pool is supplied with water pumped from the Thames, as a heavy unit and two trailer pumps draw water for supplying the branches. Trailer pumps were equipped with a special water cooling system; even so, the engine, running at high speed when pumping, became very hot, with the exhaust manifolds glowing cherry-red. Engine covers were raised to assist ventilation.

The whole of London seemed to be under bombardment. The sound of explosions came from all directions, some muffled as from a distance, others closer, bringing the fear that the bombers were retracing their flight paths, ready to add fuel to any promising fire.

Flames from the mineral water factory, contributing a splash of pink to the umbrella of crimson covering the Capital, lifted clouds of smoke and showers of golden sparks across the sky. Sub-Officer Handslip, fearing that the glare, fed by thousands of wooden bottle-crates stacked in the yard and vats of frying oil for the potato crisp section of the factory, would attract the bombers. He ran across the road to order another jet to be got to work on the building.

'Where's Leading Fireman Gothard?' he asked a fireman wielding a branch to good effect on the face of the building.

'He's just been killed,' replied the man. 'He was half-way up a scaling ladder, getting a line of hose over the factory wall when the mine went off.'

Ron Handslip's brain was in a whirl. Only minutes before he had feared all his mates had been killed; then, all seemed well. Now, he knew that one of his men was dead and there might be others before the night was through. He was brought back to reality by the situation.

'You carry on here whilst I take a look around the ground,' he told the fireman. The responsibility of watching over the safety of his men cleared the sub-officer's mind of everything but the job in hand.

The Luftwaffe continued its ferocious attack, and some explosions were too close for comfort, but the Albany Road area received no further hits. The reinforcing pumps arrived and a district officer took charge of operations. Extra crews were detailed for firefighting; others were organised into squads to help with rescue work.

The hours passed unnoticed by the toiling men until the sirens sounding the All Clear recorded the departure of the raiders. The factory fire and the smaller outbreaks had been extinguished and a steady stream of people were dug from the ruins of their homes. Some were taken to hospital by ambulance, others were removed in mortuary vans. Gradually the site was cleared.

Most of the debris had been searched for bodies; what remained would be sifted by the Civil Defence rescue crews, who had been slogging away all night at their back-breaking and often harrowing task. Firefighting equipment was made up and appliances were ordered to their home stations.

Ron Handslip glanced at the haggard, grimy faces of his crews as they climbed aboard their vehicles. There was none of the usual banter as he gave the order 'Home, lads.' They sat with elbows on knees, heads drooping as the appliances bumped and rattled over the debris-strewn Albany Road and turned into Villa Street.

'Oh, blimey!' ejaculated Bill Seabrook. 'Look up there. The roof of the Paul's alight.' The Paul was their local; they couldn't possibly allow it to burn down, miserable and exhausted as they were. They hammered on the door without reply. A ladder was extended to the roof whilst the knocking continued. Presently, an upper window opened and the landlord appeared.

'What's up?'

'Your bloody roof's alight, that's what's up. Come down and let us in.'

The men were ready with a line of hose as they heard the sound of bolts being drawn and the door was flung open. After their earlier problems, the roof presented no difficulty and it was all over in a few minutes. Although it was against regulations, the lads had no qualms about downing the pints donated by the grateful landlord.

'We'd had a bad night,' he told Bill Seabrook, 'and we only went up to bed after the All Clear sounded.'

'So you had a bad night,' retorted Bill.

The jets seen here, at work on buildings in Eastcheap, May 1941, show what can be done when ample water is available. It was not possible to prevent a building from being set alight, but it could be stopped from spreading along the street. Radiated heat from the building on the right threatens to spread fire across the road; cooling jets are employed to prevent this happening.

Chief Superintendent C. P. McDuell, Officer in Charge of the London Fire Brigade 'A' District covering the West End, had been standing by in the watchroom at Manchester Square Fire Station since the alert had sounded around 11 p.m. With him was Robin Duff, the B.B.C. news commentator, who had enrolled as a part-time fireman, and Firemaster Milne of Dunfermline, who had come to London to gain Blitz firefighting experience. Their driver, Leading Fireman Dave Millar, from north of Inverness, stood ready to transport them to any serious incident in the district.

They had not long to wait.

'Palace of Westminster, Jock!' yelled a watchroom attendant and, within a minute, the Chief Superintendent and his party were on their way, closely followed by the fire control van. Diversions in Park Lane, forced by bomb craters and U.X.Bs, resulted in some weaving and turning but little delay. The normally traffic-jammed streets, now deserted except for fire appliances and Civil Defence vehicles, allowed more room than usual for manoeuvre.

Buckingham Palace, bathed in a flickering red glow reflected from the sky, looked stark and deserted as the fire cars, bells ringing and warning lights flashing, swept into Birdcage Walk. They were now within sight of Parliament Square, all eyes peering intently forward, anxious to gain a glimpse of the famous tower. There it was, apparently undamaged, lit brightly by flames from several fires burning on the roof of Westminster Hall and adjoining buildings. Coming closer, several small offices facing the Oliver Cromwell statue were seen to be well alight. Fire crews were at work with about thirty men in the courtyard between Westminster Hall and the House of Commons Chamber.

On arrival, it was Mr McDuell's practice to reconnoitre the fire area. As he approached Parliament Square, he saw flames rising from the roof of St Margaret's Church. The fire had also been spotted by the crew of a passing fire pump which had pulled over to deal with the outbreak. Finding the door securely fastened, the officer in charge had given instructions for it to be forced and a fireman stood ready with a large axe. At this moment, along came the Chief Superintendent and, from the opposite direction, a verger. Sizing up the situation, the latter took a stand before the entrance, with an arm flung protectively across the door like Horatius Defending the Bridge.

'You must not break down this fourteenth century door,' he cried.

'Tell us what you want us to do, then,' replied Mr McDuell. 'Shall we save your fourteenth century door or your fourteenth century church?'

The verger moved aside and, a moment later, firemen were inside dealing with the blazing roof.

In view of its importance and the propaganda value to the enemy if it was destroyed, the Chief Superintendent and his driver had made frequent exploratory visits to the Palace of Westminster and had become familiar with means of access between various parts of the complex.

Following usual practice, Dave was despatched to reconnoitre the area to gather information for transmission to control, which had been set up in Old Palace Yard. An important part of his duty was to collect the tally carried by the officer in charge of each appliance, containing details of the station and crew involved. These tallies were displayed on the map of the fire area chalked on the operations board in the Fire Control. Thus, the control officer had precise knowledge of the firefighting force engaged. He would know exactly who to search for if a roll call, following an explosion or building collapse, revealed that men were missing.

Making his way through several corridors, Leading Fireman Millar entered the Commons Chamber. Looking down from the Strangers' Gallery, he saw that everything appeared normal. Turning to leave, he closed the door behind him. As he did so, a tremendous explosion flung him several yards along the passage. Shaken, but unhurt, his first thought was to report to control before a search was mounted for him, since he was known to be in the building.

After reporting to control, he encountered the Firemaster and Robin Duff and directed them to internal hydrants. Together, they got two jets to work into the blazing Chamber from the door behind the Speaker's Chair. Soon, reinforcing pumps arrived and more jets were brought to bear on the fire. Then came another crash as a delayed action bomb went off, bringing down a section of wall onto the men working in the courtyard below. Amazingly, none was seriously hurt.

The Victoria Tower was under repair and partly encased in scaffolding. Several incendiaries lay burning on the roof and upper platforms. An officer led his crew up the internal staircase, extinguishing the fires before serious damage had been done. About to return to ground, he noticed a hole he had not seen before and traced it, floor by floor, to the basement where he discovered a large unexploded bomb and a badly-injured House of Commons custodian lying nearby.

Bombs were still falling and burning embers from the Chamber had started fires in other parts of the building but there were sufficient fire crews now available to tackle them all without delay and they were soon under control.

Shortly after, the fire in the Chamber was extinguished and Millar set off to report this information to control.

The southern end of the Commons Chamber roof on the morning of May 11th, 1941. The Victoria Tower, on the right, was undergoing repair and stands encased in scaffolding. The internal lift gave access to the lower three floors only; from there, it's Shank's pony to the top! When a number of fire bombs were seen burning on the upper platforms, a fire crew, carrying first aid fire equipment, set out on the long climb and succeeded in extinguishing the fires before serious damage was done. The H.E. bomb that wrecked the Chamber was seen to ricochet off the roof of the Clock Tower.

He was then instructed to check the area around Westminster Abbey and Westminster School. Another shower of incendiaries had started more fires and several pumps were rounded up to deal with these outbreaks.

Entering the Abbey, Millar and Duff found it full of smoke, with fire glowing faintly from the roof, 150 feet above. They had a clearer view from the outside and could now see that the fire involved that part of the roof known as the Lantern. The only way up was by means of the 200 or so stairs and along various catwalks. The Firemaster and the Leading Fireman ran up to get a closer look and found that workmen, carrying out repairs to the roof, had rigged a pulley, complete with rope. Millar came down and found a crew from Wembley looking for a job and, with much coming and going, a line of hose was hoisted to the roof, using the pulley, and carried along a catwalk to where it could command the fire area.

Leaving the Wembley men to get on with the job, the Firemaster and Millar returned to ground, just as the Lantern came crashing to the Abbey floor on the spot where King George VI and Queen Elizabeth had stood at their Coronation in 1937. The collapse left the fire crew stranded, their escape cut off by the hole in the roof. Fortunately, they had been well-trained and adopted an oft-related method of escape; they lashed their hose and, using it as a safety line, slid down to the ground.

Debris from the roof litters the floor of Westminster Abbey following the May 10/11th air raid.

Whilst taking a breather after his exertions, Dave Millar had a cup of tea thrust in his hand. Thanking the girl, Dave, who had been a chauffeur in civilian life, recognised her as a fellow member of the household staff in pre-war days.

'My goodness,' he remarked. 'We do meet in strange places.'

'Drink it up,' she replied, 'and come around the corner to the van; I've got some chocolate.' Dave followed her to the canteen van, was given another cup of tea and a much prized bar of chocolate. After a short chat they returned to the centre of action.

A few days later, he was told by a mutual friend that this brave girl had been killed a few hours after their meeting. She had persisted in her voluntary task of bringing refreshment to firefighters and Civil Defence workers operating in the front line, in complete disregard for her own safety.

Yet another of the unsung heroines and heroes thrown up by the Blitz.

Meantime, the fight to save historic Westminster Hall had been given top priority. Colonel Walter Elliott, M.P., who had been present from the onset of the raid, had been liaising with the Chief Superintendent, vigorously urging that every effort be made to save Westminster Hall. Mr McDuell had reached the same conclusion; the Chamber had already been destroyed whilst much of the Hall was still to be saved.

And saved it was, by the skill, tenacity and selfless toil of the firefighters. It had been a difficult task, due to the height of the roof. The only way to douse the flames was by means of powerful jets working from within the smoke-filled building. Fortunately, the water supply from the Palace's internal hydrant system was sufficient to meet all demands. Part of the magnificent roof had gone and some of the famous hammer-beams were damaged. Debris from the roof was floating on the lake which covered the floor of the Hall to a depth of some six inches.

The House of Commons Chamber had been blasted out of existence and part of the roof of Westminster Abbey had been destroyed. Serious damage had been inflicted on the Deanery and Cloisters and on Westminster School. But when the debris was cleared it was seen that damage was considerably less than had appeared likely when the fire control van and its staff had arrived in Old Palace Yard.

Surveying the Westminster area next morning, the Chief Superintendent was met by the Dean of Westminster, Canon Paul Labilliere, and presented with a carved linen-fold panel from St Margaret's Church as a mark of appreciation of the activities of the fire service the previous evening.

20th April, 1953

Dear Mr. McDuell,

I learn with regret that you have had to retire from the post of Deputy Chief Officer of the London Fire Brigade on the 31st March due to the serious injuries you received during your very fine work at the Broad Street Station Goods Depot on the night of the 21st December, 1951.

I also recall the very excellent work you carried out on the night in May, 1941, when the Palace of Westminster was bombed and the roof of Westminster Hall was set on fire, and how largely by your exertions this great Hall was saved from destruction.

I feel that both Houses of Parliament owe you a great debt of gratitude and thanks for what you did on this occasion, and on behalf of both Houses of Parliament, I would like to take this opportunity of expressing our deep appreciation of your services.

Yours sincerely,

Cholmondeley

Lord Great Chamberlain

C.P. McDuell, Esq. O.B.E.
c/o Headquarters, London Fire Brigade,
Lambeth, S.E.1

Three firemen were killed and others injured whilst fighting the fire at Broad Street Goods Depot, when a wall collapsed. The Deputy Chief Officer, C. P. McDuell, OBE, received injuries which necessitated the amputation of a leg. When the House of Commons Chamber was rebuilt after the war, there was talk of a commemorative plaque, recording the work of the Fire Service on the night of the bombing, but nothing came of it. Hence the tardy acknowledgement. This letter is reproduced by kind permission of Major R. C. McDuell.

It was one of the most punishing nights that London firemen had experienced and nowhere was it more cruel than in Southwark and Lambeth.

It started with a heavy fall of H.E. and incendiaries in the vicinity of the Elephant and Castle, the famous south London pub at the junction of Old Kent Road and Newington Butts. Freeman, Hardy and Willis's boot and shoe warehouse; Spurgeon's Tabernacle and Deans Rag Book factory were ablaze and the area had all the makings of a conflagration from the start. The first pumps to arrive set in to a nearby 5,000 gallon emergency dam, whilst orders were given for water relays to be started from the Manor Place Baths and the converted basement of the Old Surrey Music Hall at St George's Circus, both about 800 yards distant. The first jets emptied the 5,000 gallon dam in just five minutes, bringing firefighting to a standstill until fresh supplies became available. Meanwhile, fire crews had worked frantically to set in their pumps to the swimming pool at Manor Place and to the basement dam at St George's Circus. Firemen nearing exhaustion, somehow found reserves of energy and ran their hose lines along the curbside towards the great raging inferno.

The Elephant and Castle area around midnight, May 10/11th, 1941. Lots of pumps, very little water!

The wrecked trailer pumps and the bodies of their crews have been removed from the emergency water basin at the Old Surrey Music Hall. A trailer pump removes the last of the water to uncover anything that may be submerged.

Pathetic relics at the scene of the Old Surrey Music Hall tragedy: a shattered length of suction hose; a fireman's axe and his respirator, torn from its case, lying jumbled together with pieces of rope and a piece of pump casing.

Then disaster struck.

A large H.E. bomb exploded among the cluster of pumps crowding around the Old Music Hall dam, killing seventeen firemen and creating such havoc that access to the dam was completely blocked. The fire was now out of control and rapidly spreading, as enemy pilots, recognising a promising target, set about stoking it up to even greater fury.

More water relays were put in hand from the Thames at London, Waterloo and Westminster bridges and from the Surrey Canal, over distances ranging from a mile to a mile and a half. Slowly, jets were brought to bear on the fringes to stop the spread. More jets became available as relays were completed and now the firemen began to get on top, driving the fire back to its centre. But another set-back occurred in Newington Butts when the walls of a blazing building collapsed, burying the newly laid hose lines under tons of red hot bricks just as they were beginning to carry water to the Elephant and Castle. But the grit, determination and spirit of the men eventually triumphed and the great conflagration was isolated and brought under control with water pumped through nine miles of hose.

It had been a night of unprecedented blood, tears, toil and sweat. Nearly two thousand five hundred fires were started in the London Region, adding to the enormous damage caused by high explosive bombs. The British Museum Library was an early casualty; damage there included the loss of a quarter of a million books. Five of the city's telephone exchanges were disrupted and thousands of other buildings were demolished or severely damaged, including eight of the capital's main line rail terminals.

Nearly fifteen hundred Londoners died on that night of terror, thirty-five of them firemen.

Numerous fires were still burning, out of control, as dawn broke on the Sunday morning. Exhausted firemen found it hard to raise a cheer when sirens sounded the All Clear, and barrage balloons climbed slowly into the clouds of smoke that were obscuring an otherwise clear sky. Vast numbers of Londoners found themselves without water, gas and electricity when they emerged from shelters, many to say a silent prayer of thanks for having been spared the wounds that so many of their friends and neighbours had suffered. But the Nazi's didn't have it all their own way. The night fighter boys claimed twenty-eight raiders shot down with the aid of the new airborne-interception radar equipment in this, the last major air raid on London.

During the period September 7th, 1940 to May 10th, 1941 London had received severe damage. Many thousands of buildings had been demolished and famous landmarks including Buckingham Palace, the Houses of Parliament, St Paul's Cathedral and several other Wren churches, the Guildhall and many other historic and architectural treasures had been severely damaged. The Germans had killed over fourteen thousand civilian men, women and children; many thousands more had been seriously injured. Nearly four hundred members of the London Fire Forces had been killed by enemy action. Many provincial cities and towns suffered similar attacks, and their people met them with the same spirit and determination as their London brothers and sisters. Reinforcing fire pumps reached London from Merseyside, Birmingham, Bristol, Portsmouth and other Regions. Convoys from London returned the aid when those places were hard pressed.

With the lull in the bombing, the fire service took the opportunity of catching up on the long neglected maintenance of appliances and equipment. Uniform was cleaned of paint and tar and leather fire boots were thoroughly dried out. Much time was spent in the testing and repair of fire hose,

Fires still blaze on Sunday morning after the May 10th raid. Ex-servicemen watch firemen at work in Carter Lane, as they assemble for a service in St Paul's Cathedral.

which had been in use almost continuously for eight months. But of all the relief that came with the lull, none was more welcome than uninterrupted sleep. At first, we were afraid to undress and slept rough, as we had learned to do whenever the opportunity for a nap came. But, as weeks passed without a visit from the Nazis, beds were made again upstairs and life took on a rosier hue.

On the day following the destruction of the House of Commons Chamber, Tom Stothard, now wearing his Ministry of Works hat, had arrived to survey Church House, Westminster, which had been earmarked as a possible alternative meeting place for Parliament in the event of the Chamber becoming unusable. His job was to provide essential items of furniture like tables, chairs, carpets, filing cabinets etc.

Unfortunately, Church House, too, had been severely damaged the previous night when a H.E. bomb exploded in the lovely panelled circular Chamber, the meeting place of the London Diocesan Council.

'Dangerous Wall' notices were displayed to warn people against entering the building. Tom's fire service experience had made him wary of 'live' walls and he stood well clear as he surveyed the damage.

From behind came a voice:

'Do you know your way about this building?' Turning, Tom found himself face to face with Lord Beaverbrook and Clement Attlee, the Deputy Prime Minister.

'Yes, sir,' replied Tom.

'Well, show me around,' said His Lordship as he stepped briskly beyond the limit set by the 'Dangerous Wall' boards. Disciplined Tom, who had learned to obey orders, especially notices of this nature, had no option in this particular instance but to follow on.

'It occurred to me that he was leading me round rather than the reverse,' said Tom, relating the story. 'My toes were curling in my shoes as I skirted those walls.'

But it was abundantly clear that Church House was in no condition to house the Mother of Parliaments and the Minister of Aircraft Production strode from the building into the street.

'How are we doing, Your Lordship?' enquired the man at the news stand.

'We're doing fine,' came the reply. 'Just fine.' And Tom's apprehension about the walls was vindicated next day when a demolition squad moved in to pull them down.

6

Brief Respite

DESPITE the grim days and nights, the food shortages and all the other trials and tribulations that beset the population, the traditional cockney humour was never entirely submerged. People made light of the bombing, always quick to see the funny side of otherwise tragic incidents. The story of a man providing a pep talk to a somewhat nervous individual went round the pubs.

'So Jerry decides to send 'is bombers to Lunnon. Lunnon's a big place and Bermonsey's only a little corner of it. But suppose they do come over Bermonsey, they've got to find Abbey Street, where you live. Even supposin' they find Abbey Street out of all the fahsands of streets, they've got to pick out No. 22. Nah, it'll be real bad luck if they do pick out No. 22. won't it? Even then, chances are you'll be up the pub 'avin' a drink, so wotcher got ter worry about?'

It was about this period that London Transport introduced an advertising campaign designed to assist Londoners in overcoming transport difficulties. The central character was a cheerful, bowler-hatted little man called Billy Brown of London Town, who delivered his message in rhyme. Billy Brown's smiling face was to be seen on posters at underground stations, at bus stops and on hoardings. One of the early posters carried an instruction on how to hail a bus at a request stop. 'Face the driver, raise your hand. Be sure that he will understand.'

Others followed and 'Billy Brown says' became a catch phrase. Many casualties had been caused by flying glass following bomb explosions and, to reduce the risk to travellers, a strong, net curtain type of material had been stuck on bus and train windows. Unfortunately, this had the effect of preventing passengers from checking their where-abouts so they took to cutting out small squares with a razor blade or peeling the corners to provide peep holes.

The Authority took prompt measures to discourage this practice with a new poster which I spotted in a tube train on the District Line. The poster portrayed a passenger in the act of peeling away the net from the corner of a window, with Billy Brown wagging an admonitory finger and delivering his rebuke.

'I trust you'll pardon my correction. But that stuff's there for your protection.'

An irrepressible cockney humorist had been unable to resist the temptation to answer back. Underneath he had pencilled his salty comment: 'I thank you for your information. But I can't see the bloody station!'

On June 22nd, 1941, the reason for the Luftwaffe's neglect of London became apparent, for on that day Hitler committed what Mr Churchill later described as one of the outstanding blunders in history; he invaded Russia. To our great surprise and delight, Britain had acquired a powerful ally right out of the blue.

Within a few days the capital was flooded with Red Flags, flying from mastheads over public buildings and forming the central motif in many window displays. Cinema audiences cheered newsreel coverage of Red Army units and applauded any reference to Stalin and the Russian people.

Whitewashed slogans proclaiming 'Stop the capitalist war,' daubed on walls at many street corners in the East End, were hastily scrubbed out and replaced by a new message: 'Start the second front now.'

People in heavily bombed areas were now quick to appreciate that the welcome and peaceful raid-free nights they were enjoying they owed to the Red Army and Air Force that were keeping the Luftwaffe at full stretch along the 1,800-mile Russian Front.

British civilians, after eight long months of uncomfortable nights spent in air raid shelters, were now able to enjoy an unbroken night's sleep in their own beds. But their relief was tempered in the knowledge that our new allies were exposed to an ordeal even worse than ours had been. We, at least, had been spared the horror of facing an invading army!

Adversity, indeed, made brothers of us all.

With the lull in enemy activity, life in the fire stations reverted to routine matters. Although it was a relief to be free from the threat of sudden death from the sky, the intensity of events during the past eight months contrasted strikingly with the comparative dullness of the raid-free days and nights now being experienced. Firemen attended the occasional 'peace time' fire and concentrated on essential maintenance of fire hose and other equipment, long neglected during the Blitz period. Many were kept busy in the surge to provide more emergency water supplies; erecting steel dams on every available open space and helping to convert the basements of wrecked buildings into large storage basins, some holding a million gallons of water. During the Blitz some water relays had broken down due to faulty pump operating. It was realised that there was need for special training in matters relating to water supplies in general; accordingly, a special section was established at the Strand School, Brixton, for selected officers. Water storage basins were charted and linked and the information collated in water vans, ready to attend, with a local water officer, any fire reporting a shortage of water.

In the watchrooms, firewomen found the days passing slowly. Said Betty Barrett, 'Even when our fire appliances had been out for days on end, we were still kept busy passing to and receiving messages from Control and dealing with callers. Our watch was over before we realised it. We were tired out at the end of the day or night and, after a meal, crept up to bed to fall asleep the moment our heads touched the pillow. But now the hours passed slowly and we began to devise games and diversions to help time pass more quickly. One of our fantasies was what we called an 'opera day' when any conversation between us had to be sung, not spoken. We were not allowed, for instance, to ask 'pass the salt, please,' it had to be sung to a made-up tune. Some of the girls had nice voices and introduced good parodies. We enjoyed their contributions but some couldn't sing a note, absolutely tone deaf, and we had a few good laughs before we excused them from taking part; we couldn't stand any more!

'Playing cards was a popular pastime. We were not allowed to play for money but, since we occupied rooms at the top of the building and visiting officers had to pass through the watchroom, we arranged for the firewoman on duty to give us a ring when one was on the way, whereupon we scooped up the cash and were sitting all innocent when her ladyship entered. One evening we had the cards out and money all over the table, when in walked the Assistant Group Officer. The girl in the watchroom, perhaps, was busy on the phone, or something; anyway, we didn't get a warning and were caught in the act.

'Ah', said the AGO 'playing cards?' Seeing the cash her voice rose. 'And for money!'

We hung our guilty heads, except for Leading Firewoman Rickman who was supposed to be in charge of our watch. She was so overcome with mortification that she slipped slowly from her chair and crawled under the table. But the Assistant Group Officer was compassionate and we escaped with a warning.

'Part of my job was to telephone routine messages to Fire Control at New Cross. There was a young sub-officer there who became very chatty, telling me I was "his girl with the golden voice". One day he asked if I liked dancing and I told him I did.

"How about coming to a dance with me one evening?" he asked.

"Oh. I'll think about it," I replied. He repeated the invitation some days later and I agreed.

"Right." he said. "There's a dance at the Town Hall next Wednesday; I'll meet you there."

"Hold on a minute," I answered. "How will I know you?"

"I'll wear a white flower in my buttonhole." So I togged myself up in a nice dress; put on a bit of lipstick and off I went to meet him. I was wondering what he was like and he apparently had the same idea about me, as he told me rather more bluntly, later on.

I couldn't see anyone wearing a white button hole and was about to return home when up came a young chap. "Are you my girl with the golden voice?," he asked.

"I was just going home," I told him. "Where's your white button hole?"

"Ah," he replied. "I decided not to wear it, because if you'd been fair, fat and forty, I'd have done a bunk!"

And that was the end of that!'

7 The Firewomen

WHEN the training of volunteers for the West Ham A.F.S. commenced in March 1939 only men were considered; nothing was done about the recruitment of women other than the registering of names. But when it became clear that war was imminent, women volunteers were called up for training, the first of them reporting only a few days before the declaration of war. Now there was a great rush to instruct in the rudiments of their duties those who were to work in the control rooms. Every minute was precious, for none knew when the blow would fall.

Hitherto, the fire brigade had been a male preserve and it was difficult to see what part women could play. Firemen did all the cleaning, cooking and administrative work in the fire stations but it quickly came to be realised that there were opportunities for women in the control rooms, as clerical workers, car drivers, cooks, motor cycle dispatch riders etc., thus releasing men for firefighting duties.

The cooks made an immediate impact in the fire stations; language in the mess rooms took on a polite tone never before experienced. The fireman cooks had produced well-cooked meals but if something not entirely to the liking of the troops was served up, the cook was left in no doubt of any deficiency, real or fancied. Women cooks were spared this indignity and firemen strove valiantly to curb their free expression on matters of the day. Occasionally, someone would boil over and an apology was instantly forthcoming.

Imaginary fire situations were set up and firewomen control staff were kept busy mobilising appliances and learning control room routine. The girls were intelligent and worked hard to master unfamiliar fire service jargon. As they became efficient, they were introduced to operational control rooms and gained experience of dealing with the real thing. Inevitably, there were a few gaffes and one young woman produced a gem during her first spell of duty in the Homerton Fire Control, when she took in a 'stop' message from a fire.

'From Station Officer Brooks.' dictated the fireman at the other end of the line. 'Stop for Hackney Marshes. About half an acre of furze and undergrowth burned on open ground, one jet in use.'

But the mobilising officer had doubts about the veracity of the message she had recorded on the slip when he read: 'From Station Officer Brooks. Stop for Hackney Marshes. About half an acre of frozen underclothes burned on open ground, one jet in use.'

It was a long time before she was allowed to forget it and the opportunity was taken to drive home the point that this was the outcome of failing to repeat a message which might not be all it appeared.

There had been no opportunity of instructing firewomen on anything other than the broad details of their duties; certainly, an appreciation of the traditions of the Service did not appear on the curriculum. Yet, many became aware that they were now part of a Service very close to the public, a body to whom people turned naturally in times of emergency and who responded promptly and efficiently when called upon. Thus, an appreciation of 'the best traditions of the Service' became a natural instinct, as countless firewomen demonstrated as the Blitz proceeded. They took on any job short of handling branches on the fireground and performed valiantly in their execution.

One of the first tasks of car drivers and despatch riders was to find their way about the district. They were exercised over

This quintet of firewomen D.R.s line up for the photographer. On dark nights, their masked headlamp gave only faint illumination to the road ahead, calling for extra vigilance on the part of the rider.

the ground, delivering stores and messages to fire stations, and, as they became familiar with local topography, were required to travel further afield, following alternative routes in anticipation of bomb damage to roads. The black-out and severe weather during the winter of 1939-40 combined to make life hard for those engaged in mobility exercises which took them to strategic locations in neighbouring areas of high fire risk. The time gained by the absence of enemy activity during the Phoney War period was put to good use and when the Blitz commenced almost a year later, our firewomen had become familiar with their various responsibilities.

On September 7th, 1940 the period of make-believe came to a sudden end and we were all brought face to face with the violent reality of bombardment from the air. No longer were the control room personnel dealing with simulated incidents involving ten or twenty pumps; the messages they were now receiving reported dreadful tragedies and enormous damage. The worst hit areas were calling for assistance measured in hundreds of pumps. It was difficult to concentrate on detail, for control rooms were continually rocked by blast. The D.Rs now came into their own. Telephones were disrupted over a wide area, isolating fire stations and preventing officers in charge of fires from sending assistance and informative messages. The D.Rs moved in to fill the gap, carrying

messages back and forth through streets littered with glass and rubble. Bomb craters in the roads were but one of the hazards they faced. Blazing buildings on both sides of roads created lanes of fire, and tangles of fire hose brought many a D.R. to grief. The scream of falling bombs and the rattle of shrapnel from anti-aircraft gun-fire brought fear to the stoutest hearts, but the messages were delivered, thanks largely to the courage and tenacity of the firewomen D.Rs.

The officers' car drivers, by the very nature of their job, were constantly in the centre of the action. They had to battle not only with physical fear, as bombs came screaming down and buildings collapsed all around, but also with nausea brought about by scenes of ghastly mutilation and suffering. Yet, with very few exceptions, they bore up under the greatest strain.

Firewoman Peggy Muirhead, who drove my staff car when I was attached to Clerkenwell Fire Station, positively enjoyed being in the thick of operations. She missed no opportunity of backing up a branchman struggling with a line of hose, and I have no doubt she would have been delighted to splash a branch about for the duration of the raid, even on the coldest

No punches pulled for women dispatch riders. This girl comes to grief in the mud of No. 36 Area's (north-east London) motor cycle training ground. She must be prepared to ride through streets with bombers cruising overhead as she negotiates lines of fire hose criss-crossing the road. She must learn to dodge around bomb craters; piles of smoking debris and to speed through blistering heat, radiated from blazing buildings, to deliver vital messages. This firewoman has the right spirit; she can still manage a smile!

of nights, had she been allowed to do so. There were many adventurous spirits like Peggy Muirhead among members of the wartime A.F.S. and some banded together to form pump's crews composed entirely of firewomen. But these were isolated cases; there was no official move to encourage women to engage in active firefighting with major equipment. But there are numerous cases on record of firewomen, using stirrup pumps and buckets, extinguishing incendiary bombs which would otherwise have destroyed many a building.

Commander Firebrace, then London Regional Fire Officer, was fond of telling the story of the drama at Redcross Street Fire Station on the night of the City Blitz. The area had been subjected to a hail of fire bombs; tall office buildings and warehouses surrounding the fire station blazed out of control. All fire appliances had been ordered out during the first minutes of the raid, when City fire stations were overwhelmed with calls. Firewomen remained to operate the switchboard, maintaining a vital link in the chain of communications. As the fires crept closer, senior officers were debating evacuating the station when the control room door was flung open and a Civil Defence warden burst in.

'Hey! Your bloody roof's on fire,' he yelled, disappearing as quickly as he had come.

'Whoopee!' cried a firewoman, grabbing a stirrup pump and making for the stairs, followed by others with buckets of water.

They caught the fire in its early stage and did an expert job in extinguishing it. However, they must have considered their sterling work a wasted effort when it was decided, a few minutes later, to evacuate the building. But, against all the odds, the fire station survived to stand, with Whitbread's Brewery, as a monument in the desert of rubble that was once the prosperous area of Cripplegate.

Another of Commander Firebrace's oft repeated stories tells of a visit by a lady V.I.P. to a small fire station where she was invited to stay for lunch. After an enjoyable meal, she asked to see the kitchen and was shown into a small, hot room. Congratulating the firewoman cook, she asked: 'However did you manage to make such delicious pastry in this hot little kitchen?' 'No trouble at all, madam,' came the reply. 'When we have special visitors like yourself, I pop next door into the mortuary and use one of the marble slabs. Nice and cool in there.'

Firewoman Muriel Nyman relaxing on the balcony of Whitgift House, Lambeth, the quarters of the drivers pool, March 1943. The W. H. Smith building on Albert Embankment can be seen in the background.

Muriel Nyman was just twenty-one when she joined the A.F.S. and was posted to the driving pool at London Fire Brigade Headquarters. Said Muriel: 'Most of our work consisted of driving officers to various fire stations in the London Region but, occasionally, duty took us further afield. One such occasion was when three of us were detailed to drive open lorries laden with stores to Edinburgh and to return with cars. It might have been a pleasant change from routine work but this was in February, a cold, bleak February, with icy winds blowing through our open cabs. But orders were orders and we prepared for our journey.

'I had a large green woollen scarf which hardly matched my navy blue uniform; I knew I should not be allowed to wear it had I been seen by an officer, so I smuggled it into the cab.

We were given a route and set off on our four hundred mile trip. About an hour out of London, one of the lorries broke down and it was beyond our combined mechanical skills to get it going again. So we foraged around, found a length of rope, made a tow and started off again. The rope did not seem very secure but it was the best we could do.

'Hazel Charaton started the tow; Joan Rosher came next with the breakdown and I followed up close behind, ready to give the vehicle in front a nudge or two to help it up the hills. Eventually, we reached Birmingham where we sought help from the first fire station we saw. The N.F.S. workshop patched it up and we resumed our trip.

'After a slow, laborious and uncomfortable journey, we delivered our lorries to their destination. They gave us overnight accommodation in a sparsely furnished hut at the rear of the canteen and, with nothing to do, we went to bed early. During the night, I woke up with the need to visit the toilet, but there was no toilet, so, in the middle of the night I dressed, put on my shoes and overcoat, wrapped the scarf around my neck and stumbled out into a field at the back, in the blackness of a very dark and very cold night. Next morning, after an unappetising breakfast, we collected a car each and arrived back home without further incident.'

'There were twenty-one of us women drivers in the pool at Lambeth and we were accommodated in a block of Council flats at Whitgift House, close to the Newport Street depot where our cars were garaged. The large dormitory where we all slept was on an upper floor and our mess room, on the ground floor, had a great long counter, which was used to lay out our food. Each morning, a badly crippled man delivered the morning papers. One of his arms was almost useless and dropped below the level of the other and he obviously found it difficult to walk. He was always accompanied by a small black dog.

'One morning, we had just come down to breakfast; some of us were buying a morning paper and others had moved over to the counter when there came a shattering explosion from the direction of Black Prince Road and, obviously, very close. We dived under the counter as the ceiling came crashing down, filling the room with debris. Then there was silence, broken only by the whining of the dog, and we emerged to a remarkable sight. Our news seller was wedged in a corner, literally standing on his head, his papers still under his arm. We ran over and turned him right side up whereupon, to our utter amazement, he walked briskly from the room with no trace of his disability, his dog trotting along behind! We had witnessed a miracle.'

Not least of the troubles of the day, especially for firewomen, was the problem of clothes rationing. Like their male colleagues, firewomen were called upon to surrender a significant proportion of their meagre issue of clothing coupons for their uniforms. Most of the girls were acutely clothes conscious and went to considerable lengths to maintain a smart appearance. The standard issue jacket and skirt was often poorly cut and made up of inferior serge material. Those who could afford to had their uniforms made up privately via the black market, but the majority had to fall back on their skill with scissors and needle. The black market flourished in the East End; clothing coupons could be bought for cash, and material purchased from certain shops and stalls without coupons, for a little extra payment. Some of the firewomen had been tailoresses or dressmakers in civilian life and these were in constant demand for their expertise. One way or another, the women managed to make the best of their appearance whilst keeping within the regulations. Of more concern to a firewoman at Wellclose Square Fire Station than her personal safety, was the damage she did to her stockings when diving for shelter under the control room table as a bomb came screaming down.

One advantage enjoyed by firewomen over their male colleagues was the issue of three bed-sheets. When I was serving at Whitechapel Fire Station, Assistant Group Officer Adams, who was in charge of the firewomen, told me of an incident when she was conducting a kit inspection. These inspections were carried out in Service fashion with the kit laid out on the individual's bed. A.G.O. Adams, reading from her list, came to sheets. 'Three bed sheets,' she read, whereupon the firewoman produced a neatly folded pile which struck the A.G.O. as suspiciously thin. Closer inspection revealed two complete sheets and a remnant consisting of about a square foot of sheet material. 'C'mon, where's the rest of it?' she demanded. 'I'm wearing it,' replied the firewoman, unbuttoning her jacket to display her home-made shirt!

Nellie Durrant was a single girl living with her parents in a small house off the Portway, West Ham. She was born in the borough, attended the local school and worked in the district before joining the A.F.S. She had not much to say for herself, but her intelligence was apparent in the speed with which she grasped the significance of essential points in her training. There was also the twinkle in her eyes behind the spectacles in quick appreciation of a joke. Firewoman Durrant was trained as a telephonist whose duty it was to despatch and receive messages to and from fire stations and the various controls. She was on duty at the London Fire Region's 'J' District Control at Abbey Road School, West Ham, one hectic night when the borough was receiving a particularly heavy pounding. She had been on duty for several hours, seated at the switchboard, receiving and sending messages. The control room was shaken repeatedly by explosions but Nellie, with her colleagues, carried on, methodically recording the messages and placing them in trays for attention by the controllers. Presently, one of the firewomen approached the mobilising officer. Could he allow Nellie to go home? She had just taken in a message from the local wardens, calling for assistance at a land mine incident in the street where she lived with her parents. He went over to the switchboard.

'I'm terribly sorry to hear the news, Nellie. Would you like to go home?'

'No, I don't think so,' she replied. 'The wardens will be busy and there's not much I can do.'

She was a little paler than usual but quite composed and immediately returned to her seat. The mobilising officer told the senior firewoman to keep an eye on her and to allow her to go home if she wished. It was about 11 p.m. when she was persuaded to walk around the corner to her home during a lull in the bombardment; a forlorn little figure in her steel helmet and respirator. She was back in a couple of hours.

'The house is down,' she reported. 'But mum and dad are alright. They've gone to the rest centre.'

She was given a cup of tea and sat down at the switchboard to resume duty. And she was there when the All Clear sounded at about 7 a.m.

Nan More was a fireman's wife who joined the A.F.S. as a cook. Nan was among those for whom time had no meaning during the terrifying events of September 7th, 1940, with West Ham in the front line from the first minutes of the attack. Every available fire pump was ordered out to Silvertown or the docks together with hundreds of appliances from the London Fire Region and beyond. There was little for Nan and her colleagues to do; no point in preparing a meal, for there was no one to eat it.

After the first week, the shock had been absorbed and a reasonable relief system evolved, with each fire station settling down to a routine fashioned by experience. Firemen, enjoying a brief respite, told of their feelings whilst fighting fires on a scale even the regulars found beyond their experience. For many of the auxiliaries, this was their first glimpse of a fire, and what a baptism it was! All had stories to

tell and, most of all, they talked of working twelve hours or more without food or water. Most of the water mains had been fractured and water for firefighting came from the river, docks or ponds, none of it drinkable. Despite their ordeal, there was little grumbling and what there was diminished as Nan, with her small band of helpers managed, somehow, to conjure up hot, satisfying meals without gas or electricity, doing their cooking on unfamiliar paraffin burners.

Towards evening, preparations for the nightly activity began. The firewomen control operators prepared their message slips and checked emergency lighting. The D.Rs were overhauling their motor bikes and the fire crews looked to their pumps and hose. The cooks were cutting sandwiches for the men to take with them and preparing for a cooked meal on their return from the night's action.

West Ham had received a canteen van, a gift from the people of Guelph, Ontario, Canada and it was operated solely by crews of firewomen. Nan and her colleagues were always looking for the chance to provide refreshment for hungry firemen at work in the docks, or wherever West Ham men were engaged. As nights grew colder, Nan developed strong views on the value of tea and biscuits as adequate refreshment for firemen, often soaked to the skin.

His Majesty chats to Firewoman Vera Lynfield whilst inspecting Firewomen at Lambeth Headquarters on October 16th, 1940. These are the women who took their canteen vans into the front line, night after night, to bring refreshment to the Blitz firefighters.

'What they need is a basin of soup or a nice, hot stew,' she declared. But the ingredients were hard to come by in those days of shortage, despite her winning ways with tradesmen. But on December 29th, 1940 she had been able to find the materials for a 'nice hot stew' and her first stop, that night, was to feed West Ham crews working on the burning Woolworth's store at Aldgate. Then on to the City, where they were received with cheers by all and sundry. The canteen van was emptied in record time and the party returned to Stratford Fire Station to hang up their steel helmets and respirators and prepare a meal for the starving hordes returning from the night's operations. They had achieved what they set out to do, and, like so many other firewomen canteen van crews, had placed themselves in the thick of the battle, alongside the boys.

When the fire services were nationalised in 1942, physical training was one of the ancillary activities brought under scrutiny. Intelligence reports indicated that the enemy was planning the use of secret weapons in a series of heavy bombing attacks on civilian targets. It was foreseen that the fire service would be called upon to perform duties that would require extreme physical effort. Accordingly, Captain E. N. Hebbert of the Army Physical Training Corps, was appointed by the Home Office to organise Fitness Training for Fire Service personnel; he lost no time in raising a cadre in each Fire Force. The No. 36 Area Fitness Training H.Q. was

Lancaster bomber of the R.A.F. 'O for Orange', spreads its wings before the National Gallery in Trafalgar Square as the No. 36 Area Agility Team parades, preparatory to presenting a display in support of 'Wings for Victory' week.

established at the Trafalgar Gardens School in Stepney. A team, consisting of seven firewomen and thirteen firemen, was selected; all were amateur P.T. enthusiasts with the exception of Fireman Alf Maloney, a professional acrobat who had been a member of a successful theatrical troupe.

The main purpose was to introduce organised P.T. training schedules into operational training at fire stations; the newly-raised squad was designed to raise the general standard. Visits to stations proved very popular with the troops, since the team included several shapely young ladies, clad in shirt and shorts, who demonstrated exercises to assembled fire crews. Any activity likely to maintain civilian morale was vigorously promoted; a performance by an agility team was seen as a popular event. So it was decided to widen the scope and Alf Maloney volunteered to train the team on professional lines. Split-second timing of the sequences was essential for thoroughly professional performances and to avoid injury to those taking part. Alf kept his team hard at work practising until all had mastered the art of tumbling. The girls found the going hard, but they persevered until their trainer was satisfied with the standard.

Reward for their hard work came when the team appeared at fund raising events for Service Charities and 'Salute the Soldier' and 'Wings for Victory' appeals, etc. Their quick fire acrobatic routine proved a show stopper and the team was in constant demand.

From time to time the fire service showed off its skills at demonstrations held at Lambeth Headquarters in the presence of V.I.Ps such as King Haakon of Norway, Mr Maisky, the Russian Ambassador, General Smuts and others. On these occasions, the Area Agility teams combined to present attractive displays which unfailingly proved to be one of the most popular items.

In December 1944, H.M. Queen Elizabeth, accompanied by our present Queen, then H.R.H. The Princess Elizabeth, visited Lambeth and were entertained at a display which, fittingly, was an all-woman affair.

The day was bright, but bitterly cold and, because of the importance of the occasion, the drill yard was given special treatment. It was hosed down at 7 a.m. and, although most of the water was broomed away, what remained froze. This brought consternation to those in charge of the firewomen, for whom a spectacular exercise had been planned. One formation sequence involved sitting on the ground whilst carrying out rhythmic arm and leg movements. Those taking part were wearing white cotton shirts and shorts made from black-out curtain material, hardly sufficient, as Leading Firewoman Connie Jay put it, 'to keep out the light, let

alone the cold'. It was too late to reorganise the programme, but one of the leaders had a brain wave. The first aid store was raided and large rolls of cotton wool issued to the girls to pad their shorts with. So the day was saved and, in the best tradition, the show went on, including the sit-down sequence. 'And that's where I acquired my frozen assets,' remarked Connie Jay.

Senior Women Fire Officers parade at Lambeth for inspection by Her Majesty The Queen and Princess Elizabeth. Chief Woman Fire Officer B. Cuthbert, C.B.E. and Chief of the Fire Staff Commander A. N. G. Firebrace, C.B.E. accompany the Royal Party. Home Secretary Herbert Morrison, M.P. looks on.

Six hundred firewomen took part in the display at Lambeth fire headquarters in the presence of Queen Elizabeth and Princess Elizabeth on a raw December day in 1944. The scantily clad girls needed no bidding to 'put a bit of steam in it' as they doubled round the yard.

The flying bomb did not carry an incendiary device and large fires, like this one in Calvert Avenue, Shoreditch, were unusual. Sometimes, the components of an instant blaze were present in a building and fire followed the explosion. This V1 fell on the block of flats opposite, reducing the building to rubble. The marks on the right of the picture are those of the censor's blue pencil. The tree on the left, in full leaf on August 22nd, was entirely stripped by the blast. The flying bomb did not always fly on a direct course, nor did it always dive immediately the engine cut out. I was working in my office in Barking Fire Station one fine Sunday afternoon when a V1 cut out overhead. I dived for cover but the explosion did not come until about a minute later, and I was ordered out to Wanstead. The bomb had glided a distance of four to five miles, catching people unawares as they sat in their gardens. On another occasion, one came over Stratford Fire Station on a cloudy day; we saw it only momentarily as it flew through a break in the clouds. To our relief it passed over and we heard its engine fading into the distance and resumed what we were doing. Then we heard the engine noise again approaching Stratford and, still out of sight, it flew over the top again, and away into the distance. We breathed again, but only for a moment for the beast did it again, as if determined to locate our station. Everyone in the locality thought their street was the intended target! Something had happened to affect the steering but, this time, it finally resumed its course and flew away, to crash far outside our area.

Muriel Nyman has vivid memories of a day in August 1944.

'I was detailed to drive two women officers to Shoreditch Fire Station. We were in sight of Shoreditch Church, just passing Calvert Avenue, when a flying bomb exploded on a block of flats on the corner of Boundary Street. I was driving with both side windows wide open and the blast literally lifted the car from the road and let it down after we had floated several yards. I drove on to Shoreditch Fire Station and requested permission to return to Calvert Avenue to give what assistance I could. Yes, I could go and use the car as an ambulance for sitting cases. I reported to a Warden and offered help. He was very grateful; told me where to park and gave me a large flask of coffee. "Pick up anyone who looks in need of attention; give them a cup of coffee and take them to hospital if you think it necessary."

'It was a ghastly scene; bits of human bodies lying all over the road and dazed people sitting about. One man about forty was sitting on a piece of concrete. I took him over a cup of coffee and was treated to a flow of bad language such as I had never heard before. I put my arm around him, held his cup while he drank, then put him in the car and off to hospital. I was told he had lost all his family, wife and two daughters. I did some first aid work and drove several people to local hospitals, staying about two hours and helping wherever I could.

'It was my first close-up experience of a bad incident and I felt sickened and exhausted. So I made my way back to Lambeth where Group Officer Gold was waiting for me; my officer passengers had telephoned from Shoreditch to report where I was. G.O. Gold brought me a cup of tea and something to eat. I was glad of the tea but could not eat. After drinking I was violently sick and was put to bed.

'Since then,' said Muriel, 'I have grown much tougher. I have had quite a few narrow escapes, missing injury by a hair's breadth, but I did not escape entirely scot-free. Later that year I was driving an officer back to Lambeth from Bow Fire Station. It had been misty all day but the fog really came down as I was passing Mann, Crossman's brewery in Mile End Road. There was nothing for it but to stop as it was impossible to see a yard in front of the car. Suddenly, a huge dray horse reared up beside the car and there was I, looking up at his belly, convinced he was about to fall on me. One of the shafts came through my window, struck me on the temple and knocked me out. I soon recovered and although my passenger, Column Officer Richmond, wanted to take over as driver, I carried on when the fog lifted sufficiently for us to resume but he directed me to his home, where his wife made me tea and bathed my head. Rested, I drove back to H.Q.

8   The National Fire Service

DURING the Blitz, serious operational problems arose, caused mainly by differences in the organisation and equipment of the fourteen hundred separate fire brigades then existing in the country. Expressions of concern came from informed observers. Questions were asked in the House of Commons and letters, critical of the fire service, appeared in *The Times* newspaper. The Minister for Home Security, the Rt Hon. Herbert Morrison, M.P., called in his fire advisers to consider what should be done to remedy the situation. After long discussion, during which every alternative was examined, it was decided that the Service should come under the direct control of the Minister, i.e. that the fire service should be nationalised. Mr Morrison conveyed his decision to the House on May 13th, 1941 when it received almost unanimous approval. Legislation was rushed through and the Fire Services (Emergency Provisions) Act became Law seven days later. The Appointed Day was announced, August 18th, 1941, and on that day all fire brigades were amalgamated into one huge organisation, with standard uniform, standard drill procedure and, above all, unified command. Senior officers were appointed by a Home Office Committee; these, in turn, interviewed officers for junior posts in the new Service. The change-over was quickly under way, for none knew if or when the Blitz might be renewed.

I attended an Appointments Board, presided over by an officer who was to exert considerable influence over my future career, Fire Force Commander C. P. McDuell. I received a letter a few days later, appointing me Company Officer in the National Fire Service, a rank equivalent to

It was not until the Luftwaffe demolished buildings that their basements became available for conversion into water basins for firefighting. With the lull in the bombing, an elaborate scheme to augment London's emergency storage capacity was put into operation. Eventually, nearly 200 million gallons of water was provided in improvised dams and basins, placed strategically in high fire risk areas. These were linked by a network of 180 miles of steel pipe-lines of varying diameters, to be supplied from the river and other sources. Borehole pumps, capable of supplying 3,000 gallons of water a minute at any state of the tide, were set into the river. The riser pipes were fixed to the piers of bridges and connected to 12 or 18 inch diameter pipes, as shown in this picture of an installation on Blackfriars Bridge. The valves enabled water to be diverted to the north or south, as required.

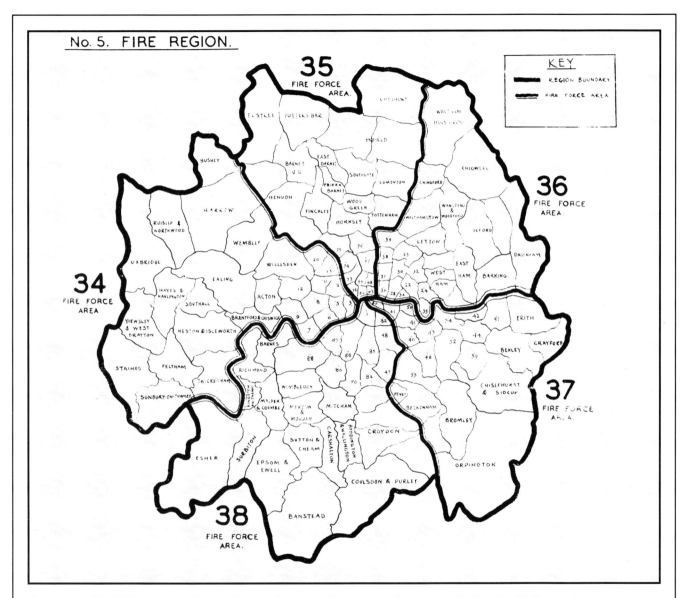

No. 5. FIRE REGION.

The London (No. 5) Region after Nationalisation, August 18th, 1941. Originally divided into five Fire Forces, No. 35 Area, for administrative reasons, was absorbed later, half into No. 34 Area and the remainder into No. 36. The numbers in the centre are those of the London Fire Brigade stations. The Region covered a total of 720 square miles.

Station Officer. I was transferred to Whitechapel Fire Station just before Christmas 1941, where the officer in charge, Column Officer Bill Ayers, welcomed me and immediately set about fitting me in to the pattern followed by the London Fire Brigade.

Although the N.F.S. hierarchy differed from the old L.F.B. and West Ham ranking systems, there was little change in the modus operandi; the L.F.B. system of doing things still prevailed. West Ham Fire Brigade had been modelled on the London Brigade and most of the West Ham officers and many of the firemen had transferred to West Ham from the L.F.B. before the First World War. Pay and conditions of service were identical; the attraction to the London men was the availability of quarters for married men in the West Ham stations. Many married members of the L.F.B. had been forced to live in single men's dormitories. My old Chief Officer, Henry Johnson, had adopted many of the London Brigade orders in West Ham and our training manual was the L.F.B Questions and Answers book. Therefore, I spoke very much the same language and the transitional period was not difficult. I found Bill Ayers a congenial colleague and we saw eye to eye on most things.

Whitechapel had five satellite stations on its ground and part of my job was to oversee three of them.

The streets off Commercial Road had been heavily bombed and many of the basements had been converted into emergency water supply (E.W.S.) dams. It was realised that a large expanse of water would be attractive to children and every effort was made to make each site as safe as possible by fencing them off. Some were surrounded by brick walls but most were enclosed with timber from bombed houses; doors, flooring etc. with a row of barbed wire on top. Despite these precautions, several youngsters were drowned in emergency dams. Usually, they had broken through the fence and gone sailing on the dam, using an old door as a raft. In the light of these tragedies, a Fire Force Order was issued setting out instructions for the regular inspection of all emergency water basins.

I was at No. 36 B1V Station, Fairclough Street, one morning in 1942 during the school holidays, when a very irate father came in, complaining about the E.W.S. site a hundred yards or so along the road. He had no specific complaint, just seemed to object to the dam being sited there; a danger to his son.

I asked him to accompany me to the site, where I pointed out the precautions the Service had taken to keep the kids out; the high fence, the barbed wire. I showed him entries in the station log book, reporting hourly visits by firemen from 8 a.m. to dusk, to check security and the action taken when a fault was discovered. He appeared unimpressed so I asked him what he did to warn his child of the danger. He had nothing to say, so I concluded by telling him that I was doing more to safeguard his youngster than he was. I asked him why I should be concerned if he wasn't?

There was a change of Officer in Charge of B Division shortly after I arrived at Whitechapel. Charles B. Stonham, M.C., was replaced by Divisional Officer Horace Charles Minister, a tough, dyed-in-the-wool London Fire Brigade officer who had spent the blitz period in the West End of London. I quickly recognised his method of control for I had had experience in West Ham of officers of similar style. Our first encounter ended with a vague threat from the D.O.: 'Everyone on his toes, or look out for trouble.'

His next visit came when the Watch was at escape drill in the school yard; he arrived as a neat carry-down was in progress. I decided to try him out!

'Everything satisfactory, sir?' I asked, knowing he would find it hard to find fault.

The station complement No. 36 Area B1V, Fairclough Street, Whitechapel, in August, 1942. A bit of indiscipline during my early days as Officer in Charge but, with some plain speaking and minor relaxations here and there, they moulded into a fairly solid bunch. We practised water relaying in the moat of the Tower of London, pumping from the flooded Traitors Gate, and exercised turntable ladder operators, who lowered volunteers by line from the roof of the White Tower.

'Not bad,' he replied. 'Not bad.'

I knew then that his bark was much worse than his bite and we became quite friendly as we learned more about each other.

I was in the habit of walking across to the Divisional Office at Camperdown House in Leman Street on Sunday mornings, to hear the latest 'buzzes' from Fire Force H.Q. The D.O. was in his office as I reached the entrance door. He was singing hymns in a loud voice that reached me two floors below my destination. I entered the main office as Mr Minister commenced a new hymn.

'Onward Christian So-o-o-oldier's' when he broke off in mid tune to yell: 'Feldman, where are those blankety-blank fire report forms?'

Company Officer Feldman, his staff officer, yelled back, 'Coming sir,' whereupon, the D.O. recommenced his devotion. 'Marching as to-o war . . .'

Which taught me a bit more about my boss.

The personnel attached to B1V station were predominantly Jewish, a pretty good all-round bunch, although I never had the opportunity of judging their ability on the fireground. The nearest we came to action was when placed on stand-by to go to Norwich following one of the Baedeker raids, but it came to nothing. I mustered all hands on my first day at the station to introduce myself and set out my method of working.

'We stick to Fire Force Instructions,' I told them, 'so you know where you stand.' I discovered that this station, like most, had a few bolshies but since I had tried most of their little tricks myself, years ago, I knew the answers and they did not get far. I was fortunate in having a strong Section Leader in Mark Glazer who maintained discipline with but little need for intervention on my part.

One morning there was a knock on my door and Fireman Assenheim entered. I recognised him, having seen him selling ice cream from the well known stall in Petticoat Lane.

'I've come to ask a favour, Mr Demarne,' he began. 'You know our business in The Lane?'

'Oh, yes,' I replied. 'I've often sampled your hokey pokey on a Sunday morning.'

'Well, that's what I've come to see you about. Both my brothers are in the Army and my father is too old to carry on. Sunday is our only day for business and I wonder if you could let me have every Sunday off if I give up a leave day in the week?'

It seemed a reasonable request and, although irregular, could be arranged without creating problems.

'Yes,' I told him. 'A day for a day. Have a word with Section Leader Glazer and tell him it's O.K. with me.'

'Thank you very much,' he replied and off he went.

About five minutes later, there came another knock on my door. It also was a request for a favour. This man had a business in Walthamstow where Thursday was early closing day. It would help him if he could change Thursday leave days for Saturdays, when business was better.

'No,' I replied. 'Can't be done.'

'Why not?' he queried. 'You did it for Assenheim.'

'No I didn't. It's just been cancelled.'

He seemed a bit nonplussed, leaving without comment.

Five minutes or so later, Assenheim was back. 'Is it true you've cancelled my leave change?'

'Yes,' I replied.

'But you promised.'

'I know I did. But you went downstairs and shot off your mouth and now they all want to pick their leave days. It can't be done.'

A few minutes after he had left Mark Glazer came in. 'Had a spot of bother, sir?'

'Yes,' I said. 'I can't let them all pick what leave day they fancy so Assenheim is unlucky.'

'Well, he is a genuine case. If you will reconsider his request, I'll see that there are no more applications.'

'Alright. But I don't want to hear any more about it otherwise I'll stop the change.'

And I never did hear any more on that subject. I am sure there were others who would have made similar requests had I allowed the second application. Mark Glazer, obviously, had made it plain that further concessions of that kind were not on. There was no feeling of resentment among the troops and, a few weeks later, I was invited to have Christmas dinner in the mess room with the lads and lassies. Strictly Kosher, of course, with lokshen soup and dumplings, salt beef and all the trimmings, with the Spirit of Christmas strongly prevailing!

In June 1945 my mother died and I covered the second button on my uniform jacket with a piece of black cloth, the traditional mark of mourning. I was out walking in Back Church Lane one morning and met Joe Assenheim, now demobbed. He greeted me warmly and, noticing my mourning, asked who it was for.

'My mother,' I replied.

'Oh, I'm so sorry,' he said. 'Excuse me asking, but these are difficult times. If I can help you in any way, I shall be only too pleased.'

Which I thought was a very kind gesture.

One of the great worries of the day involved the Tilbury Depot, a huge complex of buildings and railway sidings just off the Commercial Road at Aldgate.

This massive warehouse, with its labyrinth of corridors, passages and vaults in the basement, offered shelter to thousands of local residents. It was said that eight thousand sought refuge there nightly during the Blitz; some estimates put the figure even higher.

Bill Ayers was very concerned about the high life risk that would result from a direct hit on the warehouse. The recent Baedeker raids on Bath, Norwich, Exeter and other Cathedral cities had caused alarm and many people, fearing London would again become the target for the heavy bombers, resumed residence there. In view of the risk, we decided to hold exercises designed mainly for rescue purposes, covering the entrances and exits of the building.

Bill and I made a tour of the warehouse one evening, as people were settling in for the night. The shelter wardens had imposed reasonable discipline, turning the blind eye on those who were out to make a more or less honest penny in trading enterprises, foremost among whom were the Whitechapel ladies holding court in smaller vaults they had claimed as their own.

With Column Officer Ayers I dreaded to consider the possibility of the Tilbury receiving a direct hit from a one thousand pounder and, thankfully, the situation did not arise. The Tilbury Depot always came to mind whenever I saw the 'Wayside Pulpit' in later years, proclaiming 'Don't worry. It may never happen.' But, at the time, we were very concerned.

Shortly after Christmas 1942 I was detailed for another training course, this time at the N.F.S. College at Saltdean, Brighton, where I spent a further four weeks. Training was centred on technical matters and the control of Blitz situations. I realised that these two courses, in quick succession, indicated the prospect of promotion and I worked hard to achieve a good result.

Whilst I was at Saltdean there were several tip-and-run raids by German aircraft which approached the coast at low level in an attempt to beat the defences. We had no warning and the first we knew was the sudden roar of aircraft engines and, sometimes, the sound of bomb explosions nearby. One day the gunners on the sea-front were not caught napping by a low-flying raider and scored a direct hit as he passed over the college. The Dornier crashed in a field a mile or so inland on rolling uplands behind the College.

A minute later the college duty fire appliance came roaring up the hill. It was the first time I had seen it, a former West Ham pump escape which had been transferred to Saltdean. It was our last acquisition before the war, the pride and joy of Stratford Fire Station and instantly recognisable to me, despite the West Ham coat-of-arms having been given a coat of 'crab fat' — Admiralty grey paint. I had driven it to many a fire on its own ground; it appeared strangely out of place in this rural environment.

I wondered what had replaced it, this powerful fire pump, capable of delivering eight hundred gallons of water a minute and built for service in its highly industrialised home area. What thinking lay behind its transfer to the Fire College, where it was unlikely ever to be utilised to its full potential?

But it looked good and was, perhaps, the latest of its type in the country; none like it would be produced during the war. In fact, none like it were ever produced. The post-war pattern of fire appliances incorporated the limousine type body giving protection to the crew not only from the weather but also from the risk of falling from the machine en route to the fire.

Following my return from the Fire Service College I was ordered to Headquarters for an interview with the Chief Regional Fire Officer, Mr F. W. Delve. An Inspectorate team was being formed and my name had been submitted.

Mr Delve outlined the work of the Inspectorate and I was asked if I would like to become a member of the team. I

This is the West Ham pump-escape in its original livery before being daubed with grey paint and transferred to the N.F.S. College at Saltdean. It saw service in dockland and in the City during the Blitz. It came back to Stratford after the war, resuming service on home ground for several years before retirement at the ripe old age of 20.

The Headquarters of the London Fire Brigade, Albert Embankment. At the left of the building, deep underground, was the Control Room from which the co-ordination of movement of appliances between the eleven London fire districts originated. Should all the London Region's resources be insufficient to satisfy calls for assistance, reinforcement would be called for from the Home Office Control, which was kept informed of the fire situation throughout the country. Appliances would be mobilised from the nearest region with equipment available.

replied that I would and was posted to Regional Fire Headquarters, Lambeth, as from March 5th, 1943.

I found the work interesting and gained satisfaction in the knowledge that I was contributing, in a small way, to the smooth transition of the sixty plus fire brigades covering the seven hundred square miles of Greater London, into an integrated fire region.

The Inspectorate team occupied quarters in the training block at Lambeth and we were on call for staff duties at night in the event of an alert. This was during the period when batteries of sixty-four anti-aircraft rocket launchers — the so-called 'Z' batteries — were being installed in strategically-placed parks and open spaces throughout London. These promised a warm reception for raiders, the 'scalded cats' that frequently disturbed our nights.

The sirens sounded one evening and we hurried to our action station. As we were crossing the yard, a battery in Hyde Park opened up with a salvo of sixty-four rockets, such an unearthly din heard for the first time that my feet hardly touched the ground over the last twenty yards.

'What the hell was that?' we asked ourselves before it occurred to us that it was one of the new batteries. That same roar, in the East End, was responsible for one of the great tragedies of the war in London. Hundreds of people were streaming down the stairs, seeking shelter in the uncompleted underground station at Bethnal Green when the battery in Victoria Park opened up. There was a surge forward at the frightful noise; someone at the front stumbled and fell and a great heap of bodies piled up under pressure from the rear. When it was cleared it was found that more than one hundred and seventy men, women and children had died, having been crushed and suffocated.

On another night during a thunderstorm, a barrage balloon had been struck by lightning and set on fire. It fell blazing on a pub roof near the Black Prince Road and a pump from Lambeth turned out. The balloon was tethered to a platform in an open space to the west of the track out of Waterloo Station and the cable trailed across the railway line. The fire crew was at work on the roof when a train leaving Waterloo caught up with the balloon cable and the resulting jerk threw two of the firemen off the roof to their death on the pavement thirty feet below. I knew both these young chaps and we all were saddened at this unfortunate accident. Why them? might have asked their loved ones. I don't know; it was just the luck of the draw.

In June I was nominated for promotion to Column Officer rank and attended a Board at the Home Office. A few days later I received news of my success and remained with the Inspectorate in my new rank. Promotion brought my pay up to £500 a year. Most welcome!

There was a shortage of section leaders and leading firemen in the London Region and Fire Force Commanders had been asked to submit names of suitable men. The chosen were summoned to Headquarters for examination in drills, including squad drill, to assess their ability to control men.

Column Officer Paddy French was a former Army drill instructor, now attached to Edgware Road Fire Station. A few months earlier, Paddy French was awarded the George Medal for his work at an incident on Hungerford Bridge when a land mine fell across the electrified rails and became welded to them by the short circuit.

He was ordered to Lambeth H.Q. to put the squad through its paces. He was faced with a motley crew, all likely lads, of differing shapes and sizes. Paddy lined them up and addressed them.

'I'm going to move you around the drill ground and I want you to remember the movements and commands. After that, I want each one of you to take over the squad.'

He got them moving nicely; right turn, left wheel, into line right turn, left form etc. He gave them good instruction, repeating all the movements before bringing the squad to the halt.

'Now,' said Paddy 'It's your turn.' 'You,' pointing to a little man at the end of the line. He marched out stiffly, and turned to face the squad. He was at a loss for words and stood gazing at the sky for inspiration, but none was forthcoming. His lips moved but without sound.

Paddy was compassionate; he would give him a nudge to start him off.

'Cover them off,' he suggested. Ah, yes, that's it. Cover them off. He turned and marched to the head of the line and, in a gentle voice instructed the squad: 'Cover off . . . please.'

'Nooo!' moaned Paddy. 'Don't talk to them like THAT!' 'Caw blimey, they'll be getting their bleedin' fags out next.' Poor little bloke; he finished up with the squad looking like a ball of wool the cat had been playing with. Not exactly what we were looking for.

On the first of December 1943, the Inspectorate team was summoned to the office of the Chief Regional Fire Officer for a conference. Mr Delve began by referring to press reports about Hitler's latest 'secret weapon.' It was not just another rumour, he said, but a very formidable weapon, capable of causing severe damage and casualties. Intelligence reports indicated that the enemy was about to launch pilotless aircraft carrying a ten-ton warhead, designed to crash and explode on selected targets in Britain. The main weight of the attack was expected to fall on London and the south-eastern counties.

Although the size of the warhead was exaggerated, the weapon, otherwise, was accurately described. When the first V1 arrived in mid-June 1944, seven months after we had been told of its existence, it carried a warhead of about one ton. The original design was ten tons but, for technical reasons, it had to be modified, much to our relief. Mr Delve gave details of the estimated damage and casualties each explosion would cause.

As the result of this new threat, it had been decided to reorganise the fire service to meet the changed situation. Since the weapon carried a very powerful explosive but no incendiary device, emphasis was to be laid on rescue work rather than on firefighting. For this purpose, the Service would be divided into two sections, Home and Task. The Home Divisions would comprise the regular fire stations whose responsibility it would be to deal with 'peace-time' fires and enemy-action incidents on the station's ground. The

Task Divisions were designed to bring aid to badly blitzed towns and cities throughout the country and would be entirely self supporting, thereby relieving the burden on the stricken town. Special programmes were in preparation for the training of crews for their new activities, including instruction in Incident Control for fire officers. It was not known when the bombardment would commence so there was no time to be lost in perfecting plans. Inspectorate visits to Fire Forces were suspended and the team concentrated on the organisation of the new system.

Towards the end of December a vacancy arose for a Divisional Officer within the Region and I was among those nominated for the post. I was instructed to appear before a Selection Board at the Home Office Fire Service Department. I arrived at the appointed time and found myself seated before a high powered Bench consisting of Chief Regional Fire Officers and Treasury Officials, presided over by the Chief of the Fire Staff. It was not my first appearance before an august assembly but I must admit my heart was beating just a little faster than usual. However, I was set at ease by Sir Aylmer Firebrace, who commenced with the usual 'settling in' conversation. I remember reading in his memoirs some years later, his comments on Selection Boards in which he wrote: 'Unless a candidate gets good bowling he cannot exhibit his style and capacity for making runs.'

He certainly was good to me on this occasion, tossing up a few lobs which I had no difficulty in despatching to the boundary. I got off to a good start, quite fortuitously, when he asked what had induced me to choose the fire service as a career. I told him frankly that I was seeking a job that was secure and offered scope for promotion, mentioning, in passing, that I had been turned down by the London Fire Brigade before being accepted at West Ham.

Sir Aylmer, formerly Chief Officer of the L.F.B., smiled as he looked around at his colleagues on the Board who seemed to find the conversation amusing.

'It wasn't me that turned you down, was it?' he asked.

'No, sir, it was your predecessor, Major Morris.'

I did not know at the time that Commander Firebrace and Major Morris were not quite the best of friends and the story seemed to please Sir Aylmer for he was gracious in telling me that London's loss was West Ham's gain. From that moment I was on good terms with the Board and quite enjoyed the exchanges. I came from that interview well pleased with myself and received news of my appointment to the rank of Divisional Officer a few days later.

This was followed by my transfer to No. 36 Fire Force under my old F.F.C., Mr C. P. McDuell. I was sorry to leave Regional Headquarters and my colleagues on the Inspectorate team, with whom I had enjoyed such cordial relations. It had been ten months of hard work but I had learned much from the experience; staff work had given me an insight to much that was entirely new and the knowledge I gained was of enormous value.

I was posted to No. 36 'D' Division then comprising the boroughs of West Ham and Leyton, an area I knew so well. The highest risk in the Division, of course, was the dock area, which had now been increased by the cargoes of munitions and explosives entering the port daily from the U.S.A., together with naval vessels undergoing refit in the ship repair yards.

The No. 36 Fire Force contingent on parade on Albert Embankment to mark the second anniversary of the formation of the National Fire Service. The Rt Hon. Herbert Morrison M.P., Home Secretary and Minister for Home Security, takes the salute at the entrance to the headquarters building, London Fire Region.

Leading the parade is Fire Force Commander C. P. McDuell, OBE; behind (right) is Deputy F.F.C. Vic Botten, M.B.E., Area Officer Mrs Swann (centre), and Assistant F.F.C. Sid Barnes, G.M. (left). Lambeth Palace stands in the background; the tram lines have long been removed!

9   The Baby Blitz

MY first operational turn out in the new Division was to a fall of incendiaries in the vicinity of Leyton High Road. It was a night of minor activity but notable in that it was my first experience of the phosphorus bomb. The fire service had been appraised of the problems arising from the firefighting aspect of dealing with these nasty devices and were warned that phosphorus, in contact with the skin, would cause deep burns which were difficult to heal.

The German method was to mix phosphorus with a rubber-based solution. The compound was sealed in a bomb casing with a small explosive charge, designed to scatter the incendiary material on impact. Exposure to air caused the mixture to ignite, setting fire to any combustible material it contacted. Magnesium bombs had started roof fires and firemen were at work when I arrived.

My attention was drawn to a brown, sticky mass on the pavement and my first impression was that it was a phosphorus compound, although I began to have doubts. If it were phosphorus, I reasoned, it should be burning or, at least, smoking. But it was doing neither, not even glowing in the dark.

I decided to test it to see if it did burn, so I probed the mass with a piece of stick. It was rubber-based, for it came away in elastic threads, just like the rubber solution I used on my bike tyres, and it smelled of petroleum.

I struck a match and put the flame to the blob on the end of my stick. It ignited at once, giving off heavy black smoke. Immediately there came a bellow from an air raid warden, 'Put that light out!'

'Which one?' called my D.R., pointing in turn to two of the blazing roofs.

It was a phosphorus bomb, without doubt, but something had gone wrong with the mix; not enough phosphorus content, perhaps. My impression was that Jerry should stick to his two pound magnesium bombs; they were far better fire raisers.

Although the docks constituted the greatest risk in the Division, there were a number of other industrial undertakings which justified inclusion in the list of 'Vital Points' maintained in fire control rooms. In highly industrialised areas like West Ham, activities of great importance to the war effort were being conducted; the purpose of the VP list was to ensure priority of fire attendance to these addresses.

Practically all the factories in Carpenter's Road, Stratford, known to the locals as 'the street of a thousand stinks,' were engaged in work of a hazardous nature in peace-time, when a fire call to any address in the road was given special attention. West Ham firemen were accustomed to seeing workpeople fleeing from a blazing factory thought to be in danger of exploding, as they arrived to deal with the outbreak. Now, under war conditions, some of the firms continued as before, others took on new production. Some of these were of high fire risk, others not necessarily so but of vital importance.

One such was established in an inconspicuous factory building in Carpenter's Road. It housed a laboratory, busy manufacturing the newly discovered drug Penicillin. Thousands of bottles were set out on benches, cultivating the life-saving antibiotic, at that time in great demand for the treatment of war wounds.

The pharmaceutical chemists, May & Baker, occupied extensive premises at Dagenham. They, too, were engaged in producing vast quantities of life-saving drugs of the Sulphonamide group, among other pharmaceutical items. But most urgent was the production of the anti-malaria tablet, 'Mepacrin'. With General Slim's XIVth Army in close pursuit of the fleeing Japs through the Malayan and Burmese jungles, the overriding need was for large and continuing supplies of 'Mepacrin' to protect the troops from the debilitating effects of malaria.

Early in 1944, the May & Baker factories were the target for a concentrated fall of fire bombs which started a number of fires among the cluster of buildings. The firm was high on the list of priorities and ten pumps were despatched on receipt of the call with a column officer in charge. Confronted with a number of fires burning among the production buildings and bearing in mind the importance of the works, he sent back a message calling for the attendance of fifty pumps. This was an overkill but he felt it better to be safe than sorry; in any event, it would result in the attendance of a senior officer!

When I arrived there were several fires still burning, only one of them serious. A forty-four gallon drum that had been punctured by a bomb splinter was lying adjacent to one of the larger buildings, with a jet of flame about three feet long roaring into the doorway. Fire already had entered the building as an official of the firm came running up.

'For Heaven's sake, save this building. The others don't matter but this one is vital. We make "Mepacrin" in here and without it, the advance in Burma will come to a halt.'

Beside me stood a fireman using a good jet on some loose fire but ignoring the blazing drum.

'I've been warned not to put water on that drum or it will blow up,' he reported.

'Who told you that?' I asked.

'That man in the white coat, over there,' he replied.

I ran over and asked the man what the drum contained. He mentioned a chemical I did not recognise and repeated his warning: 'You musn't put water on it or it'll explode.' Here was a dilemma. 'You must save this building.' 'You mustn't use water.'

It had long been my practice to take note of the advice of works chemists but there are times when a fire officer has to make his own judgment of the situation, even if it goes against expert advice. I decided to have a go at the drum so I took the branch, sent the fireman back out of the way and swung it directly at the jet of flame for an instant, then away. Nothing alarming happened, so I gave it another drink. Still no blast so I hit it fair and square and out it went! A quick splash around the burning entrance and that was the end of everybody's fears. After sending the stop I looked around for the man in the white coat but he was nowhere to be seen. Perhaps it was just as well for I might have said something I should have regretted later. However, I couldn't let him get away with it. I returned to the factory next morning for a general look around and a word with the white-coated gent. I met the works manager who was full of praise for the fire service, making special mention of the 'Mepacrin' building. I told him of the 'no water' incident and asked to see the man concerned. The manager was at a loss to know who it might be. That may have been a diplomatic answer and I never did trace him.

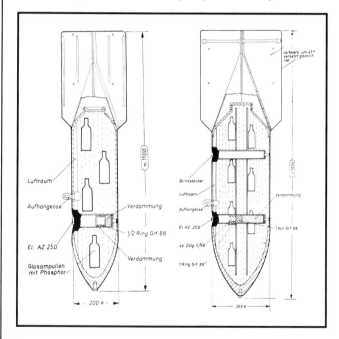

There were two main types of phosphorus bomb (known to the Germans as Phosphorbrandbombe). At the left of this diagram is the smaller version, similar in dimensions to the 50kg bomb. On the right is the larger version which had a much weaker mix of phosphorus to rubber. It was comparable in size to the 250kg bomb. The Civil Defence designation for these was Ph.I.B. (Phosphorus Incendiary Bomb).

I was invited to take a look around some of the buildings, which proved to be an eye-opener in more ways than one. It confirmed my belief that we'd better come running if M & Bs received a further visit from the bombers.

One of the buildings I was shown was furnished with six ten-gallon carboys suspended from the ceiling. When I asked what they contained, my guide grinned and replied: 'Ah, that's our own patent automatic fire extinguisher. The materials in this room are highly flammable so we've come up with the idea of putting up those carboys filled with C.T.C. If a bomb drops nearby. it will shatter the carboys and drop the C.T.C. which will extinguish the fire automatically.'

'Well,' I replied, 'I'm sorry to disappoint you but you'd better get them down straight away, unless you want to be responsible for the death of a couple of dozen of your workers and any unfortunate fireman who comes to put your fire out. Carbon tetrachloride is deadly and in that concentration will kill anyone within range of the vapour.'

That wiped the grin off his face and he promised to remove the carboys forthwith. I felt he should not have needed telling, but then, the fire service had removed C.T.C. fire extinguishers from its appliances only two years ago!

Early in 1944 the Liberty Ships, bearing military stores of all kinds from the U.S.A., were queueing to enter the Royal Docks. The N.F.S. provided a fire crew for each vessel carrying hazardous cargo, during the period of unloading.

Explosives were limited to 2,000 tons per vessel and each presented a grave risk to the surrounding area. The *SS Fort Stikine* was a 7,000-ton freighter which blew up in Bombay Harbour during the war. She was carrying 1,400 tons of explosives and the blast devastated a large part of the city of Bombay; the ship's hull was blown out of the water and came to rest on the quayside. In another incident following a German air raid, several ships blew up in Bari Harbour in the south of Italy, in a chain reaction following a direct hit on one of the vessels, an example of what might happen in a similar event in the Port of London.

I was at stand-by in the West Ham Control at Stratford when a heavy fall of incendiaries was reported from the Royal Victoria Dock. I glanced at the list of hazardous cargoes and checked the position of vessels carrying H.E. Seven vessels, each with 2,000 tons aboard — the makings of quite a big bang — and it only needed an unlucky hit from a small bomb to trigger off what surely would have been the biggest single disaster of the war in Britain. There was, in fact, a near miss. A one-ton container of incendiary bombs failed to open and

crashed through a railway truck standing only sixty yards from one of the vessels carrying explosives.

As soon as the fall of incendiaries was reported, I made for the Victoria Dock and saw the characteristic white glare of burning magnesium lighting up large areas of the dock as I approached along Silvertown Way. The white glare was a welcome sight, indicating that the bombs had fallen on open ground but, ominously, patches of pink were appearing among the tall buildings. A fire on one of the upper floors of the giant Co-op flour mill had taken hold but a local crew had pounced on it and had it surrounded. No need for me to remain here; the local officer had it in hand so I ran off to a glare coming from behind the mill. It was a long, single floor office building on the quayside, alight from end to end. There was no hope of saving it but the flames were so bright that we were afraid Jerry would stoke it up. A pump was at work, with jets knocking down the fire, when I heard a series of small explosions like firecrackers against the din. Men were going down all round me. I saw my despatch rider, Charlie Irvine, who was a few yards ahead, clutch his leg and run hopping along, as I recognised the sound of exploding incendiaries. Small pieces of shrapnel were scattered far and wide causing flesh wounds, unless one was unlucky enough to be close at hand when more serious injury might be inflicted.

This Liberty ship arrived at the Royal Docks early in 1944 with a cargo of army lorries, each one fully loaded with military stores to make full use of all available space. During unloading, fire broke out and spread rapidly among the canvas hoods, but, with a fire crew on the spot, the outbreak was held in check and damage confined to the hold involved.

I ran over to Charlie who had pulled off his boot and was examining his leg. He had several pieces of metal embedded in the limb and I sent him off to hospital. I was one of the few in the vicinity who escaped injury; most of the others had collected at least one small wound.

Despite this interruption, the jets began to subdue the office building fire and I went on to a blaze in a nearby timber yard. It was here that I heard of the incendiary container incident in the Albert Dock. The timber yard fire was coming under control and I went along to take a look at the near miss in the adjoining dock. We had been very lucky, that night, only relatively few fires, one or two potentially serious but, bearing in mind the risk, we had escaped lightly. During the night, three fire bombs landed on the deck of the Port of London Authority's giant floating crane, *The London Mammoth*, as she was being towed across the Royal Victoria Dock. The intense white glare illuminated the huge superstructure towering above and silhouetted a tug, slowly passing in the opposite direction. The tug skipper altered course to bring his vessel alongside and, as she glided past, a deck hand leaned over the side and casually swept the bombs overboard with a flick of a broom. No noise; no fuss and no excitement. It was made to look as routine a job as tying up or casting off. The incendiary container had crashed with such force as to open a crater fifteen feet wide, fracturing a water main a foot or two under the surface, and the thermite and magnesium bombs bubbled and frothed all night.

Several hours had elapsed since the exploding incendiary casualties had gone to hospital and I was surprised to see Charlie Irvine coming to report.

'What are you doing here?' I asked. 'I thought I sent you to hospital.'

'Oh, that was nothing,' he replied. 'They took four pieces of shrapnel from my leg and when I got back to the station, they told me my house had been hit. I went to have a look; it's knocked about a bit but nobody hurt. So I thought I'd report back to duty; the bastards can't do this to me.'

Charlie Irvine, formerly a bacon hand with the London Co-op, was typical of the people Hitler sought to overcome with his Blitz. And there were many more ordinary folk in the East End who showed similar spirit after suffering injury and the loss of their homes. Like the old man we discovered in the ruins of his house in East Ham. We got him to his feet after a brief examination and found that shock had deprived him of speech temporarily, a fairly common condition. After plucking numerous small splinters of glass from his face and bald head, we wiped the dust from his eyes, nose and mouth. He had not uttered a sound since we had found him but, suddenly, in a loud voice, gave vent to his pent-up feelings in two words: 'Sod 'im.'

Not very impressive, perhaps, in cold print, but you should have heard him. Laurence Olivier could not have got more into it!

Earlier that same night, Tom Stothard, now Company Officer, and his crew of part-timers had been ordered to Victoria Dock where an officer directed them to Messrs Silcocks' cattle cake mills in North Woolwich Road. Entering the large, cavern-like factory they were able to see all around by the light of several fires burning separately among large stacks of bags containing various grains. Two other crews were already at work and a party of soldiers was busy in one corner of the building.

'Before I had the chance to make up my mind where to start,' said Tom, 'I was approached by a Major of the Royal Engineers.

"Do you think you can lend a hand over here?" he asked. I walked over with him and was shown the area of fire he wished extinguished. I called the lads over and we soon had a jet working. But the fire was deep-seated in a most foul-smelling stack and we had no option but to climb up and break down the bags, one by one, to get at the fire. Consequently, it was not long before we all were stinking like the rest of the pile. When we had knocked down the fire the major re-appeared and assembled three or four of his men. They set up sheer-legs in the corner and two of his chaps disappeared down a hole we had not seen. It was not long before one of them came up and the rest of them began hauling on a rope over a pulley on the sheer-legs and up came a blooming great bomb!

'We went back to finish off our job and were told to report to a pub along the street where the landlord had made some arrangements for tea and sandwiches. So off we went, more than ready for a cup of tea and a bite to eat, but as soon as we entered the place there was a yell from all those inside. "Get out of here, you stinking so and so's!"

'There was nothing for it but to make our way home. We drove into the station yard and parked our appliance before entering the mess room.

'"Phew" said Frank Barnes. the Oi/c. "You can't come in here smelling like that." So we had to strip down to our underwear in the station yard, lay our tunics and trousers out and give them a good scrub with water and stiff brooms before being allowed in to don our spare clothing.'

10 Enter the Robots

AFTER only a few months in my new job, the reorganisation of the National Fire Service to meet the threat of the V-weapons was put into operation. I was appointed to the newly formed 'C' Mobile (Task) Division based at Ilford. My Divisional H.Q. was situated in a large Victorian house in Coventry Road and I occupied a small private room over my office. Several staff officers shared a dormitory in the same building, which also contained mess room and kitchen; all very plain and unpretentious, almost austere. Firewomen occupied a similar house opposite and my staff car was garaged some twenty yards along the street.

I was introduced to my drivers, Firewomen Ball and Bradley, the latter known to all as 'Goldie' from the pony tail of golden hair which she persistently wore over the collar of her tunic, much against the regulations. As the D.O.'s driver, she felt privileged in this respect and I left it to the women officers to keep the drivers in order over uniform matters.

Both were accomplished drivers and maintained the staff car in immaculate condition. They had been well trained in turn out procedure and never kept me waiting, even in the middle of the night. They were, of course, given a short start, since the control room staff always warned them that the car was required a moment before they rang me. But I was a professional fireman, accustomed to a sub-minute turn out, yet I would see one or other leaving her quarters across the road as I was leaving mine, and hareing along to the garage.

They took advantage of my visits to the regular stations to use the cleaning facilities and, winter and summer, could be seen washing and polishing, taking enormous pride in their vehicle. Each had a good knowledge of the very large district and rarely had to check the location of any but the most remote streets. Their tour of duty was forty-eight hours on and twenty-four off, while I did seven days on continuously, with one off. The girls shared the driving and both were of even temperament, showing no sign of nervousness under fire.

During the early part of 1944, the R.A.F. and the anti-aircraft defences were knocking down German aircraft almost nightly and several had fallen in the Dagenham and Ilford area. Our spirits were high and we began to feel that destruction was inevitable for any raider daring to attack London during this period.

Our joy and optimism was unbounded when the great news came of the Normandy landings. We knew invasion was imminent, of course, from the feverish activity taking place in the areas converging on dockland. Monty had been along for pep talks to the dockers, who had cheered him to the echo. All firemen stationed in the docks were impounded and not allowed past the guards posted at the dock gates, for two weeks prior to D-Day. Large prisoner-of-war cages had been built on Wanstead Flats, among other places, and roads leading to the docks were choked for hours on end, day and night, with convoys of troops, tanks, artillery and military stores of all kinds.

Some of the lorries bore slogans, chalked by the troops, 'Look out, Hitler. Here we come' and 'Berlin or Bust' were typical. These brought cheers from the people of West Ham gathered en masse to greet the troops.

'Give 'em one for me, boys,' shouted a stout matron, whilst others pointed to demolished buildings and called 'Pay 'em back for this,' bringing broad grins and V-signs from the troops. I had not seen a bar of chocolate for years, but the

Another combined operation following a V1 blast. Firemen and Civil Defence rescue workers have located casualties buried under debris on the second floor of this severely damaged building. A victim has been secured to a stretcher and is being lowered to ground level whilst the search goes on for others. The precarious position of all engaged in this rescue is plain to see; their skill in reaching those trapped and their devotion to duty is not so apparent.

women had managed to find some and presented them to the lads, together with cakes, fruit, sandwiches and any other suitable gift they could lay hands on, as the convoys rolled slowly into the reception area.

As night fell, the air was filled with the roar of hundreds of aircraft en route to the northern coast of France, to bomb fortifications, bridges and marshalling yards, and to carry the war into Germany itself.

Now, the Germans were reaping the whirlwind, and Churchill's promise of ten tons of bombs for every one dropped on the British Isles was being fulfilled.

It became almost nightly routine to be ordered out to a crashed German raider and one evening, a week after D-Day, a raiding aircraft was reported down at Samuel Williams coal depot on Dagenham Marshes. Whilst there, I heard that another aircraft had crashed with its load of bombs at Grove Road, Bow.

Next morning, I met Assistant Fire Force Commander Vic Botten and cheerfully said:

'Another two last night.'

He grinned and said: 'No. Only one.'

'Two,' I replied. 'One at Dagenham, one at Bow.'

'No. Only yours, at Dagenham.'

The penny dropped.

'Not one of those?' I queried. He nodded and suggested that the aircraft had been spotting for the V1; it was important for the enemy to know where it had fallen.

And that was the first of many hundreds that fell on London and its environs, killing and maiming thousands of men, women and children and creating havoc in the congested areas covering the entire Region. No part of the capital escaped but the south London boroughs, particularly Croydon and Bromley, Kent, were very heavily punished.

One of the early disasters occurred when the Guards Chapel, in Birdcage Walk, received a direct hit. It was a bright Sunday morning and the Chapel was filled with Service personnel and their families attending Morning Service. Over a hundred bodies were recovered from the rubble.

The East End of London again came in for heavy bombardment. It became apparent that forecasts of the damage were accurate. Few fires were started but the blast effect of the V1 was severe, resulting in long hours of excavation, working to release those buried in the debris of their homes and workplaces.

When the Nazi plans to use V-weapons against Britain became known, the N.F.S. was given special training in rescue work; my job was to organise fire service operations at the scene. Fire, of course, remained our prime responsibility

Combined operations at a flying bomb incident near Manor Park railway station in July 1944. A woman, buried in the kitchen of her demolished home, is just visible. A fire officer is ready with oxygen equipment, a police inspector holds her hand and shields her head from falling rubble whilst the rescue officer removes a key piece of debris enabling her release. I watched this rescue, impressed by the patient skill and gentleness of those engaged and by the calm acceptance of her predicament by the victim.

A few days later, the happy sequel! Her soldier husband came home on compassionate leave. Their home had been destroyed, but what matter. His wife, apparently none the worse for her ordeal, was there to greet him, and the N.F.S. photographer, who also took the grim picture opposite, was delighted to place on record their joyous reunion.

but the Service was always ready to provide every assistance in its power to alleviate the misery of the long-suffering civilian population.

The flying bomb attack built up to its peak from mid-June 1944 through July and August. At first, it took me about two hours to get the organisation working before moving on to the next job, but the V1s came so fast that I could not afford the time at each site. Of course procedures became streamlined with experience and I was able to move on to each incident in much less time, unless there were special circumstances. During July, I once attended sixteen incidents in a twenty-hour period.

I had been on duty continuously for nearly a week, chasing V1s over a large area of East London and metropolitan Essex. Those aiming the buzz bombs, as they became known, were not working to union rules, for they came at all hours of the day and night, sometimes singly, sometimes in twos and threes. The menacing blast of flame from the exhaust pipe and the ear-shattering bark of the rocket engine struck fear in the hearts of all as a V1 approached.

All Londoners developed an ear tuned to the note of the exhaust and, whenever the signal was picked up, those with the sharpest hearing yelled 'There's one coming' and led the dash for the shelter.

My overpowering need was for sleep. I had been without adequate rest since my last leave day and was very tired, but I was due for twenty-four hours leave next day and that cheered me up.

Regular meals became a thing of the past; I existed on sandwiches, bolted whenever the opportunity came. I tended to generate stomach acid after dealing with a particularly distressing job and really had no zest for food; even a cup of tea lost its appeal.

I returned from an incident near the Wanstead Golf Course and settled into my chair for a snooze. I had been asleep for about an hour when I was awakened by the roar of an approaching V1 and moved to a corner of the room, away from the window. The bomb passed over but, almost immediately, the engine cut out and I had the feeling of being suspended in space as I waited for the explosion. It came, a resounding b o o o m, after the usual ten seconds or so pause, and not very far off. I put on my dusty old cap and buttoned my tunic as I waited for the call from Area Control.

'V1 explosion in Blake Hall Crescent, Wanstead, sir. Your car has been ordered.'

Oh, God. Here we go again. What frightful scenes should we encounter this time? We had become accustomed to rows of shattered houses and shops and the back-street factory with a dozen girls entombed. To the heart-rending cries of the bereaved and children screaming for their parents. To the torn and hideously mangled bodies to be recovered from debris and to the little corner shop, a heap of ruins, with customers slashed by flying glass, lying amid bundles of firewood and tins of corned beef.

I asked my driver if she knew where we were going. Yes, she knew and we were there in a few minutes. All the trees in the vicinity were stripped of leaf by the explosion and the pungent smell of chlorophyll mingled with the musty stink of mortar and other dusts; only the stench of blood was missing, something to be thankful for.

Several houses had been wrecked and women and children were being removed from the debris. As we worked, several V1s roared across the sky and there came a chorus of 'Sieg Heil, Sieg Heil' from hundreds of German throats in the PoW camp along the road. How I prayed for one to come down smack in the centre of that camp, but my prayer went unanswered and the bombs flew on, to crash in Poplar or Stepney or points west.

The houses in Blake Hall Crescent lay in a hollow, which restricted the area of blast. Casualties, relatively, were light and we were able to clear up rather more quickly than usual and make our way home. There was no knowing where or when the next buzz bomb would dive.

The PoW camp came near to disaster about a week later, when a flying bomb crashed on the anti-aircraft rocket installation on the opposite side of Woodford Road, killing a number of gunners and A.T.S. girls. Their shallow slit trenches proved no protection from the massive blast.

The explosion set fire to dry grass on the site and it was by a narrow margin only that the N.F.S. stopped the fire before it reached the magazines, crude corrugated iron sheds with the rockets laid out on racks and the openings screened by hessian curtains. It was a close shave but then, life was full of close shaves in those days.

The expert navigators of the R.A.F. Pathfinder squadrons had achieved great success in marking important targets in Germany for the bomber force following up. The Luftwaffe attempted to copy the technique and, in recent raids, had taken to dropping marker flares. In a move to counter this strategy, fire officers had been instructed to carry six sandbags on each appliance, to be used to smother the flares. My first experience of this tactic came with an incendiary attack on the eastern outskirts of the Region, when I was on hand to witness a Nazi muck-up. There had been a fall of fire bombs in the vicinity of Manor Road, Chigwell. Several houses were alight and fire crews at work when I arrived. I was reconnoitring the area when there came a fall of marker flares in fields about half a mile to the north of the built-up area. At once, two pumps set off in the direction of the markers.

'Stop,' I yelled to the officer of the leading pump. 'Where are you going?'

'To black out those flares,' he replied.

'Leave them to burn,' I replied. 'Let them drop their loads on the fields.' So the appliances returned to the job in hand, the crews gazing, somewhat apprehensively, in the direction of the white glare, anticipating a deluge of high explosives. But there was no further bombing that night.

Somehow, the Nazi lines had become crossed. Surely the aim was to follow the markers with bombs? But the bombs had arrived first and the markers, far off target, came later. In any event, Chigwell, a dormitory suburb on the outskirts of London, hardly. presented a strategic target worthy of bombing. We had come to regard the Luftwaffe as a deadly efficient force, .but that night's experience had knocked a small dent in its reputation, to our intense satisfaction.

Perhaps we were witnessing the effect of the great losses inflicted on the enemy during the closing months of 1944. I returned to the area next morning, following my usual practice of taking a closer look in daylight, to judge the general effect of firefighting. In addition, we were always concerned to assist, wherever possible, in making houses habitable by spreading tarpaulin sheets, for example, over exposed roofs. I knocked at a door with this in mind.

It was answered by a lady whose attitude was distinctly cool. I explained the reason for my call and was met with an outburst from the occupier. The gist of her complaint was that it was bad enough to be bombed by an enemy, worse to be robbed by people supposed to be coming to help. She went on to say that a much prized silver tea service, a gift from her children for her Silver Wedding Anniversary, was missing; only firemen had been upstairs to deal with the fire; they must

Firemen clear a bomb-blasted roof of loose tiles before laying a tarpaulin. Then, gaping windows will be covered with bitumenised paper to render the house habitable. The men forming these special squads were employed in the building trade in civilian life and received extra pay for trade work.

I made a mental note to congratulate the local firemen on their judicious use of water. It was clear that they had a lively fire to deal with but had not drowned the place. The N.F.S. demonstrated its goodwill by spreading tarpaulins over the gaping roof later that day.

A most welcome memo arrived from Fire Force H.Q: the two Divisional Officers sharing operations in 'C' Division had been granted one week's leave apiece. Leslie Smith and I tossed to decide who should go first; I won and lost no time in packing my bags.

My family would have preferred a seaside holiday, but all coastal resorts were out of bounds; beaches were mined and strewn with great coils of barbed wire. Instead, we arranged to visit a relative in Cambridge and set off from Liverpool Street station on the Saturday morning.

The train had just pulled out of the station when we heard the roar of a V1 and watched it dive in the vicinity of Mile End Road. I was, perhaps, half a mile away but the scene, vividly, was before my eyes. The cloud of choking dust and the smell of freshly spilled blood. The shocked, dazed people; the shattered buildings and the frenzied rush to assist those in the stricken area. I experienced all the sounds and smells and horrible scenes as I sat there in the placid atmosphere of that railway carriage, rolling steadily away from it all. Great gaps among the streets of small houses bordering the railway track; demolished factories and tarpaulin covered roofs bore witness

be the culprits. I asked if I might see the room and was shown up. Part of the roof had been destroyed and the room and its contents were severely damaged. I asked to be shown where the tea service had been kept and she indicated the general area, adding that it was stored in a glass-fronted display cabinet which had been destroyed in the fire.

I foraged about in the debris and came across what looked like a blob of solder, about the size of a tablespoon, then some smaller pieces and what, unmistakably, was the brass screw for fixing the knob to the lid of the tea pot. I handed my find to her.

'Here's your tea service,' I said. 'It's been melted by the fire.'

She was profuse with her apology, saying she had been upset by the damage to her home and the loss of her tea service, which had such sentimental value.

I suppose it was natural that she suspected the firemen of stealing her property and I have no doubt that neighbours would have been given this impression albeit in good faith, had I not found the remains. The evidence might easily have been swept up and disposed of in cleaning up.

With the invasion of Europe in full swing, every effort was required to maintain output in the factories. Firemen play their part by laying tarpaulins over a roof damaged by blast from a nearby V1.

to the damage the V1s were wreaking on the metropolis. We had reached the fringe of the countryside before all traces of the bombardment were left behind.

The sun was shining from a cloudless sky as we emerged from Cambridge station into streets reminiscent of the peaceful atmosphere and stability of pre-war days. American servicemen strolled with smiling girls in summer dresses, apparently without a care in the world, in sharp contrast to the harried, beleaguered Londoners. My wife and I were the only ones who ducked as a formation of Mustangs roared low over the station, raising amused glances from onlookers. A bit of my Shakespeare returned: 'He jests at scars who never felt a wound.'

I fell asleep over lunch and had to be dragged up to bed, to sleep for twenty hours. What a tonic!

We spent tranquil, sunny days, lounging on the bank of the River Cam behind King's College Chapel and riding through peaceful country lanes on the Linton bus. But our days passed all too quickly and the time came for our departure.

Auntie Nell was helping my daughter with her jacket. 'Now you will be able to sleep in your own little bed, tonight.'

But the child had not slept in her own bed for months, unless the corner of a Morrison shelter could be so described. It was difficult to believe that people only fifty miles away could be so completely unaware of the ordeal people in London and the south-eastern counties were undergoing. We had no desire to distress the old lady with the reality and the horror. Dear old soul, she had made us most welcome and comfortable and given us a brief glimpse of a life we had almost forgotten; we were very grateful.

Leslie Smith was waiting for me when I arrived back at the office to 'book returned.' He thrust some foolscap sheets into my hand. 'Hallo, Dee. Here's your hand-over notes. See you next week.'

'Have a good holiday, Les.' I replied, addressing his back as he made for the door.

A column officer in the room is joined by a fireman to help with the search. They have no idea what they will discover; a crushed, mangled body perhaps? An unconscious person or persons, trapped under a beam, or nothing at all. The search must be carried out, however hazardous. But it's a wonderful feeling when they locate an injured person and extricate him or her from the shadow of death.

A flying bomb had crashed in a street of small houses at about midnight. The scene was one we had come to expect; several houses completely demolished, others damaged in varying degree. The road was littered with an assortment of debris; roof tiles and bricks, smashed chairs and household items, window curtains and a bed, complete with mattress, pillows and blankets, just as though it had been placed there deliberately. I was told it had been occupied by a young girl who had been removed, uninjured, after being blown from her bedroom.

Fortunately, there was no outbreak of fire and the N.F.S. was able to concentrate on the search for casualties in the damaged houses. It was the practice to chalk 'NFS' on the wall by the entrance door indicating that the house had been searched by the fire service, thus avoiding duplicated search by other services.

My D.R. and I entered a house, shouting 'Anybody there?' There was no answer but it could not be assumed that the house was empty; the occupiers might be unconscious, or even dead. So we crawled under the collapsed passage ceiling, supported crazily by one wall and forming a triangular cavity and found our way into the front room. Here, too, the ceiling had collapsed, smothering everything with a thick, white coating of plaster dust. The furniture had been tossed about by the blast and it was difficult to orientate our appreciation of what lay before our eyes. Slowly, we began to get our bearings as we shone our handlamps around the room and saw an old man lying partly buried by pieces of furniture. We freed him from the debris and got him to his feet, speaking to him all the while, but without response. He appeared to be uninjured but the shock had deprived him of speech, although he was trying to tell us something.

'Anybody else in the house?' I asked. At last, he got it out.

'Only my dog. He's here, somewhere.' So we searched around for the dog.

'Here he is,' said my D.R. His hand-lamp beam had reflected in the dog's eyes, although it was not possible to identify the animal as such. He was covered in white dust and his form blended with the irregular mass of debris surrounding him. Like his master, he could make no sound and we heard not a whimper. I reached over the remains of the table and rubbed his ear, testing his temper. He seemed docile enough, so I found his collar and lifted him free.

I don't know if dogs cry, but two tracks, washed by tears coursing down his cheeks, reminded me of a child with a grimy face.

We assisted the man into the street and saw him off to hospital in an ambulance. The dog we handed over to a fire crew, standing by to deal with any outbreak of fire. They would provide him with a temporary home at the fire station, following a fairly general practice at the time, until he could be restored to his master.

The knowledge spread among the general public that a missing animal might be found at the fire station, and those in search of a pet, lost after a local incident, often made the fire station their first port of call.

That's how a lively wire-haired terrier became a full-time member of a temporary fire station's complement, at Lovatt's Garage in Romford Road. He was rescued from the ruins of a house in Manor Park in which all the human occupants were killed. Fireman Johnny Johnson took a liking to the dog and called him Mick. The attraction was mutual and the dog took to life in the fire station as though he had been born to it. He was thoroughly at home with the men and showed good sense

in getting out of the way of the size ten fireboots when the bells went down on his first day there.

The men were at carrying down drill one morning when Mick, entirely without prompting, decided to have a go. He

The notice says it all. This damage was caused by a flying bomb in July 1944. During the Blitz in 1940 the front of a small tailor's shop in Stepney was completely removed by bomb blast. Out came a Union Jack, propped up in a heap of debris, together with a chalked notice board 'More open than ever!' I encountered this spirit many times in various parts of London, exemplified by the succinct remark of an old man we recovered from the wreckage of his home: 'Sod 'im!'

What thoughts occupy the mind of the officer in charge of the first appliance to arrive at a V1 incident like this one? First, he must put aside any feeling of dismay at the scale of the damage and revulsion at any horrific scenes he may encounter. His first action must be to get a jet to work on the most threatening area of fire to stop it spreading. He must make a reconnaissance to estimate the assistance he will require and send the message to control, all the while keeping a sharp eye open for hazards, for example, the sagging brickwork in the centre of the wall. Check for casualties and, if necessary, get a second jet to work. With a nominal crew of five, but, often, only four, it may confidently be assumed that he will be sweating, physically and mentally, by this time. Assistance should be on the way but its prompt arrival, and with it a senior officer, may depend on the availability of appliances in the locality or on road conditions. Eventually, help will arrive but, until it does, 'It's all his!'

jumped on the bottom rung of the ladder, his back paws together and stood there with his front paws hooked over the next rung. He then proceeded to mount the ladder with a series of leaps until he reached the top, whereupon he bounded to the roof and stood barking at his admiring master on the ground.

Fireman Johnson ran up the ladder and brought him down under his arm. From that moment, Mick was hooked on ladder drill, never missing an opportunity. In fact, he became a nuisance and had to be chained up whenever a ladder was in use, otherwise he would have monopolised the occasion.

Then somebody had a bright idea; could Mick be carried down on a fireman's back? The only way to find out was to try him. So up to the roof went a fireman, followed closely by the dog. Then Johnny Johnson went up and made a broad back. Mick was lifted up and stood barking and wagging his stumpy little tail nineteen to the dozen as he was carried down.

It was about this time that the 'Salute the Soldier' savings campaign was launched and the Romford Road station took part in the competition to see which station could raise the most money. A board outside the station announced that Mick, the fireman's dog, would give a private demonstration of climbing a ladder and being rescued, to any person investing £25 in Savings. Many came along with their money and Mick was kept busy doing his bit for the cause.

When Fireman Johnson was demobbed, he took the dog home. He became a well-loved pet, on good terms with all but the coalman, whom he disliked intensely until the end of his days.

Goldie was driving me along Eastern Avenue, late one evening, en route to a V1 incident at Leyton. I was sitting in the back seat, pulling on my fire boots, when she remarked:

'Shall I let them go ahead?'

I thought she was referring to a staff car following up, but could see no sign of one from the rear window.

'Let who go ahead?' I asked.

Her head jerked sideways. 'Them.'

I looked out of the side window and saw a group of three V1s flying parallel to us.

'Oh, yes,' I replied. 'Don't hold them up.'

We were booked out to our job at Leyton; someone else would have to take care of what happened when that deadly trio crashed.

General Eisenhower once wrote that he, like most people, used to mutter 'Keep going, keep going' whenever he found himself remotely in the path of a V1 thundering overhead, conscious of the fact that he was wishing death and destruction on some unfortunate citizens along the road. I confess to similar feelings and crossed my fingers.

In his book *The Battle of the V-Weapons*, Basil Collier wrote of 'the dismal rattle of the flying bomb.' I doubt if any Londoner, crouching in a shelter as one of these horrors roared overhead, with vibration rattling window frames and shaking any loose article in the house, would have considered the din a 'dismal rattle.' I would describe it as a terrifying roar. It is impossible to convey the nervous tension which enveloped one and all as a shattering roar, like that of a dozen motor cycles with open exhausts, saturated the entire atmosphere in the vicinity of the flight. Paradoxically, this was accompanied by an even greater fear that the din, suddenly, would cease, signalling the bomb's dive to earth. To those below, hoping that the continuing roar indicated the passing of their own particular peril, a sudden silence produced an almost heart-stopping shock for ten seconds or so. Then came the blast as a ton of high explosive went up, shattering everything within a radius of a hundred yards or so, and creating severe damage far beyond. Some unfortunates never heard the blast; others, over a wide area, told friends 'I thought it was coming straight down my chimney'.

The damage at our incident was widespread. The builder of the mean little houses must have used mud for mortar, for dozens of houses were demolished and it was possible to take walls to pieces by lifting brick from brick, as a child would use playblocks. A thick layer of dust covered everything and clouds rose with every step I took.

Most of the residents had taken shelter in their cellars; cries could be heard and lights seen flashing through crevices in the debris. Rescue services were methodically searching for survivors and many were released without much trouble, but there were several difficult tasks to be faced.

One house resembled nothing more than a pile of rubble, topped by roof timbers, with floor boards protruding from the bricks and slates. I heard a faint call for help coming from beneath the pile and called to the man: 'Where are you?' He told me he was lying on the cellar stairs and was trapped by heavy debris. I got closer to him by entering the cellar through the coalhole in the pavement. I found the place almost filled with rubble from the interior of the house, but was much closer to him. He could see the light of my torch through crevices, but I could not see him. He sounded very close and told me he was in great pain from a heavy beam across his legs.

As we spoke, I heard another V1 approaching and fly over, the vibration bringing trickles of dust from the rubble overhead. I crouched there, expecting the heap to cascade on me, as it certainly would had the bomb exploded nearby. I held my breath and waited for it to pass over before telling the man that I would find a doctor and the rescue leader. He

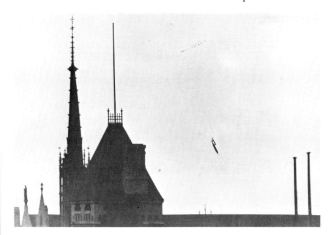

This incredible pair of photographs were the first to be released (on August 3rd) which actually showed a V1 diving onto its target and exploding. It is believed this incident is that at Wild

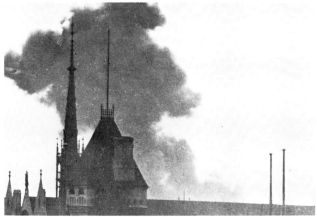

Street on June 28th which hit the Peabody Buildings. The building in the foreground is the Royal Courts of Justice situated in the Strand.

Firemen burrow beneath floor joists to reach a family trapped in the cellar of their home. After dark, rescuers would look for pinpoints of light from hand torches or candles filtering through crevices in the debris. By day they were guided by shouts.

begged me not to leave him but I told him I must, promising to be back with help. I soon found a doctor and the rescue leader and took them to the cellar. The doctor inserted a rubber tube through a crevice, guided by the light of my torch, and the trapped man was able to place it in his mouth, as directed. The doctor then administered two pints of sodium bicarbonate solution, to counter the effect of shock. We were as close as that.

The rescue leader pursed his lips when he saw the position and motioned me outside. He told me it would be a long job; the condition of the debris was such that he dare not use mechanical equipment, the heap would need to be removed by hand. I left him to it and went back to my car to prepare and send a report to control.

I had fifty men at work on the site and there was plenty of rescue work to be done; happily, no fires. I kept an eye on the place where the rescue squad was working, hoping to see the man released but progress was slow. One clumsy or unfortunate move would bring tons of rubble pouring down. I left the site at about 8 a.m. Much of the rescue work had been completed but the man in the cellar was still pinned down. I was informed that he was released about half an hour after I had left. He died in hospital at noon.

Goldie was relieved that morning by Firewoman Ball. She came to the office to report that she was taking the car to refuel and I took the opportunity of discussing with her a new Standard Message form to be completed at each V1 incident. I explained the procedure. The driver would accompany me to the centre of the damage and take down details as I dictated. She understood and there seemed to be no problem.

We had not long to wait before putting the new system into operation. A particularly nasty, gory situation confronted us following a V1 explosion in Dames Road, Forest Gate. A trolleybus, crammed with home-going workers, had caught the full blast and the whole area was a sickening sight. Dismembered bodies littered the roadway; others were spattered over the brickwork of the houses across the way and the wreckage of the trolleybus was simply too ghastly to describe. I dictated my report to Firewoman Ball who raced away to telephone the message to Control. It was not a long job; there was no fire and the casualties were quickly recovered and removed. There was no time-consuming excavation work to be done.

Next morning there came a knock at my office door; Firewoman Ball entered, nervously fingering her cap. She had come to ask a favour; could she be excused from accompanying me to the centre of damage? Yesterday's experience had sickened her and she felt she could not repeat the operation without fainting. I understood her reaction.

I cannot say with certainty that this is the trolley-bus involved in the Dames Road incident, but it is remarkably like it. The roof and upper deck, together with the passengers was blasted away. Standing passengers on the lower deck also were flung against the fronts of houses on the other side of the road. The lower deck seated passengers were all dead.

There were many who felt the same way. She had been out with me during air raids, had lain in the gutter when bombs were falling and got up with a joke, without fear for her personal safety, or, if she had, disguising it pretty effectively. So what could I do but arrange for my D.R. to take over the duty?

Little Miss Ball was very grateful, albeit a bit shamefaced. She had no reason to be.

Goldie was not affected in the same way. I kept my eye on her in somewhat similar circumstances and saw her step over bits of human bodies lying in the road without visible effect. But her weak spot was revealed in a rather different situation during the raids of early spring, 1944, when fast-flying aircraft roared over London, dropped a load of bombs and fled as quickly as possible. A number of isolated fires had occurred in the Forest Gate/Manor Park area and I found myself in a temporary fire station manned by a part-time crew, round about midnight. The firewoman on duty reported that her crew had been ordered out to a fire at the Manor Park cemetery and had been gone for three hours. I could not imagine a fire in a cemetery occupying a fire crew for anything like three hours and I had passed the place several times during the evening, observing nothing out of the ordinary. However, I had better investigate; it was not unknown for a fire appliance to be engulfed in a bomb crater.

The cemetery gates were wide open and we drove in, following the main drive until it narrowed to a single width road and terminated in a sort of round-about. The glow of a distant fire was the only light we could see as we stopped. I got out and had a look around; there was no sign of a pump or crew. I told Eddie Lambert, my D.R., to take a look along one of the paths while I walked in the opposite direction.

I was soon out of sight of the car and, passing a clump of bushes, was startled to hear a voice out of the stillness of the night.

'I wouldn't go down there,' it said, 'something's come down.' It was the cemetery keeper. I searched around with my hand-lamp and saw a cluster of shiny fire bombs lying scattered over path and graves. I picked up two and walked back towards the car. The keeper told me that firemen had been in the cemetery earlier in the evening to deal with a fire in a heap of discarded wreath frames but had left before the second fall of incendiaries.

When I came in sight of the car I was surprised to see it shining like a beacon in the black-out, with every light switched on. In front stood Goldie, crouching in the light of the headlamps, her hands between her knees, peering in the direction of my footsteps as I crunched along the gravel path.

'Here's a fine place to leave anyone at midnight,' she croaked, her voice hoarse with fright.

I can't say I was exactly cheerful myself, surrounded by marble angels, gravestones, broken columns and the like. I appreciated Goldie's feelings, stranded there alone in the darkness, with no sound other than the eerie soughing of the wind in the trees. Eddie Lambert came up a minute later and we all had a good laugh over the incident.

I gave Goldie one of the bombs and promised to have it defused and made up into a table lamp, adding 'You'll be able to tell your children and grandchildren how you came to get your novel table lamp,' and, I guess, she has told the tale many times since.

The missing pump turned up eventually. It was manned by a part-time crew who reported for duty one night a week. Their instructions were to report back to their station after dealing with the fire to which they had been sent. But business had fallen off since the heady nights of the Blitz and they wanted to make the most of their 'good luck' in finding themselves on duty on a night of considerable activity. So, after dealing with the cemetery fire, they chased after one showing a light at Manor Park, then to others, finally arriving back at their station at about 1 a.m., tired out but happy with their taste of action.

The Victoria Dock was the centre of mysterious activity in early 1944. Vast concrete structures were being erected by a labour force of thousands, mainly Irishmen, engaged in work around the clock. There was much speculation as to the purpose of these strange concrete rafts, the most likely of which seemed to be that they were gun platforms, to be submerged in the Channel and used in the bombardment of the occupied French coast.

The keels of the platforms were laid on the mud flats of the River Thames at Barking. When a suitable height in the construction of the superstructure had been reached, they were floated off by the rising tide, assisted by N.F.S crews using powerful jets of water to cut away the mud. The craft were then towed to the nearby Victoria Dock where the superstructure was built up to a height of some thirty feet. As the height increased, ballast became necessary to afford stability. Again the N.F.S. were brought into action to pump water into the shells at various stages of construction, until the weight of the concrete provided its own stability, whereupon the water was pumped out again.

It was, of course, a construction site for sections of the Mulberry Harbour and the scheme remained a very well-kept secret, for nobody I knew had any idea of what these objects, which looked like floating warehouses, really were until the news broke, following the invasion.

I visited the sites frequently to inspect N.F.S. crews at work and was impressed by the manner in which work was proceeding.

The project, obviously, was important to the war effort and very hush-hush. All concerned were keen to take part in anything that would help speed victory.

One of the features which made obvious the priority of the project was the fact that the sites were floodlit throughout the hours of darkness, the only time I knew the black-out rules to be lifted, apart from emergency lighting during rescue work following an air raid.

The 'scalded cat' raids were occurring at frequent intervals and a simple signal was used to give warning of the approach of raiders. Floodlights were blinked once if raiders came within fifty miles of the dock. This was a preliminary warning. If the enemy came within twenty-five miles, the lights were blinked three times at ten-second intervals, remaining blacked out after the third time. This system gave men working deep in the interior twenty seconds to find their way over the scaffolding to the safety of the shelters.

I was present on a number of occasions when warnings were received after black-out time, and was fascinated to see hundreds of men swarming like ants up, over and down the scaffolding before the lights went out. There were always a number who failed to make it; some received injury as the result.

A pair of caissons for the Mulberry Harbour near completion in the East India Dock. I watched the build up of Mulberry Units, quite unaware of their purpose, until the East India Import Dock was packed solidly with these concrete monsters. Returning a day or two later, they were all gone!

The invasion had seen activity in the Royal Docks reach its peak. Landing craft were embarking men and stores for passage to the Normandy beaches, returning packed with German prisoners.

I was in the Royal Albert Dock a few days after the D-Day landings. Liberty ships were unloading thousands of tons of bombs and shells, with a fire crew standing by aboard each vessel in case of mishap. I noticed a convoy of army lorries with an armed escort, lined up at the quayside with a very smart sergeant-major in charge.

'What's all this in aid of?' I asked the local officer.

'Oh, it's a load of Jerry prisoners coming in on a tank landing craft,' he replied.

We watched as a L.C.T. (Landing Craft Tank) nosed into a ramp, saw its massive door lowered and I found myself looking into the black cavern of its hold, eager to catch a glimpse of the tough enemy troops I had heard so much about. Words of command in the German language rang out and we heard the tramp of marching feet. Out of the darkness came a motley crowd of men, blinking in the afternoon sunlight.

It was an uncanny experience, standing there watching this column of men wearing the grey uniform I had only seen on the cinema screen. Some were hatless; others wore soft pill-box caps and nearly all looking dejected. My first impression was one of surprise at their generally poor physique; I had expected to see sturdy, fit-looking men but these were anything but shock troops. Some looked very frightened and one little man peered about him through thick, pebble glasses, as though he feared a vicious British mob might set upon him and beat out his brains. The column was halted near me and I saw apprehension on many faces.

But there was one who was not cowed. A handsome, well-set-up youngster, wearing an Afrika Korps cap, stood out among his comrades. He looked around contemptuously as he felt for his cigarette case; selected a fag and tapped it deliberately on the case and slowly put it in his mouth. His look was one of sheer insolence as he turned his gaze on me, his expression fixed. He lit his cigarette, took a long pull and, with a curl of his lip, blew the smoke almost in my face. This was the most articulate dumb insolence I had ever seen. I felt grudging admiration for his show of spirit and a strong desire to kick his backside. The whole episode had lasted but a minute or so and my attention had been rivetted on the young Nazi.

I did not notice the marshalling of the lorries and escort but I was soon made aware of their presence. The sergeant-major quickly had the prisoners sorted into convenient lorry loads.

'Come along there! Come along!' he shouted in his most aggressive parade ground manner, and if the language was not understood, there was no doubt about the intent. The prisoners jumped to it, including my arrogant young Nazi, who hopped into the truck as smartly as any and I didn't blame him; that sergeant-major was only a pace or two behind him, ready to bite any dawdler!

One of my most harrowing experiences followed the explosion of a flying bomb in Barking Road, Plaistow, at about 7 p.m. on a summer evening. Houses in the area were of the late Victorian type of structure; three floors and semi-basement. The blast had demolished several of these old buildings and nothing but a heap of rubble confronted the rescue teams who were quickly on the scene. It was feared that many were buried in the debris and firemen worked with the rescue teams, since there was no firefighting to be done.

Try to imagine a ten-foot-high pile of bricks, mortar, masonry, furniture, timber floors and doors, all inextricably mixed; about seventy feet long and thirty feet deep, with taller columns of brickwork, the remains of chimneys, rising gauntly from the heap. Where on earth does one start to search for those buried?

It was in such circumstances that the local knowledge of the wardens was of such value. They were able to recognise small clues which led, for instance, to the front path of a house, leading in turn to the front door which gave a guide to the situation of the rooms. This enabled rescue workers to concentrate the search on the most likely areas.

One of the houses was occupied by a part-time member of the N.F.S. whom I had trained before the war. He was a key worker at Messrs Tate & Lyle, the sugar people, and had gone to work on the night shift an hour or two earlier. The dreaded message from the wardens brought him hurrying home.

Progress had been made in tunnelling into the mass of debris, with separate parties searching in each of the demolished houses. He stood on a heap of debris beside what had been his front door, giving what guidance he could to the rescue squad. He appeared quite calm, smoking a cigarette. Presently, there was a pause and he was called forward. He glanced at a body on a stretcher and identified a son. He waited, quietly smoking, as the body of another of his children was recovered. Some time later came the body of his wife. Welfare workers urged him to wait at the Working Men's Club across the road but he declined, saying he would 'see them all out'.

The arrival of the RAF-trained 'sniffer dogs' always introduced an extra measure of drama at an incident where people were buried under debris. I was often present, particularly during the V1 and V2 periods, when large buildings were reduced to great heaps of rubble. The Heavy Rescue Leader would call for silence, his call taken up by those working on the site. A hush would descend, whereupon the leader would shout 'Can you hear me?' 'Where are you?' and all would strain their ears to catch the slightest sound from underground. Sometimes there would be a response, but often none. Then came the dogs. The handler would consult with the rescue leader who would indicate the area of search. The handler would lead his dog to the spot, then slip the lead. With hope of recovering a victim alive fading, it was electrifying to see a dog, moving apparently at random, suddenly start to paw the ground. Immediately, the dog would be leashed and rescuers move in to dig on the spot. In my experience, the dogs never failed, although the search sometimes brought forth only a body.

Daylight faded and the work continued by the light of fire service floodlights. After the frenzy of activity following the first shock, operations had settled down to a systematic search fashioned by long experience. The harsh glare of the lights focused attention on the critical area, illuminating the highlights of bricks and floorboards, tiles, heaps of dust and rubble, casting deep shadows behind. Toiling rescue teams came wriggling from tunnels bored into the debris, carrying large baskets filled with bricks and rubble. The sound of sawing came faintly from under the heap as pieces of floorboard were cut to provide shoring for the roof of the tunnel. Then came a grim little procession of stretcher bearers carrying the body of the last of his family. He broke down and finally allowed himself to be led away.

Meanwhile, other rescuers were recovering bodies from the ruins of adjoining houses. As the hours passed, an even greater tragedy, next door, was revealed. An entire family of six had been wiped out and there were more dead in the other houses. It was 3 a.m. when the rescue men completed their gruesome task. They had recovered eighteen bodies from this short stretch of terrace houses.

These were the scenes I was witnessing several times a day and I was becoming emotionally involved. I had to take a grip on myself and cultivate an air of indifference, otherwise my work would suffer. But it was hard to shut out all human feeling and I found myself most affected when children were involved. With two of my own at home, I could feel for others.

I recall another incident at Dagenham at breakfast time. A father had recovered the body of his three-year-old from the ruins of his home and, clasping the child to his breast, ran, demented, down the street. As he passed, I heard his anguished moaning and was haunted by the sound and sight of the baby's chubby little legs, jogging up and down as he ran.

Scenes like this — and they were common — aroused in me feelings of cold hatred towards the enemy and I vowed I would kick to death with my heavy fireboots any German airman falling into my hands. The opportunity did not arise and I doubt if I should have reacted in that manner if it had, but that's how I, and many of my colleagues, felt at the time.

This was the period of heavy and mounting raids by the R.A.F. and American Air Forces on German cities. I listened to the roar of the aerial armada, flying low over London on their way to the Continent, with a feeling of grim satisfaction. I had been a close witness for more than four years of the brutal terror, the agony and destruction unleashed by a ruthless enemy on innocent men, women and children and now he was being given powerful doses of his own medicine.

But my thoughts turned to Hamburg or Frankfurt or the Ruhr towns, where old men and women and mothers, clutching their children, would be scurrying to the shelters as German sirens sounded the approach of the Allied bombers.

I visualised the scene in fire stations, as my German counterparts prepared for the onslaught. Many would be affected by nervous dyspepsia, as I was. Their thoughts, like mine when the position was reversed, would turn to the chances of survival.

Will this be the night I bought it? Shall I end up under tons of rubble in a demolished building? If I am lucky enough to hear the All Clear sound, will my wife and children and our home have come through unscathed?

I couldn't help feeling a grain of pity for those who would feel the weight of the attack, that night, and I was very thankful we were not to be the target.

The V1 attack on London showed no sign of abating. Bombs dived on the closely built up area at random intervals throughout the twenty-four hours and continued to do so, week after week. The strain on those living in the target areas became a matter of great concern to the civic authorities.

The use of air raid sirens was abandoned when it became obvious that the Capital was under constant alert. Instead, use was made of the spotter system in order that work in the factories might continue uninterrupted, even when the fearsome bark of a V1 exhaust could be heard. When a missile was seen to be approaching in direct line, the spotter would sound his local alarm, usually a klaxon horn, as a signal to the workers to take cover.

Nervous strain sent the absentee figures soaring and normal life was seriously affected. Many mothers were unwilling to send their children to school; others were too nervous to leave home to do their shopping, for none knew when the next flying bomb, or two or three for that matter, might appear in the sky overhead.

The strain on the rescue services was particularly acute. Not only were they and their families exposed to the general tension; their duties called for long hours of back-breaking toil, tunnelling into debris in search of those buried. As they worked, more bombs roared across the sky. Some passed over, others crashed in nearby streets, compelling rescuers to make a dash for safety. But not all were in a position to do so. It was not uncommon to find oneself crouching in a narrow cavity with tons of loose rubble piled overhead, trying to reach some unfortunate fellow citizen. Nothing then concentrated the mind on the slender thread between this life and the next, more than the harsh note and vibration of an approaching V1, bringing mortar dust trickling on the back of one's neck!

The strain began to show. Personnel were seen to be in need of a complete break from the mental and physical fatigue brought about by the barrage of these atrocious weapons. Accordingly, a plan devised by senior fire officers was inaugurated early in September 1944. An area of countryside at Upshire, just north of the Wake Arms pub, was taken over for development as a camp site for firemen and firewomen from the East End. It was an imaginative scheme, planned with a dual purpose in mind.

Personnel were withdrawn from the front line to enjoy a period of rest in the peaceful environment of Epping Forest, only a few miles beyond the boundary of the target area.

The crew of a Mobile Kitchen parade for inspection by Her Majesty, Queen Elizabeth, at Lambeth Fire H.Q. December 6th, 1944. Those wearing white overalls are the cooks; on the left is their driver, an all-women unit. These firewomen stand ready to accompany their Division to reinforce any badly blitzed town or City in the country, providing up to one thousand meals for hungry firefighters. They were accompanied by a stores van carrying the necessary food. Meanwhile, they gain experience in the use of their equipment at the Upshire Camp.

Additionally, it provided an opportunity for a practice run in exercising the troops in the problems involved in supporting a badly blitzed city, the purpose for which the Task Divisions had been formed. Each Division comprised 100 pumps, with a hose-laying lorry carrying a mile of hose and a steel pipe-laying unit.

A small administrative unit was included to take care of pay, welfare, provisioning and mobilising. Also included was a mobile kitchen carrying its own fuel supply and a stores van, with two complete crews of kitchen staff, capable of providing meals for the thousand personnel required to operate the Division. There was a field telephone unit equipped with telephone cables and portable exchanges for connecting operational centres and base. Canteen vans were included to provide on-the-job refreshment for crews working at incidents; mobile workshops would be available to repair any breakdown of equipment which might occur. In short, a Division would in this way be equipped to live off its own fat, without being a burden to the stricken city it had come to support.

Half a division at a time was withdrawn from the most heavily bombed area and moved into camp at Upshire. Mobile kitchens had preceded the pumps and a hot meal awaited the troops as they moved into the tented accommodation.

Of all the restrictions imposed on N.F.S. personnel, none was more acutely felt than lack of sleep so, with the immediate prospect of an uninterrupted night's rest, and more to follow, weary crews promptly made up for lost time.

The weather, like that of the first days of the Blitz four years earlier, was hot and sunny and the clean, sweet air of the Essex countryside provided an exquisite luxury to be savoured and enjoyed, in contrast with the dust and stench in which rescue crews were obliged to work, following a violent explosion among Victorian terraces.

A substantial breakfast awaited the campers after the first restful night they had enjoyed in weeks. After eating, squads were introduced to planned training courses in which the activities envisaged in a reinforcing project, were simulated.

The men worked stripped to the waist and pale bodies soon developed a healthy tan under the hot sun. Crews competed in water relaying exercises from a pond and the field telephone boys laid miles of cable, using trees for support; the control room firewomen followed up with a communication exercise. A commando style obstacle course, using sheer legs and a ropeway over a stream, enabled competing crews to match their ability against others in crossing the water, carrying lengths of hose and other weighty equipment.

Man-handling trailer pumps across rough country at the Upshire camp, a practical form of physical training. The trees were used as supports for field telephone lines laid by the specialised crews attached to the Division.

The cooks and kitchen staff, of course, had been familiarising themselves with the intricacies of their ranges and the stores procedures. Impromptu games of football and cricket, together with orthodox fitness training sessions attracted willing volunteers until lunch time, after which all hands were free to follow their own inclinations.

During evenings, the large marquee was filled for concerts given by No. 36 Area's own concert party, 'Blitz and Pieces.' The improvement in physical well being and morale was astonishing after only one week in the country.

In course of time, all personnel attached to No. 36 Area Task Divisions were given a week's respite in the peaceful forest setting, returning to their stations mentally and physically refreshed for the task ahead.

I would have been happy to settle for just twenty-four hours of rest in leafy Epping Forest but my twenty-four hours leave entitlement came after seven days and nights continuously on duty; I snatched a nap whenever I could. Frequently, I was so exhausted when I got home that I fell asleep over breakfast, which didn't please my wife and children. It didn't please me either, but there is a limit beyond which nature takes over and I just could not keep awake. It troubled me that we were unable to enjoy even the rudiments of family life. My wife, understandingly, did not complain, but it all amounted to an extra measure of strain on us all.

Men of the No. 36 Fire Force Mobile Divisions undergoing commando-style training at Upshire Camp. The man carrying four lengths of fire hose, a total weight of some 200 lbs, is Column Officer Jim Dale, the Camp Commandant. The exercise demonstrates a method of carrying fire equipment across a stream, part of a toughening up preparation enjoyed, yes, enjoyed, by the troops.

I had been thinking about this and resolved that I would fight off sleep next leave day, at least until after lunch. Arriving home that fine summer morning, I told my wife we would take a bus ride into the country for a picnic, immediately after breakfast. She opened a tin of Spam, cut sandwiches and, with a bottle of orange juice, we set off for a short trip into the Essex countryside. We had heard a few explosions before leaving home but I paid no heed; nothing to do with me, this was my leave day!

We left the bus at Abridge, then truly rural, and strolled along a quiet country road towards Passingford Bridge, enjoying the warm sunshine and summer breeze. We had not seen a single person since leaving Abridge and we all felt relaxed in the peaceful, pleasant surroundings.

A large fallen tree lay in a quiet pasture beside the road; just the place to enjoy our picnic. My younger daughter, then aged ten, was tucking into her sandwich and failed to notice the wasp, also with a taste for Spam. I spotted it, but too late; Margie bit and the wasp responded. She let out a sustained yell, with her mouth opened so wide that I could see the sting embedded in her tongue. I had pulled it out without difficulty when, in the midst of all the kerfuffle, there came the harsh bark of a V1, coming straight at us. It passed over, but only just, for the engine cut out directly over us. Long experience had sharpened my reaction.

'Down!' I yelled, and we all lay behind the tree trunk, as the fiendish weapon dived, the explosion scattering the soil a few fields from where we lay. We gave up in disgust; packed our small bag and were back on the bus before we saw the funny side of it. But it really was a narrow escape. That fallen tree probably diverted us from straying into the danger zone.

Relations between the Fire and other Civil Defence Services, on the whole, was good; nevertheless, differences sometimes became apparent. The Fire Service operated beyond local boundaries whilst other C.D. services, generally, operated within their local districts, under the control of local officers. On the vast majority of occasions, services worked side by side on an incident amicably and with complete co-operation.

Occasionally, friction arose, sometimes as the result of a clash of personality. The Controller of Civil Defence, in a borough far to the east of Aldgate Pump, regularly took charge of incidents in his area. A somewhat pompous individual, he was in the habit of summoning officers of other services to his Control Point by loud hailer: 'Will the Officer in Charge of the electricity service report to the Control.'

One night, an enemy aircraft had crashed in flames and, although damage was relatively light, the spectacular event attracted the local Controller and the Fire Force Commander, among lesser lights of the services. The fire had been extinguished and casualties recovered from the damaged houses when, in his usual haughty tone, the Controller broadcast his Summons to Court: 'Will the Fire Officer in Charge report to the Control.' Fire Force Commander McDuell, who was standing by his Control Point, turned to a young messenger boy. 'Go on, that's you. Go and report to His Lordship.' The Controller continued to make use of his loud hailer at incidents, but I never heard him summon a fire officer after that.

A rather more serious difference arose at a flying bomb incident in the East End. A number of people were buried under a considerable pile of debris and progress in tunneling was slow. There was no fire and firemen worked alongside the rescue squads. As darkness gathered, I was approached by the leader of the rescue squad who informed me that he was withdrawing his men for the night. I asked if he was satisfied that all casualties had been cleared.

'If there's anyone left in there, they are dead,' he replied.

'How do you know?'

'Experience.'

'Well, we will continue until we've cleared it all,' I replied. 'I've just ordered emergency lighting and the canteen van.'

A few minutes later I was asked to speak to a local Assistant Controller who tried to get me to change my mind, but that was out of the question. All my fire service training and, now, experience of incidents of this kind, was to continue until all bodies had been recovered. I had seen people brought out alive after being buried for days.

The atmosphere was hardly cordial when he announced that his men would continue. So we set up the lights; the canteen van arrived and we all enjoyed a well-earned cup of tea which eased the situation somewhat, and got on with the job. Three more bodies were recovered and the rescue leader was proved to be right; they were all dead. I told the Fire Force Commander what had happened, in case there were repercussions, and as I expected, was given his full approval.

During one of the last raids, there had been a minor fall of incendiaries in the vicinity of West Ham football ground. Only slight damage had been caused and the few fires were soon extinguished. It was about midnight in a street off

Barking Road; I was about to return to H.Q. when I heard the thin whistle of a bomb falling from what seemed a great height.

We were a party of three; my driver, the D.R. and myself. The sound of the bomb became louder and we all lay in the road, waiting for the explosion, with ample time for the action we had been instructed to take in such circumstances. I raised my chest from the ground in the 'press up' position and opened my mouth to reduce the effect of blast. Closer and louder it came and I had no doubt that it would strike in the middle of my back, a feeling shared by us all.

After what seemed an age, we heard it strike the ground with a heavy thud. I cringed as I waited for the explosion. A minute passed. We raised our heads and took a furtive look around, to see where it had landed. Still no bang and we rose, apprehensively, to our feet. Was it a dud, or fitted with a delayed action fuse?

'It's in the football ground,' said my driver.

'No. It's behind us, somewhere,' said the D.R.

I thought it was in a different direction altogether. Back at Stratford Control I reported the U.X.B. and had the information passed to Civil Defence H.Q. They knew all about it and had wardens out searching.

Next morning, I was informed that a pump was standing by at the site of an unexploded bomb near West Ham Park. I went along and spoke to the officer in charge of the Bomb Disposal Squad. I explained that the firemen had been on duty all night and I wished to get them back to their station as soon as possible for a meal and some rest, ready for what lay in store that night. He told me that his men had uncovered the bomb and took me to the side of the house, where I saw the fin of a fifty kilo bomb which had struck in the angle of a wall and the concrete path.

The Valetta Grove bomb awaits defusing in 1974

'It's almost ready,' he told me. 'We shall be finished in about twenty minutes; I think you can withdraw your chaps now.'

'Thanks,' I replied; 'I'll do that if you're satisfied they are no longer required.'

We said 'Cheerio' and I instructed the fire officer to return to his station and I drove back to Stratford. I had just entered my office when a sharp explosion rattled the windows. I did not wait for the message from Control; I knew exactly what had happened and made my way back to the scene. The Captain and two of his sappers were dead.

We would never know the precise details, but it appeared that the bomb had exploded as it was being withdrawn from its small crater. Those who had been connected with this incident and had been speaking to the B.D. boys only a few minutes earlier, were shocked by the tragedy. We were no strangers to the emotional reaction to the loss of comrades, and the death of these gallant men affected us as if they had been our own.

My thoughts returned to the big bomb we had heard hit the ground the previous night, and I wondered if it had been located. The Wardens Service, too, was puzzled. They had received many reports of the bomb but there was no clue as to where it had struck. All reports indicated that it was a big one, but it was not the first time that a U.X.B. remained unlocated and the search was discontinued; there were many other urgent items to be dealt with.

A possible solution to the mystery came with the discovery of a German H.E. bomb in August 1974 during excavations for a building site in Valetta Grove, Plaistow. The Bomb Disposal Squad was called and identified it as a 'Hermann' which weighed in at over a ton.

It was considered too dangerous to move and the B.D. men decided to steam out the explosive on the spot. The occupiers of houses in the neighbourhood, including the tenants of three tower blocks totalling a thousand people, were obliged to leave their homes whilst operations proceeded. Trains on the adjacent District Line, part of London's Underground railway system, were halted to prevent vibration.

When the fuse was detonated, many windows in the area were broken and pieces of shrapnel were scattered over a wide area. It was, for many of the older folk, an event reminiscent of the days and nights of the Blitz. In those times it was usually the warden's knock that roused the occupiers and sent them hurrying to the rest centre. On this occasion it was the policemen, but the message and effect was the same. One shudders to think of the consequences if the bomb had remained undetected.

11 Vengeance Mks 1 and 2

'ARE you there, sir?' said the operator over the phone. 'The Fire Force Commander wishes to speak to you. I'm putting you through.'

'Doing anything special this morning?' asked F.F.C. McDuell.

'Nothing that can't wait, sir,' I replied.

'Well, call in during the morning, I want to speak to you.'

I knew the F.F.C. very well; 'Sometime during the morning' meant NOW. I lost no time in making my way to F.F.H.Q. at Gants Hill and was ushered in to the Commander's office.

I knew the drill. He would chat about this or that, matters always affecting the Service, before coming to the point. I listened intently for a clue, seeking the wind direction, so to speak, in order to gain a second or two to think over my answer if an awkward question was in the offing.

But today he was quite affable and asked how long I had been in charge of 'C' Division, as if he didn't know!

'Nearly eleven months, sir,' I replied.

'How would you like a change?'

'I wouldn't mind a Home Division,' I answered.

'How about the "A"?'

He was watching me closely and paused in the act of lighting a cigarette.

'Oh, I'd like that, sir.'

'Very well. You are transferred forthwith. Report to Hatton Garden ['A' Division H.Q.]; they'll be expecting you.'

'Very good, sir, and thank you.'

A curt nod of his head and I was dismissed. What had happened to the former incumbent I had no idea. I would find out in due course, when the Commander would invite me to his quarters for a midnight chat over several cups of tea, after which I could reasonably expect to get to bed by 2.30 a.m!

I left his office feeling elated and was met by Assistant F.F.C. Barnes. He grasped my hand in congratulation and told me he was on the way to Clerkenwell Fire Station and would give me a lift to my new H.Q. Sid Barnes was my new superior officer; the 'A' his most important Division, covering much of central London and the City. He wanted to brief me on general procedure; the officers I knew from my previous attachment, albeit as a humble (more or less) company officer.

The 'C' Division staff car carrying my fire gear; tin helmet, tunic, fire boots, etc., was dispatched to Hatton Garden, the equipment to be handed over to the 'A' Division staff officer and placed in my new car.

Sid Barnes was chatting to me as we drove along the Mile End Road when a loud explosion shook us. A moment later came a radio call 'V2 explosion in Middlesex Street' [Petticoat Lane] 'On my way, with D.O. Demarne.'

'I've got no gear with me,' I said, in alarm.

'There's a spare set of mine in the boot; use that,' came the reply.

Within minutes we were at the scene. The rocket had wrecked the Norwegian Navy Store and had damaged adjoining buildings. The Whitechapel and Bishopsgate appliances were at work, dealing with fires in the debris, as A.F.F.C. Barnes ran off to reconnoitre the incident while I grabbed his spare gear from the boot.

The A.F.F.C. was an inch or two shorter than I but about four inches more around the chest, even more around the waist. My feet were a size larger than his and I had to struggle to get into his boots, but I had no such problem with his tunic! The difficulty was how to get rid of the slack. Despite the grim occasion, the mental picture of the traditional Petticoat Lane tailor, holding a handful of slack at the back as his potential customer surveyed his image from the front, then the slack taken up from the front while the back view was examined, came to mind.

What an undignified début in my new division! That was not all. The tunic, of course, carried the rank markings of an A.F.F.C. and a row of medal ribbons including the G.M., to which I was not entitled. I was known to most of the men engaged and I collected some peculiar glances from them. I thought a word of explanation was due to friend and colleague, Bill Ayers, who had not heard of the change in command; not surprising, since it had been effected only about thirty minutes or so earlier. We cleared up the incident in a couple of hours after some trouble with a deep-seated fire and I returned to Whitechapel Fire Station that evening, for a drink with Bill and his wife in their flat. My own gear was now in the boot of my car, in case of further action.

I returned to my bed which had been set up in a spare room at the rear of my H.Q. in Hatton Garden; a very humble establishment, I reflected, in view of its location in that fabled street of diamonds and bullion.

All that remained of the Norwegian Navy store after the V2 struck on November 10th, 1944. I am standing at bottom right, in silver helmet, and the AFFC on my left, wearing peaked cap, in corner of photo.

Admiral Sir Edward Evans, 'Evans of the Broke,' was Deputy Commissioner for the London Civil Defence Region. Always a man of action, Sir Edward continued his practice of being in the forefront of operations in his Civil Defence duties. He was frequently to be seen in London streets during the Blitz and V-weapon attacks, always with a cheery word of greeting for firemen and C.D. workers.

One of his concerns was for the victims of bombing. He carried a considerable amount of ready cash on his person during his walkabouts, donated by well-wishers, which he distributed to hard-hit citizens on the spot. I frequently met the Admiral in devastated areas of the East End. I have no doubt he was occupied with administrative work during the day, for it was mainly at night that he appeared at the scene of a 'bad one'.

He was a man of rather less than medium height and compactly built. His rig was what I imagined he would have worn during his sea-going days; peaked cap, a naval reefer jacket with a muffler round his throat and trousers stuffed into sea boots, with white woollen stockings turned over at the top. He carried his fingers tucked into his jacket pockets, thumbs outside in naval officer fashion.

He always greeted me with a friendly grin and was interested in all that was going on. He liked to be told of any unusual event and, despite the grim surroundings, joined us in a laugh when something of a lighter nature came along to lift the gloom.

I used to keep an eye open for any particularly harrowing event and would tell the Admiral, knowing he would offer a few genuine and dignified words of comfort, plus a little practical financial aid. Sometimes it helped, but his obvious sincerity and humanity were not always successful in easing the distress of the bereaved or of those who had been made homeless.

I remember setting up a forward control point in the centre of a great heap of rubble, all that remained of a couple of Bethnal Green streets after a V1 had struck. Rescue squads were at work all over the area as a young girl came running breathlessly, stumbling over pieces of debris. She gained her first sight of the ruins of her home as she approached me. I saw her raise her hand to her mouth to stifle a cry and just managed to catch her as she collapsed from shock and fell to the ground.

Happily, her parents were released soon after, smothered in dust and dirt but only slightly injured, and we were all witnesses of the tearful, joyous family reunion, in which Admiral Evans happily joined.

A garden bloomed in Redcross Street, in the shadow of St Paul's. 'Dig for Victory' was the Order of the Day and the lads and lassies attached to the fire station enthusiastically answered the call. Permission had been obtained for the cultivation of a vegetable plot on land adjacent to the remains of the burnt-out branch of the Midland Bank, across the road from the fire station.

When I first saw it, espalier-trained fruit trees stood in front of immaculate rows of potatoes, cabbages, carrots, onions, etc. all looking extremely healthy and well cared for.

The venture had been started after the clearance of debris following the City Blitz of December 1940. The Government Pig Scheme aroused the interest of the firemen's co-operative and it was decided to organise a pig club. Membership was open to all personnel serving at Redcross Street Fire Station at a subscription of two shillings and sixpence a year.

The scheme involved the purchase of a number of three-month-old piglets from government sources, the club undertaking to fatten them for a further three months. The great attraction was that one half of the meat produced could be retained for distribution among the members and the remainder sold back to the Ministry of Agriculture. Swill for feeding the animals was to be obtained from the fire station mess room, supplemented by deliveries from City restaurants and canteens.

Where to house the pigs was a problem; a suggestion to keep them in the station yard was stifled at birth. Then a bright idea emerged. What about the Midland Bank, opposite? Only the carcase of the building remained but it was weatherproof, or could easily be made so. The hon. secretary was instructed to write to the Midland Bank people, requesting permission to use their abandoned premises for the purpose of keeping pigs. 'Go ahead,' came the reply. 'We have no objection.'

So the lads set to. The interior of the bank was cleared of debris and concrete divisions were constructed. Books on pig keeping were consulted and along came the first consignment of baby pigs. Bales of straw were delivered and the animals were snugly housed in their custom-built home, surely the most expensive ground rented pigsty in the country!

They deserved to prosper, and prosper they did. Willing helpers took bristle brooms to clear out the muck whilst a fire hydrant was used to flush out the effluent. All this was swept down a convenient drain to the sewer, the pigs having been turned out for drill to a neighbouring blitzed patch.

Great excitement when the first trading account was published, and happy club members queued to receive their share of the pork; not enough for a choice cut for all, but

'Dig for Victory' urged the Minister for Home Security, Herbert Morrison, M.P. and firemen and women at Redcross Street Fire Station responded with enthusiasm. This general view of the smallholding shows the fruit and vegetable section; the bomb damaged building at the rear, formerly a branch of the Midland Bank, housed the piggery and the fur and feather club; hens and rabbits. Topsoil was brought from Hampstead Heath; bricks for the ornamental plot hedging were obtained locally. A totally self-sufficient enterprise!

trotters, head and belly gave some consolation, with promise of preference, next time.

This led to suggestions for increasing the herd. Ways and means were discussed, including adjusting the lay-out of the styes. This would affect the cleaning out operations and an alternative method was suggested. Why not lay a concrete gulley from the rear of the bank, across part of St Giles Cripplegate Churchyard to connect with a convenient man-hole? This would simplify the wash-down procedure greatly.

All hands paraded for daily inspection, including livestock.

'All ship-shape and Bristol fashion'. Materials for the multi-storey rabbit hutches came from bombed City buildings. Members of the club accepted an additional fatigue, cleaning the animal quarters. But some of those who had made pets were unaccountably missing when the time came for the share-out of carcases.

No time was lost in writing to the Midland Bank for permission to carry out the necessary work.

'Sorry,' came the reply. 'We cannot give permission in this case. You must write to our landlords, the Ecclesiastical Commissioners, setting out your plans and requesting their consent.'

Promptly, a letter went to the Commissioners, setting out the plan and seeking their permission. The reply was swift.

'The Commissioners have examined your request and I am directed to inform you that the gulley you propose would cross consecrated ground. Under an ancient law, still extant, any person found guilty of desecrating consecrated ground is liable to be hung, drawn and quartered.'

The plan was not pursued.

Unhappily, the supply of pig swill dwindled and the club had to be wound up, but not before all members had enjoyed a nice profit from their investment, as befits a City enterprise, but also what was even more acceptable, a supply of choice pork extra to the ration.

The fruit and vegetable garden, however, remained productive until the end of the war.

Towards the end of 1944 the arrival of V1s over London dwindled as the launching sites were overrun by Allied Forces, advancing through Normandy. But the attack continued with the use of rockets — the V2s.

Anti-aircraft batteries had been shooting down a high proportion of the V1s and RAF fighters took their toll of those that survived the AA attack. However, nothing could be done to intercept the V2s and these continued to make life hard for Londoners and those living in south-east England, despite the cheering news from Europe and the hope that it would soon be over.

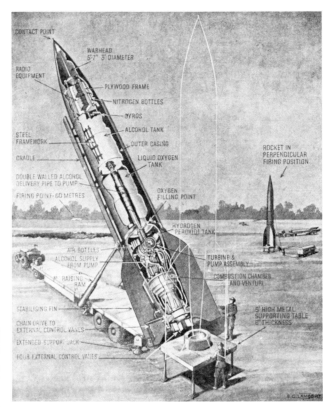

This drawing illustrates the construction of the V2 rocket. It carried a one-tonne warhead and ascended some 60 to 70 miles during its 200 mile flight.

I was present at a Boxing Day party at Redcross Street Fire Station when an explosion was heard — there was no mistaking the sound of a V2. A minute or two later I was informed that the rocket had landed at Mackenzie Road, Holloway.

It was a freezing night and patchy fog made conditions worse as I jog-trotted in front of the car with my hand lamp slung across my back for the driver to follow. When I'd had enough we changed over, taking advantage of the clear patches to drive as fast as possible.

The rocket had landed in the centre of the road at the junction with Wellington Road, and had created widespread damage. The time was coming up to ten-thirty and the pub along the road had run out of beer shortly before closing time. The customers transferred to another at the corner of Mackenzie Road and the place was jam-packed when the V2 exploded at the crossroads, only a few yards from the pub. The bar collapsed, dropping customers into the cellar, with debris from the remainder of the building falling on top.

The glow of a number of fires could be seen through swirling fog as a trailer pump operator set his suction hose into an emergency water dam. He attempted to draw water, without success. A horrible thought entered his mind; surely it was not empty? He shone his torch through the door and saw that the water was at its normal level but the surface was frozen, with the suction strainer lying on the ice. He grabbed a large axe, smashed the ice and dropped the strainer below the surface. Soon water was flowing and the branchmen were bringing the fires under control. The mains had been fractured by the explosion and the large crater was filling with water.

It was difficult to obtain a clear appreciation of the extent of the damage since the fog effectively blotted out the scene. I had to run around the centre of the area to find where the problems lay. I was attracted by loud shouting and went over to see what it was all about. A fireman, manning a fairly long line of hose alone, had called upon bystanders for help in dragging the hose nearer the fire. They had responded with such vigour that they had dragged a trailer pump away from the crater from which it was drawing water. I found a fire crew to put the matter right and, despite all the problems, we quickly had the fires under control.

It was clear that the casualty list would be long, with those trapped in the pub cellar providing the most difficult job. A long slog of rescue work lay ahead. It was one of those incidents calling for great care in removing debris; a careless move could dislodge piled rubble and bring it crashing down on victims and rescuers alike.

When a V2 exploded at the rear of the 'East End Mothers Lying-in Home' in Commercial Road, Stepney, on March 17th, 1945, it caused serious damage to the wards. Mothers, with their new-born babes, were littered with plaster from walls and ceilings. Some had been cut by fragments of flying glass and a large hole was blown in the floor of an upper ward. Fortunately, there was no fire so fire crews were put to work removing beds from precarious positions and wheeling them to corridors etc. Then the tidying-up began with the removal of debris and a general sweeping up. Firemen joked with young mothers, some tearful but, by and large, remarkably calm considering the anxiety felt for the babies. The Matron, a virago of the old school, most definitely was in charge of the situation. She bossed me about as if I were a messenger boy, privileged to be allowed to enter her hospital! I couldn't help smiling inwardly — I dare not *show* amusement — at her assertion of authority. I made a face at Company Officer Jack Milbery, behind her back, of course. He hung his head and pursed his lips as he busied himself with the job in hand. As work proceeded, I was approached by a priest from the Roman Catholic Church of St. Mary and St. Michael just along the road. He explained that his church had been damaged and was littered with debris, and a wedding service was due shortly. 'Can your men lend a hand to clean up?' he asked. Of course we could. Some twenty firemen moved in with brooms and debris baskets and the church was made as tidy as possible, in the circumstances, in time for the wedding. This picture shows the men sweeping the pews; all had removed their helmets, deferentially. I was not there to see the bride arrive, but we could not allow Adolf to spoil her day, now could we?

Pitiful cries for help were heard coming from the cellar, as Civil Defence rescue squads worked alongside firemen, tunnelling into the debris. It was a long, arduous and anxious job, fraught with danger to those striving to reach the people trapped below.

The dawn of a grey, cheerless morning was breaking over the desolate scene as the last of the bodies was recovered. Over sixty people had been killed that Boxing Night, with many more seriously injured.

I was leaving the scene of a V2 explosion when a local woman enquired about the number of casualties. I gave her the situation as I knew it but I gained the impression that her interest did not lay entirely in that direction. She wanted to chat, perhaps tell me her bomb story!

'I don't like these 'ere rockets,' she told me, in conversational tone. 'I'd sooner 'ave the old buzz bombs; you can 'ear 'em comin'.'

Fair enough, I suppose, but my choice of a substitute differed from hers.

I was attending a fire in Hackney one morning just as dawn was breaking. The eastern sky was lightening with the promise of a bright day when Column Officer Charlie Brooks drew my attention to what seemed to me to be nothing more than a rift in the clouds.

'That's a rocket on its way,' he remarked.

'Can't be,' I replied. 'The rocket sites are now in Holland, over two hundred miles away.'

'That's a rocket,' he repeated. 'I've seen one before.'

I looked again — it appeared not to be moving — just a vertical, irregular rift in the clouds. Before I could make further comment, he said: 'You've only to wait a few minutes for confirmation.'

It was a sobering thought and I stood waiting, somewhat apprehensively. Sure enough, there came the sound of an explosion a good way off, followed by the rumble of the missile's approach, which always reminded me of a tube train running into a station.

That was my first, and last, sight of a rocket going up and I never met anyone other than Charlie who had seen the trail of a rocket on its way. But several people have told me that they have caught a glimpse of a V2 falling to earth, as a flash from the corner of an eye. I never did, but I had plenty of opportunities of seeing the effects of their landing, close up and within minutes of the explosion.

V2 rocket trails as they appeared in Holland — in this case of a pair of V2s being launched from Wassenaar — the one on the right has just been launched, whereas that on the left has obviously been launched some minutes before. The photograph was taken early 1945 by a local Dutchman, B. P. Visser, at great personal risk.

One of the most remarkable effects was in Beckton Road, Canning Town, when a V2 landed in an allotment garden, creating one of the largest craters I had seen. The clay sub-soil was broken into uniform rectangular blocks which immediately brought to mind the Giant's Causeway.

Column Officer Jones of Dagenham came running to report to Fire Force Commander McDuell as he stepped from his car. He opened his mouth to speak but was cut short by the Commander.

'Phew. You've been eating onions,' he said.

'No sir, not me,' replied Jones. 'It's the allotment.' The

Can the Giant's Causeway have been created by a massive explosion in pre-historic times? This photograph, taken the day after a V2 had wrecked an allotment garden in Beckton Road, Canning Town, bears a resemblance in miniature to the famous tourist spot.

rocket had pulverised what had been a substantial onion bed, for the whole area reeked with the characteristic odour.

Poor old Jonesy; I shall never forget his look of amazement at the F.F.C.'s greeting.

The morning was dull and grey as I looked from the window of my room at Kingsland Road Fire Station. The night had been without incident and I had enjoyed an unbroken night's rest, a great relief, for they had been few and far between, lately. I was about to go down to breakfast when the room lit up, as though the sun had come out. I turned again to the window and saw a great plume of flame rising from the gas works, barely two hundred yards away across the Kingsland Road. A V2 had crashed fair and square in the centre of a large gas holder. I reached for the telephone and told Control it was the gas works.

The area inside the works was a bizarre sight. The steel plates of the holder lay around the pit like the petals of a huge tulip, blown open by the sun on a hot day. The oil on the surface of the pit was blazing but this was quickly brought under control and the search for casualties began.

It seemed to me that the plates covered an area of about an acre and they had to be lifted in sections to see if any casualties were buried underneath. In the meantime, I spoke to the works manager and asked him to carry out a roll call of his staff. This did not take long as only a small night shift was present; the day shift had not yet arrived. All but one were accounted for and we checked again the area beneath the plates. The manager confirmed the man was missing, his hat and coat were hanging in the office.

A thorough search of the whole area failed to locate him and I concluded he may have been blown or drawn into the gas holder pit and drowned. There was nothing for it but to pump out the water; the body must be recovered. Four pumps were set in and began pumping out water at about three thousand gallons a minute; there were hundreds of thousands of gallons to be cleared but it had to be done.

I returned to the fire station and a late breakfast. It was not until the afternoon that the pit was emptied but there was no sign of the man's body and a further search of the whole yard was made, without result. The fate of the missing man remained a mystery.

It was about a week later that I heard that he had been located in Southend. Apparently, he had good reason for disappearing and had taken advantage of what he must have considered a Heaven-sent opportunity of leaving his cares behind. Unfortunately for him, he did not go far enough away, for he was spotted by an acquaintance. Now, he had to face up afresh to his domestic squabbles.

I set out one morning from Clerkenwell Fire Station to visit stations in the City. I had eaten a plain, but substantial, breakfast and was well wrapped up in my greatcoat against the cold of the February day. Passing Smithfield Market I noticed a queue consisting mainly of women, waiting to purchase food; perhaps a little off the ration. Snow was drifting about in the icy wind, as those in the queue huddled together, heads down against the snow flurries.

We all had our problems in these hard times but I could not help feeling a trifle guilty; warm and well-fed, sitting in the back of my car whilst those women stood uncomplaining, seeking food for their families. It made me feel quite miserable, but there were many things requiring my attention and the mood passed.

The month of March came in with a spell of fine weather. Everyone was feeling cheerful with the warm sun on their backs. Spring was well and truly in the air and the Allied armies were sweeping through Germany. The Fourteenth Army was advancing through Burma, with the Japs in full retreat. Hope and longing for the end of the war was in the minds of all.

I was in a barber's shop in Kingsland Road at about 11 a.m. when the thunder of a V2 explosion, not very far away, brought us all to our feet. I ran back to the fire station to receive the report. Smithfield Market!

I was there within five minutes. The rocket had landed in the centre of the island site occupied by the market and had penetrated the floor, exploding in the underground railway network beneath. All the market buildings collapsed into one huge crater, with the shops fronting Farringdon Road reduced to rubble. The extensive wrought iron work which formed a feature of the façade lay scattered around and I noticed several people pinned down under the heavy sections. Fire crews came running to release them and others laying injured on the pavement. Only one small fire had been started and a crew was dealing with that, leaving the rest of the firemen to help with rescue work.

Apart from those buried under rubble on the Farringdon Road side, all the casualties seemed to be located in the crater. Many had been in the market and I was told that there was also a substantial queue standing outside when the explosion occurred and many were buried by debris which poured over the pavement as the buildings crumbled.

My thoughts returned to that February day and I wondered how many of the women I had seen standing in the snow lay beneath that great heap.

The death toll was even greater than at McKenzie Road. One hundred and ten were killed outright and many more severely injured.

The deep crater inside Smithfield Market. The rocket struck here, penetrating the floors to the railway subway below. Firemen and Civil Defence rescue squads search for casualties buried in the debris, as a fractured main spills water on the spot where a rescue party appears to be concentrating its search. It was in this area that many of the victims were located. I am standing at the bottom of the picture — the officer in the silver helmet.

The pump-escape from Clerkenwell Fire Station at work on a fire in the debris at Smithfield Market. The London Passenger Transport Board's mobile tower (on the right of the picture) is being set into position to clear trolley-bus cables brought down by the explosion on the Farringdon Street corner of the market building visible behind. The crowd of onlookers is milling around, unaware of the danger from live cables, aside from the fact that they might be in the way!

Column Officer Vic Blewden (centre, wearing light-coloured helmet with dark stripe), perched precariously on the edge of a cavity, supervises his crew from Clerkenwell Fire Station as they recover the body of a victim from debris at Smithfield Market. Over 100 people were killed in this particular incident, many of them housewives shopping in the market.

The scene following the V2 explosion at Hughes Mansions, Vallance Road, Stepney. The rocket buried itself in the foundations of the centre block of three, demolishing it and severely damaging its neighbours.

A search, in difficult conditions, through one of the Smithfield shops. There had been no reply to their shouts 'Anybody there?' but it could not be assumed that the place was empty, so it must be searched. This picture conveys the difficult nature and the risks involved, but the job was never shirked.

The last V2 of the war fell at Orpington at the end of March, but, a few days earlier, on March 27th, London had its second worst rocket incident when a V2 wrecked council flats in Vallance Road, Stepney. There were three separate buildings on the estate, each of forty flats contained on four floors. Families were eating breakfast or getting ready to leave for work when the rocket buried itself in the foundations of the centre block, with devastating effect. The whole block just crumbled and the other buildings were severely damaged by the blast.

When I arrived, firemen from the temporary fire station just across the road, were working to free some of those lightly trapped but they were hampered by the frenzied action of distraught relatives and friends of entombed victims, pouring on to the piles of debris. Their intention was to help but they only succeeded in adding to the crushing load on those beneath the rubble. Some of the women were hysterical. One screamed into my face, as I tried to lead her off the rubble: 'My family's in there!'

It really was a frightful scene, but order must be maintained and some force had to be used to clear the area, for rescue work was being obstructed. The heavy rescue services were arriving with their specialist equipment and rope barriers were set up to keep those not engaged in rescue work clear of operations. Casualties were being recovered, but few were carried to ambulances; most were taken to the mortuary vans.

Work continued throughout the day, and when the mountain of rubble had been cleared, one hundred and thirty-four dead had been recovered; others succumbed later to their injuries.

12   **Victory in Europe**

WITH the enemy being routed on all fronts, it became a matter for conjecture as to how much longer the war could last, surely only a matter of days.

I was driving along Commercial Street, Shoreditch, when I saw an operation which convinced me, and all passers-by, that the end of hostilities was in sight. It was a borough council street lamp tower being set up, with a workman preparing to fit a bulb to a lamp standard. The lights were going up, at last! I let out a mild cheer. People on the street below made V signs to the workman who was conscious of the significance of his job. He held up the lamp for all to see, in the manner of the captain of the winning cup team holding aloft his trophy at Wembley, and ceremoniously screwed it into the socket. What a relief it was; no more creeping about after dark by the dim light of a pocket torch, that is, if you were influential enough to obtain a battery. More comforting, it was confirmation of the end of the 'sudden death from the sky' fear we had lived with for nearly a year. It was just a few days before street lighting was restored.

The feeling of victory was in the air and Londoners prepared to celebrate. Derelict premises were raided for timber and huge bonfires were prepared on bomb sites and on roadways, ready for lighting when official news of the German surrender was announced.

We senior officers of No. 36 Fire Force had as much to celebrate as any and we jumped the gun, treating ourselves to a celebration lunch at the Crown and Castle pub at the corner of Dalston Lane and Kingsland Road on the day before Victory in Europe Day.

On V.E. Day, celebrations erupted all over town. As night fell, bonfires were lit in almost every street. I took my wife and daughters on a tour of the eighteen fire stations in my Division, to congratulate all hands on coming through safely. We all went up to the roof of Cannon Street Fire Station in the City, where we looked out on a scene reminiscent of the worst nights of the Blitz, the sky a brilliant pink and visibility restricted by the dense pall of smoke rising from thousands of bonfires, fed mainly by timber from bombed premises, old rubber tyres and anything that would burn.

We had driven up Ludgate Hill towards St Paul's. The dome was floodlit by four searchlights, two on the east side, two on the west. and the shadow of the Golden Cross stood out on the clouds, high above the Dome like some great Omen, a symbol of Peace.

The night, most certainly, was not without incident. Many of the bonfires got out of hand and needed the attention of firemen, who soon discovered that the public are a fickle lot. A few weeks ago, we were being cheered and lauded to the skies; now the men were soundly booed and, in some cases, threatened with violence as they doused those bonfires that were damaging road surfaces or threatening buildings. One individual, carried away by excitement, drove a lorry to the centre of a large bonfire in Kingsland Road and left it there, to add to the blaze. Firemen came in for violent abuse when they arrived.

But all good things come to an end, and we were allowed peace from about 3 a.m. The bonfires, slowly decreasing in number and size, continued for several more nights before the East Enders began to think of the homecoming of the lads and lassies from the Forces, and set about organising street celebrations of another kind.

One of the more modest fires lit to celebrate VE Day — in this case in West Croydon.

This picture, taken on April 23rd, 1945, shows the devastation surrounding St. Paul's Cathedral. On the right, Queen Victoria Street curves towards the Mansion House. Fire laid waste the solidly built-up area of tall office blocks, travelling northwards to cross Cannon Street, consuming on its way the buildings in Friday Street, Watling Street and Bread Street before it was stopped at Cheapside. To the left of the Cathedral, the congested area between Paternoster Row and Newgate Street was left a wilderness of rubble. This is the ground over which firefighters fought the battle for St. Paul's, armed with ample courage but inadequate water. Above, to the left of the picture, the devastation extends from Aldersgate Street to Moorgate, space now occupied by the Museum of London, the Barbican and the modern London Wall. It is most appropriate that the City of London Corporation has donated a site on Old Change, just across the road from the Cathedral, for the erection of the Firefighters Memorial sculpture, for it is here that one of the sternest battles of the Blitz was fought.

The Auxiliary Fire Service under training, Hyde Park, June 1939 (during the London Fire Brigade review) and, right, firemen under fire themselves. In this case we see the rubble which was Soho Fire Station in Shaftesbury Avenue until struck by a German bomb — luckily nobody was killed, although members of the Control Room staff were trapped until rescued by their comrades.

Just as the outbreak of war had seen a fifteen-fold increase in the strength of the Fire Service, so the cessation of hostilities had witnessed an equally rapid contraction. Many auxiliary firemen were anxious to return to civilian life and sought early demobilisation. Others developed a liking for the Service and applied for permanent employment.

Following the vast reduction in manpower, more officers than posts were available and all officers were required to attend Boards for re-classification. Many, through no fault of their own, suffered reduction in rank, leaving them, understandably, bitter.

And a large number of auxiliaries left on a sour note. Many wished to retain their axe as a memento of service, but all items of uniform and equipment had to be handed in for eventual sale at auction. The country was broke and every asset, however small, had to be realised. I felt this to be rather stingy, particularly when the axes came on sale at Gamage's and similar retail stores, at one shilling and sixpence each.

Now began the task of forming the post-war Service. The organisation followed the N.F.S. pattern, now centred on the regular fire stations. Steel joists, used to stiffen fire station buildings, were being removed and protective netting stripped from windows. Paint, other than Admiralty Grey, was in very short supply but, as supplies became available, the drab appearance of many a station improved out of knowledge with a lick of cream and brown.

But political pressure was being brought against the N.F.S. When the Service was nationalised, the Home Secretary, Mr Herbert Morrison, stressed that the change was due to wartime necessity and he pledged that the Fire Service would return to local authority control after the war. In the view of many, including Mr Morrison, nationalisation had been so successful that it would be in the national interest if it were to remain in operation after the war. The local authorities, however, were determined to hold the Home Secretary to his promise and the necessary legislation was eventually passed in July 1947.

So the National Fire Service, having served the Nation well, came to the end of its life at midnight on March 31st, 1948 and the local authorities took over control.

Firemen stand well back from the danger of falling debris whilst damping down a persistent hot-spot in Pilgrim Street, May 11th, 1941.

It will be appreciated that the events set out in this book cover but a tiny segment of the activity of the Fire Service during the war. Most of what has been written is a record of my own experience; the remainder is made up of material given me by former colleagues, men and women, who took part in the events described. My endeavour has been to present some of the incidents of those fearful days as seen through the eyes of members of the Service.

We experienced the blood, toil, tears and sweat we had been promised. We had witnessed the agony of civilians and been inspired by their fortitude and undaunted spirit. The terrifying, sleepless nights did not deter them from the daily business of producing the paraphernalia of war and the no less vital task of supporting the family unit.

Many provincial cities and towns suffered similar attacks and their citizens met them with the same spirit and determination as shown by Londoners, but theirs is another story.

Firemen had been force-fed with the firefighting experiences of a lifetime, crammed into the space of eight months. Even under the heaviest attacks, morale remained high and camaraderie flourished, despite reports of bad feeling between regulars and auxiliaries, emanating from certain quarters. Throughout the Blitz, the vast majority of both sections stood shoulder to shoulder, carrying out their duties in mutual respect and harmony. And with the advent of the National Fire Service, they were absorbed into a unified service.

The colours of the Women's Section of the Auxiliary Fire Service flew high. Firewomen took on any job with the exception of operational firefighting, displaying a robust sense of duty and efficiency in everything they undertook. Many were decorated for outstanding deeds but the majority simply soldiered on, quietly performing the support duties without which the wartime fire service could not have functioned as it did.

I conclude with a memory typifying the spirit of the W.A.F.S. It is the story of a young firewoman who had driven her van, loaded with five hundred gallons of petrol in two gallon cans for supplying the pumps, along streets lined with blazing buildings, from Whitechapel to Stratford. She joined the queue of officers in charge of appliances reporting for instructions at West Ham Fire Control on the first night of the Blitz. When she reached the desk, her report was terse and to the point.

'Five hundred gallons o' petrol. Where d'ya wannit?'

And she was quite prepared to deliver it to the pumps working on dockland fires, if called upon!

The grim sight of standard Civil Defence issue tubular steel stretchers being unloaded in Goodge Street at the scene of a V1 explosion, June 1944. The usual assortment of curious bystand- ers, wardens and British and American Servicemen is evident, plus a bowler-hatted vicar by the lamp post, middle right, in front of the group of firemen awaiting orders.

Postscript

Towards the end of 1945 I was given the job of conducting parties of overseas fire officers around the worst damaged areas of the City, among them a senior officer of the Hamburg Fire Department. We met at Redcross Street Fire Station and set off around the Cripplegate area.

I used to make a mild joke when pointing out to visitors that only two buildings remained intact between Redcross and Chiswell Streets, namely the fire station and Whitbread's Brewery. I advised them that no undue significance should be placed on that fact but my German counterpart remained singularly unamused.

We walked across to the burnt-out shell of St Giles Church and stood gazing at the wilderness of rubble and the carcases of office buildings and warehouses in Jewin Street. His face showed no change of expression as he surveyed the pulverised acres beyond Aldersgate Street and St Martins le Grand to the waste of Paternoster Row, with St Paul's Cathedral rising beyond. After a moment, he turned to me:

'Is this the worst?'

'Well,' I replied. 'There are a number of similar areas but this is as bad as any.' He made a dismissive gesture with his hands.

'It is nothing.'

I had reservations about that at the time, but after reading the Allied Commission Report on the Effect of Bombing on German Cities and Towns, I had second thoughts.

The Wilderness — Fore Street (opposite and above left) and Bridgewater Street (above), in 1945.

The report revealed that some 40,000 people were killed on July 27/28th, 1943, in Hamburg, the night of the terrible firestorm when more than four square miles of the city were destroyed, together with practically every living thing within.

Tragically the almost bomb-proof bunker shelters proved a death trap. Thousands of citizens flocked to the shelters when the warning sounded, confident in the light of the safety they had enjoyed during previous raids.

This raid, however, was to be an exceptional one. The hot, dry weather; the congested blocks of six-floor buildings and an extra heavy concentration of explosive and fire bombs combined to produce an inferno of unprecedented fury. As the firestorm developed, the wind howled with hurricane force through the narrow streets, carrying oxygen to feed the flames. It snapped stout tree trunks and swept into the inferno all debris, including human beings, like leaves before a gale. The sheer power of the wind sucked air from the shelters, replacing it with deadly carbon monoxide gas which rapidly overcame thousands of shelterers, unaware of the insidious gas creeping silently upon them.

It was destruction on a scale never seen in Britain and it was grim irony that the code-name assigned to the R.A.F. raid invoked a Biblical overtone: Operation 'Gomorrah'.

The bodies of Firemen George Cert and Edward Rosebridge rest in St Mary's Church, Plaistow. Both were killed in a V1 explosion at Abbey Road School on August 24, 1944.

Roll of Honour

The Charter of the Imperial War Graves Commission (the name was changed to Commonwealth in 1960) covers all war deaths occurring prior to December 31, 1947, civilian deaths, which include firemen, being commemorated on the Civilian War Dead Roll. This Roll of Honour was compiled by the London Fire and Civil Defence Authority HQ and forms the basis of the Firemen's Memorial beside St Paul's Cathedral.

17·09·40 Abrahart, Alfred G., Fm.
20·04·41 Aitchison, Percy C., Fm.
23·12·40 Albert, George, Fm.
10·04·41 Aldridge, Arnold, Fm.
10·09·40 Aldsworth, Thomas C., Fm.
25·04·41 Alexander, Douglas F., Fm.
21·11·41 Alexander, Philip, Fm.
06·07·43 Allen, James, Fm.
22·11·40 Allen, Percy F., Fm.

30·12·40 Ambridge, Edwin W., Fm.
23·12·40 Anderton, William H., Fm.
16·11·40 Andreazzi, Cecil R., Fm.
04·02·42 Andrews, David J. H., Fm.
09·05·41 Andrews, John W., Fm.
14·11·40 Appleby, David, Fm.
02·12·41 Appleby, Frederick G., Fm.
09·03·41 Arber, Albert E., Fm.
10·09·40 Archer, Richard, Wroom Att.

09·05·41 Arton, Leslie B., LFm.
18·09·40 Ash, Arthur, Sub.O.
14·11·40 Ashby, David, Fm.
20·06·42 Ashcroft, Rhoda, Fwm.
02·05·41 Ashley, Albert R., Fm.
02·04·45 Ashton, Thomas E., Fm.
17·07·43 Astle, Samuel E., Fm.
14·11·40 Atkins, Frederick, Fm.
03·01·43 Attrill, Robert W., Fm.

05·07·41 Auchterlonie, William C., Fm.
16·11·40 Aust, Derek E., Fm.
28·11·40 Austin, Francis W., Fm.
14·11·40 Axcell, John A., Fm.
11·05·41 Ayers, Maurice C., Fm.
01·11·42 Aylott, Charles, S.Ldr.

08·12·40 Badland, Edward W., Fm.
08·05·41 Bagnall, William, Fm.
07·02·43 Bailey, John W., S.Ldr.
20·04·41 Bailey, Ronald M., Fm.
22·04·44 Baines, Cyril L., Fm.
17·09·40 Baker, Alfred L. K., Fm.
10·05·45 Baker, Christopher L. J., Fm.
20·04·41 Baker, Lilian S., Fwm.
21·02·40 Baker, Percy J. S., Fm.
19·09·41 Baker, W. Young, Fm.
06·11·40 Baldesarre, Victor, Fm.
20·04·41 Baldwin, Douglas B., Fm.
24·12·40 Baldy, James H., Fm.
16·06·43 Ball, Walter, Fm.
23·12·40 Balme, Ernest, Fm.
20·04·41 Barber, Alan C., Fm.
03·02·45 Bardsley, Wilfred G., LFm.
20·06·43 Barker, William J., Fm.
08·05·41 Barnes, Albert, Fm.
20·04·41 Barrell, John C., Fm.
14·11·40 Barrow, Charles W., LFm.
18·09·40 Bartlett, Joan F., Fwm.
21·04·41 Bartlett, Mark A., Fm.
17·09·40 Batchelor, Arthur E., Fm.
06·01·42 Batchelor, David W., Fm.
16·08·41 Bates, Arthur, CFO
17·09·40 Bathie, Jack, LFm.
04·03·43 Beacon, Percy W., LFm.
17·04·41 Beacon, Richard, Fm.
20·04·41 Beadle, Ernest R., Fm.
16·11·40 Beard, William, Coy.O.
20·10·40 Beaumont, Arthur T., Sub.O.
27·07·41 Bedford, William R. J., Fm.
17·10·40 Beer, William A., LFm.
11·04·41 Bees, John, Sergeant
12·04·45 Beeson, Leonard C., LFm.
04·01·41 Belinski, Solomon, Fm.
17·10·40 Bell, George A., Fm.
17·10·40 Belton, William F., Fm.
11·03·41 Benn (BEM), John E., Stn.O.
04·04·45 Bennett, Harry, Col.O.
10·01·44 Bennett, William H., Fm.
16·08·41 Bennett-Snell, William, LFm.
18·04·41 Benney, William T., Fm.
 · ·   Benton, John
02·04·40 Berkeley, John A., Fm.
02·11·40 Berkon, Samuel, Fm.
09·05·41 Best, Herbert H., Fm.

23·11·40 Best, Reginald J. L., Fm.
09·04·41 Bickerton, Alfred E., LFm.
10·01·41 Biggs, Bernard, LFm.
16·08·44 Billings, Harry, LFm.
31·01·44 Bilton, David M., S.Ldr.
27·10·43 Binda, Henry E. C., Fm.
11·05·41 Bines, Joseph C., Fm.
21·12·40 Birch, John I., Fm.
12·02·45 Birch, William C., Fm.
09·08·45 Birchenough, John W. L., Fm.
14·03·41 Bisland, Walter E. M., Fm.
06·09·43 Biswell, Ernest H. L., Fm.
14·11·41 Blakeman, Charles C., S.Ldr.
29·12·40 Blundell, Herbert T., Fm.
07·05·42 Blundell, John H., Fm.
16·05·41 Blunt, Victor H., LFm.
14·12·43 Bocutt, Alexander H., LFm.
16·11·40 Booth, Edwin J., Sub.O.
20·10·43 Botcherby, Harold L., S.Ldr.
23·12·40 Bothwell, F., Fm.
20·01·40 Bouch, Henry J., Fm.
19·09·40 Bowen, George, LFm.
20·04·41 Bowles, Kenneth J., Fm.
29·01·44 Bradburn, William, Fm.
18·07·42 Bradbury, Ronald S., Fm.
20·04·44 Bradshaw, Peter, Col.O.
14·01·44 Brampton, Reginald, Fm.
08·05·42 Braybrooke, Bernard H., Fm.
11·05·41 Brazier, John W. F., Fm.
10·10·44 Breed, Ernest, Fm.
23·09·40 Briggs, Christopher J., Fm.
03·01·41 Bright, Henry, Fm.
19·09·40 Brightwell, Henry C., Fm.
09·09·43 Broadfield, Roger W., Fm.
29·04·42 Broadhead, Arthur, Fm.
30·10·40 Brocklehurst, Edward R., Fm.
11·01·41 Brooker, Albert F. S., Fm.
14·07·45 Brookes, Frank W., Fm.
23·04·41 Brooking, Francis J., Fm.
02·10·41 Broomhead, William, Mesngr
03·01·43 Brown, Alfred B., LFm.
23·04·43 Brown, James J., Fm.
28·09·40 Brown, Thomas W., Fm.
23·05·44 Brown, William F. T.
28·09·40 Brown, William H., Fm.
16·11·40 Brum, William G., Fm.
28·10·40 Bryan, Patrick, Fm.
21·03·41 Buckingham, Thomas, LFm.
09·04·41 Buckler, Sydney, Fm.
11·05·41 Burch, John H., Fm.
20·04·41 Burden, Charles F., Stn.O.
08·07·42 Burgess, Charles F., Fm.
18·03·42 Burley, Peter B., Mesngr
08·05·41 Burns, Thomas, Fm.
23·12·40 Burrows, Raymond, Fm.
19·11·40 Burrows, Raymond A., Fm.
27·04·42 Bussey, Sam, S.Coy.O.

06·11·40 Butcher, Henry H., Fm.
09·09·40 Butler, Richard H., Fm.
23·11·40 Byfield, Edward, Fm.

21·04·43 Calder, William, LFm.
13·04·44 Callaway, George W., LFm.
29·11·40 Callicott, Thomas J., Fm.
11·04·41 Camp, Thomas L., Fm.
04·04·44 Campbell, James N., Fm.
02·06·43 Campbell, James W., Coy.O.
20·04·41 Campbell, Patrick J., Fm.
14·03·41 Campbell, William, Mesngr
23·12·41 Carberry, Ernest W., Fm.
20·04·41 Carden, Henry J. C., Fm.
19·11·40 Carless, Edward, Fm.
13·03·41 Carlile, Henry G., Fm.
06·09·44 Carrington, Dorothy, Fwm.
21·10·42 Carrington, Percival S. R., Fm.
26·01·41 Cartwright, Eric B., Fm.
10·01·42 Cassidy, George, Fm.
15·04·41 Castle, H. P., Fm.
09·05·41 Cavill, G., Fm.
24·08·44 Cert, George C., Fm.
22·05·42 Chadwick, Ernest, Fm.
23·11·40 Chalkley, Edward A. W., Fm.
17·04·41 Chalmers, David J., LFm.
01·05·43 Chamkin, Albert E. N.
09·04·41 Chater, F. C., Fm.
08·01·43 Chawner, Robert W., Fm.
10·09·40 Cheater, Oliver C., Fm.
11·04·41 Childs, Geoffrey, Mesngr
06·11·40 Childs, Walter H., Fm.
09·04·41 Chilton, Gilbert H., LFm.
14·11·40 Chinn, Eric
29·12·42 Chinnery, Benjamin E., Fm.
07·02·43 Chitty, Pearl M., Fwm.
24·04·41 Chopping, Cecil R. S., Fm.
16·02·44 Clark, Joseph, Fm.
17·09·40 Clark, Joseph W. H., Fm.
18·10·43 Clark, Thomas J., Fm.
11·12·40 Clarke, Albert E., Fm.
11·05·41 Clarke, Albert E., Fm.
30·08·44 Clarke, Harold E., Fm.
10·09·40 Clatworthy, David, Fm.
11·04·41 Clausen, William G., Pat.O.
16·09·40 Clayton, George, Fm.
13·03·41 Clelland, Alexander F., Fm.
09·04·41 Clements, Anthony R., Pat.O.
11·04·41 Clemett, George, Fm.
30·08·41 Clewes, Leslie
26·10·40 Clews, Victor L., Fm.
03·01·43 Cohen, David, Fm.
18·04·41 Coleridge, Harold G., Fm.
21·04·41 Collins, Alexander W., Fm.
30·07·45 Collins, Ernest R., Fm.
13·03·41 Collins, Harry, Fm.

19·12·44 Collop, Harold, Fm.
07·07·43 Colmer, Lionel L., Fm.
11·01·41 Conniff, Stanley T., Fm.
17·10·40 Conrad, Herman H., Fm.
11·11·41 Cook, Albert H., Fm.
20·03·41 Cook, George J., Fm.
06·10·39 Cooper, Reginald W., Fm.
28·06·42 Corke, Herbert H., Fm.
20·09·44 Cornell, Cyril A.
14·09·44 Cornwell, Norman, Fm.
01·05·45 Cossar, John, Fm.
08·05·41 Cottam, George C., Sub.O.
23·04·41 Crabb, Stanley R., Fm.
06·11·40 Crane, Percy, Fm.
23·04·41 Crapp, Alfred J., Fm.
09·05·41 Cressey, Leonard A. H., Fm.
11·02·44 Cromwell, Paul, S.Ldr.
08·03·41 Crowe, Frederick W., Fm.
09·09·40 Culley, John, Fm.
08·12·40 Cumberland, Alfred, Fm.
11·04·41 Curry, Percy, Fm.
16·09·40 Curson, Thomas W., Snr.Fm.
21·06·43 Cutmore, Charles E., LFm.

08·05·41 Daggett, Leslie J., Fm.
31·12·40 Daly, James, Fm.
26·09·41 Dance, Alfred P., Fm.
20·02·41 Daniels, Herbert R., Fm.
09·12·40 Davidson, Henry J., Fm.
22·11·40 Davies, Arthur J., Fm.
22·02·41 Davies, Daniel W., Fm.
13·03·41 Davies, Fred, Fm.
06·11·40 Davies, Marjory W., Fwm.
14·11·43 Davies, Sidney, Fm.
17·10·43 Davies, Walter, LFm.
22·08·45 Davies (GC), Frederick, Fm.
21·08·40 Davis, Frederick G., Fm.
09·01·43 Davis, William E., Fm.
20·10·40 Davy, Claude F., LFm.
28·06·41 Dawson, Cyril C., Fm.
23·12·40 Day, Allen R., Fm.
20·04·40 Day, Frank A., Pat.O.
24·03·43 Day, Hilda, A.G.O.
03·01·43 Day, Ivor C., Fm.
07·06·40 Day, Kenneth, Fm.
20·04·41 Deans, Robert J., Fm.
21·12·40 Dearing, Percy, Fm.
08·12·40 Dell, Frederick W., Fm.
12·04·45 Denning, Joseph, Fm.
17·06·44 Denoval, Roy K., Mesngr
06·03·44 Dett-Willer, Reginald F., Fm.
08·03·41 Deutch, Israel, Fm.
05·05·42 Dewey, Herbert J., LFm.
07·09·40 Dicken, Hugh, Fm.
24·04·45 Dickson, William, Fm.
29·10·42 Diffey, Ronald R. G., Mesngr

13·03·41 Dillon, Martin, Fm.
10·09·40 Dilworth, John, Fm.
17·10·40 Dinwoodie, James W. N., Fm.
14·11·40 Dixon, Henry A. C., Fm.
10·02·43 Dixon, William H. S., Fm.
13·03·41 Donald, Archibald A., Fm.
13·03·41 Donnelly, Hugh, Fm.
03·10·39 Donnelly, James, Fm.
20·12·44 Donovan, J., Fm.
11·05·41 Dormer, Bernard J., Fm.
24·11·40 Dovell, Philip G., Fm.
10·09·40 Downes, William, Fm.
04·03·43 Drake, George T., Fm.
20·03·41 Drew, Charles L. M., Fm.
26·10·40 Driver, Reginald H., Fm.
06·11·40 Du Vergier, Stanley G., Fm.
07·02·43 Duke, Frederick, Fm.
30·12·44 Duncan, Albert G., Fm.
24·07·43 Duncan, Doreen, Fwm.
30·11·40 Dunnell, Sydney H., Fm.
20·04·41 Dupree, Hilda, Fwm.
12·09·40 Durling, James A. C., Fm.
11·02·44 Duthoit, Walter, LFm.
28·11·40 Dutton, Cyril G., Fm.
17·09·40 Dyson, George, Fm.

11·05·41 East, Edward B., Fm.
17·10·40 Eaton, James H., Fm.
17·05·41 Ebery, Ernest J., Fm.
13·03·41 Edminston, John, Fm.
01·05·41 Edwards, Robert, Fm.
02·12·40 Edwards, Thomas J., Fm.
03·01·43 Eldridge, Lawrence D., Fm.
11·05·41 Elliman, Cecil A., Fm.
12·05·41 Ellis, Herbert T. W., Fm.
14·11·40 Emmett, Edmund F., Fm.
20·04·41 Endean, Frank J., Fm.
14·11·40 Endersby, Stanley D., Fm.
03·05·41 England, Frank H., Fm.
29·11·41 Entwistle, Joseph D., Col.O.
07·08·43 Etheridge, Basil B., Fm.
16·09·40 Evans, Albert B., Fm.
09·04·41 Evans, Ivor, Fm.
09·04·41 Evans, William V., Fm.
08·12·40 Eyre, Albert C., Fm.

20·04·41 Farley, Cecil, Fm.
01·05·43 Farmer, Percy D., LFm.
16·11·40 Farndon, Clifford R., Fm.
17·09·40 Farnin, Arthur, Fm.
31·05·44 Farr, Reginald H., Fm.
06·05·41 Farrow, John S., Mesngr
23·04·41 Featherstone, Guy I. C., Fm.
19·03·41 Feldman, Hyman, Fm.
22·12·40 Fell, Jonas, Fm.

18·05·43 Fenna, Charles R., Fm.
14·09·40 Fenton, John H., Fm.
23·12·40 Fenton, Kenneth G., Fm.
05·04·41 Ferrari, Arnold J., Mesngr
08·03·41 Field, Percival H., Mesngr
13·03·41 Findlay, Thomas, Fm.
26·04·45 Fisher, Robert F., Fm.
20·03·41 Fitzgerald, Denis G., Fm.
17·04·41 Flegg, Henry G., Fm.
02·03·44 Flemen, William F., Fm.
10·09·40 Fletcher, James, Fm.
23·07·43 Foley, Stephen J., Fm.
18·10·40 Ford, Arthur T., Dep.Cmdt
19·11·40 Ford, Joseph S., Fm.
11·03·41 Ford, Leslie W., Fm.
11·01·41 Forrester, Robert, Fm.
07·09·40 Forrow, Thomas, Stn.O.
23·11·40 Foster, Norman, Fm.
09·05·41 Fowler, George, Fm.
14·11·40 Fox, Edward J., Fm.
27·02·42 Fox, John, Fm.
16·11·40 Francis, Alfred J., Fm.
11·04·41 Fraser, Ian, Fm.
28·04·44 Freeman, Edwin, S.Ldr.
30·12·40 Freeman, Leonard J., Fm.
07·04·45 French, William E., Fm.
03·05·41 Fullbrook, Harry, Pat.O.
15·01·41 Fuller, William, Fm.

03·03·41 Gaccon, Frank W., Div.Cdr
08·12·40 Gage, Frederick G., Fm.
18·11·40 Gallacher, Daniel M., LFm.
04·05·41 Gallagher, Joseph, Fm.
25·04·44 Gannon, Harold, Fm.
22·12·40 Garbett, Charles, Fm.
12·12·40 Garlick, Alfred, Fm.
22·12·40 Garrett, Daniel A., Fm.
28·09·40 Garrick, David W., Fm.
15·12·42 Garvey, James H., Mesngr
24·12·40 Gaskell, Frederick J., Fm.
13·03·41 Geddes, George, Fm.
17·04·41 Gentry, Albert, Snr Fm.
17·09·40 George, Robert W., Fm.
06·06·42 Georgeson, John, Fm.
21·04·41 Gerrity, Joseph T., Fm.
09·04·41 Gibbon, Cyril, Fm.
15·10·44 Gibbons, Cyril S. W., Fm.
04·09·41 Gibson, Frank, Fm.
06·07·44 Gifford, Alice J., Fwm.
24·11·40 Gigg, Reginald, Fm.
22·12·40 Gill, Robert W., Fm.
12·04·41 Gillard, Charles, Pat.O.
18·09·40 Gillard, Harold C., Fm.
04·03·44 Gilson, John P., Fm.
14·03·41 Girvan, Matthew, Fm.
03·01·43 Glantzpigel, Harry F., Fm.

07·02·43 Goacher, Walter H., Fm.
07·06·44 Goddard, Herbert R., Fm.
17·10·40 Godfrey, Bernard J., Fm.
24·04·44 Gold, David W., Fm.
11·05·41 Golden, Herbert B. H., LFm.
27·01·45 Goldrick, John W., Coy.O.
17·04·41 Goldsmith, George E., Fm.
07·02·43 Gosden, Fred, Fm.
11·05·41 Gothard, Lionel A., LFm.
15·11·40 Gould, James H., Fm.
12·01·41 Gower, James S., Fm.
05·10·40 Graham, Hector M., Pat.O.
28·05·43 Grange, John A., Fm.
14·11·40 Grant (GM), Arthur H., LFm.
25·03·42 Gray, George E., Fm.
10·09·40 Gray, Samuel J., Fm.
16·05·42 Greaves, Richard E., Fm.
11·05·41 Greenburg, Barnet, Fm.
01·01·41 Greenburg, Joseph, Fm.
17·10·40 Greenway, Frank L., Fm.
08·05·41 Gregory, Reginald, Fm.
17·10·40 Grieve, William G., Fm.
17·04·41 Griffin, Albert W., Fm.
09·11·41 Griffiths, Alfred, Fm.
24·04·42 Gush, Emmanuel, Fm.

19·06·44 Haines, Wilfred S., Fm.
28·04·42 Haliday, Charles W., Fm.
23·12·40 Hall, Arthur, Fm.
22·05·43 Hall, Dudley W., Fm.
20·04·41 Hall, George J. J., Fm.
20·03·41 Hall, George W., Snr Fm.
04·02·43 Hall, Hilda, Fwm.
21·07·40 Hall, Robert, Fm.
24·12·40 Hall, Talbot E., Fm.
23·12·40 Hallas, James T., Fm.
23·01·40 Halliday, Henry W., Sub.O.
08·12·40 Hammersley, John S., Fm.
09·04·41 Hammond, Frank A., Fm.
16·08·41 Hammond, William D., Fm.
11·04·41 Hancock, Archibald C., Fm.
03·07·43 Hanson, Arthur B., LFm.
26·07·44 Harford, Henry J. C., Fm.
08·04·41 Harkness, Brice E., Fm.
20·04·41 Harris, Bertie J. F., Fm.
30·06·41 Harris, Cyril, Fm.
03·01·43 Harris, Edward F., Fm.
21·09·40 Harris, James C., Sec.O.
24·05·41 Harris, Patrick, Fm.
13·04·44 Harris, Richard C., Fm.
08·04·41 Harrison, Charles H., LFm.
13·03·41 Harrison, George, Fm.
13·04·44 Harrison, Leonard, LFm.
13·03·41 Harrison, Myre, Fm.
01·11·40 Hart, Walter C. W., Fm.
09·09·40 Hartwell, Christopher E., Fm.

16·08·40 Harvey, Percival H. F., Fm.
09·08·45 Hastings, William C., Fm.
02·09·43 Hately, James H., Fm.
23·03·43 Hawtin, Elsie A., Fwm.
22·03·42 Haycock, Harry C., LFm.
23·11·44 Hayden, Alexander W., Fm.
16·04·41 Haylen, Alfred R., Fm.
26·10·40 Hayward, Frederick W., Fm.
14·03·45 Hayward, Horace D., LFm.
12·12·41 Hazzard, Jack, Fm.
20·04·41 Healey, Leslie T., Fm.
03·01·43 Healy, Thomas J., Fm.
16·11·43 Heath, Frederick T., Fm.
23·11·40 Heath, James H., Fm.
05·12·41 Hembury, Reginald W., Fm.
11·05·41 Hemming, Ernest A., Fm.
07·05·41 Hendry, James, Fm.
20·04·41 Henley, Ernest J., Sub.O.
20·04·41 Henly, Herbert E., Fm.
18·04·41 Herbert, William H., Fm.
08·06·40 Hewitt, George, Fm.
13·03·41 Hewitt, William, Fm.
26·11·40 Hibberd, Joseph E., Fm.
06·11·40 Hickey, George A., Fm.
22·12·40 Higham, Eric S., Fm.
03·07·44 Highly, Charles W., Fm.
10·09·40 Hill, George W., Fm.
17·10·40 Hill, John J., Fm.
30·12·40 Hill, John W., Stn.O.
23·12·40 Hilton, Joseph H., Fm.
01·05·41 Hitchman, Harold H., Fm.
08·05·41 Hitchon, Edward A., Fm.
27·04·41 Hobbs, Edgar R., Fm.
11·02·43 Hodgson, Alfred, Fm.
30·12·40 Holder, Sydney A., Fm.
11·05·41 Hollett, Edward A., Sub.O.
22·01·41 Holloway, George H., Fm.
11·12·40 Holmes, Albert G., Sub.O.
29·10·40 Holt, Arthur M., Fm.
21·12·40 Hood, James, Fm.
23·12·40 Hopwood, Joseph, Fm.
13·03·42 Horne, Leslie, LFm.
03·12·41 Horrocks, Thomas, Fm.
07·11·43 Hose, William M., LFm.
17·04·41 Hoskins, Edward W., Fm.
03·01·43 Howard, Ruby M., Fwm.
18·11·40 Hubbard, Walter G., Fm.
17·04·41 Hudders, Stanley R., Fm.
19·03·41 Huggett, Harold, Fm.
11·05·41 Hughes, Albert V., Fm.
07·07·44 Hughes, Roland, Fm.
23·12·40 Hughes, Thomas, Fm.
22·07·40 Hume, Robert, Fm.
29·11·40 Humphreys, A. S., Fm.
12·05·41 Humphries, Eric E., Fm.
23·09·42 Hunt, Alan H., Fm.
11·04·41 Hunt, John A., Fm.

07·02·43 Hunter, John, Fm.
16·05·40 Hunter, Joseph H., Sergeant
13·03·41 Hunter, William C., Fm.
30·12·40 Hurd, Frank W., Fm.
19·12·42 Hurley, Ian E., Coy.O.
24·01·44 Hurst, Edward, Fm.
02·03·44 Hurst, Ernest A., Fm.
22·09·43 Hurt, Leonard A., Fm.
08·09·40 Hutton, Ernest J., Fm.
11·09·40 Huxley, Frances E., Fwm.
01·11·40 Hyde, Ernest W., Fm.
17·10·40 Hyde, Leslie J. H., Fm.
10·05·41 Hynd, William, Sec.O.

26·09·44 Ilett, Terence A., Fm.
15·11·40 Inman, Edgar, Fm.
13·03·41 Irwin, Alexander, Fm.
16·11·40 Isaacs, Leslie W., Fm.
08·05·41 Isherwood, Joseph, Fm.

06·10·43 Jackson, Allen, Fm.
19·09·42 Jackson, William, Fm.
14·11·40 Jackson, William A. E., Fm.
03·01·43 Jacobs, Leslie A., Fm.
03·01·41 Janes, Albert, Fm.
17·09·40 Jarvis, Sydney H., Fm.
23·04·41 Jasper, Bernard, Fm.
24·06·43 Jepson, George, Fm.
02·11·40 Jerome, Harold G., Fm.
07·05·40 Jessop, Thomas C., Fm.
11·05·41 Johnson, James A., LFm.
20·07·43 Johnson, William J., Fm.
13·09·40 Jones, Arthur H., Fm.
11·05·41 Jones, Evan M., Fm.
21·12·40 Jones, Glyn, Fm.
23·11·40 Jones, Islwyn M., Fm.
24·10·40 Jones, Leonard, Fm.
14·04·45 Jones, Robert, Fm.
20·04·41 Jones, Sidney B., Fm.
04·01·41 Jones, Sydney G., Fm.
17·04·41 Jordan, Sydney, Fm.

04·05·41 Kehoe, Robert, Fm.
17·10·40 Kelly, Charles S., Fm.
10·07·43 Kemp, George F., Fm.
25·10·40 Kendrick, Leslie S., Fm.
15·12·40 Kennard, George, Fm.
14·11·40 Kenney, James, Fm.
09·02·43 Kerley, Daisy M., Fwm.
31·12·40 Kerr-Lindsay, Robert L., Fm.
17·09·40 Kiefer, Frederick G., Fm.
06·02·42 Kilbryde, Edward, Fm.
14·11·40 Kilbuern, Frederick, Fm.
21·08·40 Kilby, Ivor J., LFm.

23·12·40 Killeen, Thomas, Fm.
09·03·42 Killick, Arthur P., Fm.
14·11·40 Kimberley, William H., Stn.O.
02·08·42 Kinchenton, Alfred H. R., Fm.
06 05 42 King, Albert E.
08·03·41 King, Charles T., Fm.
11·05·41 King, David A., LFm.
29·07·43 King, James E., Fm.
12·12·40 King, Leslie G., Fm.
14·11·40 King, Reginald F., Fm.
08·05·41 King, Walter E., Fm.
03·01·43 Kingswell, Edward J., Fm.
08·09·43 Kirby, Edward A., Fm.
16·05·41 Kirkland, James D., Fm.
20·04·41 Kite, Albert V., Fm.
27·10·40 Kneale, William A., Fm.
08·09·40 Knight, Henry W., Stn.O.
08·03·41 Knight, John T., Fm.
14·11·40 Knight, Reginald F. W. J., Fm.
11·01·41 Knight, William F., Fm.

31·12·41 Laimbeer, Albert A., Fm.
20·05·42 Lamb, Charles E., Fm.
20·03·41 Lambert, Eric W., Fm.
11·08·44 Langham, Leslie, LFm.
07·07·44 Langley, Leonard A., Fm.
09·09·40 Lavelli, Marcel, Fm.
13·01·43 Lawrenson, George, Fm.
09·02·43 Lay, Doris M., Fwm.
11·05·41 Layton, Charles L., Fm.
24·10·43 Leadbetter, Enoch, LFm.
16·11·40 Leake, Clifford M., Fm.
28·09·40 Leaver, Thomas C., Fm.
21·11·41 Lee, Robert W., Coy.O.
06·11·40 Legg, Victor H., Fm.
14·03·41 Leitch, Neil, Mesngr
31·05·42 Lennan, John, Fm.
18·06·43 Lennick, Hymen
17·04·41 Lettner, Ascher D., Fm.
05·11·42 Levenson, Albert, Fm.
12·05·41 Lewis, Abraham, Fm.
06·11·40 Lewis, Eric D., Fm.
22·02·41 Lewis, Herbert, Fm.
06·11·40 Lewis, John J., Fm.
11·01·41 Lewis, John W., Fm.
24·10·43 Lewis, Robert A., LFm.
19·09·42 Libbert, Samuel, Fm.
03·08·41 Liggat, David, Pat.O.
20·12·40 Lindford, Edward, Fm.
15·04·45 Little, John C., Fm.
08·05·41 Livesey, William, Fm.
08·02·45 Loader, Henry G., LFm.
19·11·40 Logg, Hubert V., Fm.
02·04·44 Long, Beatrice, A.G.O.
07·09·40 Long, William H., Fm.
28·07·42 Lovatt, Reginald W., Fm.

19·10·40 Loveman, Samuel, Pat.O.
11·04·41 Low, Herbert, Fm.
14·11·40 Lowe, Arthur H., Fm.
28·11·40 Lowe, George, Fm.
16 04 45 Lower, Erwin, Fm.
17·05·41 Lowrey, Joseph, LFm.
20·03·41 Lucas, William G., Fm.
08·12·42 Lunn, George, Fm.
12·10·40 Lunt, Frederick, Fm.
16·08·40 Lutman, William G., LFm.
01·12·42 Lythgoe, Fred, Fm.

13·03·41 MacDonald, James J., Fm.
19·05·43 Mace, Ronald
02·03·42 Machin, Ronald H., Fm.
12·12·44 Mack, Harry, Fm.
18·09·40 Mackenzie, Donald, Fm.
07·05·41 MacKinven, Donald, Pat.O.
10·03·41 Mallane, John C., Fm.
29·03·45 Maloney, Albert F., S.Ldr.
20·04·41 Mander, Vincent L., Fm.
07·05·41 Mann, Patrick, Fm.
17·09·40 Mansbridge, Benjamin, Fm.
24·02·40 Marr, William B., Fm.
08·12·40 Marriott, Harold, Fm.
29·05·40 Marsh, T. B., Fm.
17·06·44 Marshall, Benjamin J. T., Fm.
24·11·40 Marshall, Cyril R., Pat.O.
10·01·41 Marshall, Frederick W., Fm.
07·09·40 Marshall, Harry R., Fm.
29·06·44 Marshall, William, Fm.
08·09·40 Martin, Richard J., Fm.
10·04·44 Mason, Sidney G., Fm.
11·04·41 Matthews, Gordon, Mesngr
09·11·41 Maynard, John H., Fm.
04·12·39 McCauley, Arthur H., Fm.
10·03·41 McClean, Donald, Fm.
08·04·41 McDonald, Archibald, Fm.
20·04·41 McDonough, Francis, Mesngr
27·10·40 McElliney, Robert, Fm.
16·10·40 McEvoy, Daniel B., Fm.
08·12·40 McEwen, Ewen S., Fm.
22·12·40 McGauley, William, Fm.
13·03·41 McGibbon, Alexander, Fm.
31·08·41 McGregor, George W., D.O.
13·03·41 McGregor, William, Pat.O.
17·09·40 McHale, Samuel, Fm.
14·03·41 McIntosh, Donald, Fm.
16·12·41 McIver, John, Fm.
22·01·44 McKenzie, Clarence D. P., Fm.
14·03·41 McLaren, George C., LFm.
25·02·43 McLaughlin, Thomas, Fm.
13·03·41 McLean, John K., Fm.
11·09·40 McMillan, James, Fm.
30·03·41 Mead, Henry J., Fm.
20·04·41 Mead, John F., Fm.

01·11·40 Medhurst, Leslie C., Fm.
16·05·42 Messenger, William G., Fm.
06·11·40 Michaelson, Victor, Fm.
20·04·41 Middleditch, Vernon J., Fm.
11·03·41 Miles, Albert, Fm.
21·08·40 Miles, Clifford, Fm.
16·07·43 Millar, Alexander H., Coy.O.
11·05·41 Miller, Arthur W., Fm.
16·11·40 Miller, Josephine I., Fwm.
09·09·40 Millett, Percy, Fm.
18·02·43 Milliner, Ernest G., Fm.
02·12·40 Mills, Frank K., LFm.
17·06·44 Mills, Frederick J., Fm.
20·04·41 Minter, Alfred E., Fm.
07·10·40 Mitchell, Frederick, Fm.
11·05·40 Moor, G. L., Sec.O.
12·12·40 Moore, Arthur, LFm.
17·04·41 Moore, Charles E., Fm.
·   · Moore, Charles L.
20·03·41 Moore, Frederick W., Fm.
11·05·41 Moore, William B., Fm.
21·08·40 Morgan, Trevor C., Fm.
14·07·42 Morris, Ernest, Fm.
14·11·40 Morris, Frederick A., Fm.
14·10·40 Morris, Sydney A., Sec.O.
13·03·41 Morrison, Robert, Fm.
28·09·40 Morrow, William G., Fm.
13·08·42 Mortimore, Maurice C. L., Fm.
20·04·41 Mountjoy, Norman R. C., Fm.
17·09·40 Mullard, Phillip G., Fm.
13·03·41 Mulvaney, Christopher W., Fm.
19·03·41 Munday, John J., Fm.
18·05·41 Murphy, C. W., Fm.
08·12·40 Murray, Arthur E., Fm.
06·10·40 Murray, Victor, Supt.
30·10·40 Murtagh, Eric A., Fm.

14·07·42 Neill, William, Col.O.
29·03·41 Nelson, Edward D., Fm.
03·11·44 Nelthorpe, Robert, Fm.
14·11·40 Neville, Fred, Fm.
09·09·40 Newbold, Sydney J., Fm.
07·02·43 Newett, Frederick G., LFm.
09·04·44 Nicoll, George H., Fm.
17·09·40 Nightingale, Charles F., Fm.
23·12·40 Nightingale, Kenneth, Fm.
11·05·41 Norris, George R., Fm.
24·04·41 Northcott, Walter H., Fm.
25·02·45 Nutter, Winston

11·05·41 O'Neill, Maurice P., Fm.
25·12·43 Oak, William H., Coy.O.
21·04·41 Oakden, Leo H. P., Fm.
17·05·44 Oates, Squire, Fm.
18·05·43 Offler, Henry A., LFm.

11·04·41 Olbort, William, Fm.
23·04·41 Old, Ernest S., Fm.
30·10·40 Oldbury, William C., Fm.
19·09·40 Olney, Horace V., Fm.
30·10·44 Ormerod, John J., Fm.
07·05·41 Owen, Albert E., Fm.

13·03·41 Pacitti, Ronald, Mesngr
14·10·40 Page, Harry, Sub.O.
03·10·42 Palmer, Edward E., Fm.
20·03·41 Palmer, Leslie J., Fm.
08·12·40 Palmer, Walter J., Fm.
06·02·43 Parberry, Robert G., Fm.
20·04·41 Parcell, Frederick G., Fm.
26·04·44 Pardon, Joseph, Fm.
20·04·41 Parfett, Martin C., LFm
11·05·41 Parfrey, William F., Fm.
11·05·41 Parkes, Harold C., Fm.
11·08·43 Parkinson, Harold F., Fm.
16·07·41 Parton, Arthur P., Fm.
17·09·40 Patten, John, Fm.
29·12·40 Pattenden, Edward J., Fm.
23·12·40 Paul, Alexander, Fm.
25·10·40 Payne, Ernest W., Fm.
11·04·41 Payne, Stanley, Fm.
25·03·42 Pearce, Russell L., Fm.
19·09·40 Pearson, John C., Fm.
10·11·40 Pearton, Albert E., Fm.
16·08·41 Pemble, Robert W., Fm.
18·09·40 Pengelly, Violet I., Fwm.
16·08·40 Pennell, Jesse, Fm.
11·05·41 Pepper, Edward E. G., Fm.
25·10·40 Perry, Charles A., Fm.
02·12·40 Perry, George, Fm.
01·11·40 Perry, Harry, LFm
08·05·42 Peryer, Albert E.
29·08·43 Peters, Frederick A., Fm.
20·04·41 Peters, Winifred A., Fwm.
14·11·40 Phelan, John, Fm.
23·04·41 Phillips, Benjamin A., LFm.
08·05·42 Phillips, James E., LFm.
10·01·41 Pickett, Queenie R. C., Fwm.
10·09·40 Piller, Henry, Fm.
23·10·40 Pimblett, Charles, Fm.
20·04·41 Plant, William C., Fm.
21·05·44 Poland, Norman, Fm.
20·04·41 Porter, Cyril B., Fm.
20·09·42 Porter, Percy E.
12·04·41 Potter, George A., Fm.
29·07·41 Preece, A. W., Fm.
11·05·41 Preston, Edward J., Fm.
30·01·45 Price, Joseph A., Fm.
10·04·41 Priestly, Matthew, Fm.
02·06·41 Pugsley, Walter C., CFO
05·09·42 Purcell, Henry J., Fm.
03·01·41 Purnell, Arthur W., LFm.

28·09·40 Purslow, James H., Fm.
10·04·41 Purvis, Albert G., LFm.
14·11·40 Pyett, Percy, Fm.

26·10·40 Quinn, Eric F., Fm.

17·10·40 Rae, Frederick A., Fm.
20·02·42 Ramsay, Ambrose J., Fm.
11·08·44 Randall, Walter J., LFm.
17·10·40 Randall, William T., Fm.
17·04·41 Randolph, Stanley H., Fm.
11·12·40 Ranger, Frederick T., Sub.O.
06·11·41 Ransley, Cecil A., Fm.
20·04·41 Rashbrook, William T., Fm.
08·03·41 Rathbone, Henry C., Fm.
21·12·41 Raulston, James, Fm.
11·03·41 Rawlings, Walter C., Fm.
08·11·40 Rawlings, William, Fm.
02·01·45 Rawnsley, Malcolm, Fm.
09·11·39 Ray, Robert, Fm.
06·02·43 Read, Albert S., Fm.
10·09·40 Reardon, George, Fm.
21·12·40 Redman, John, Fm.
02·05·41 Redmond, Patrick G., Fm.
14·12·41 Reed, William H., Fm.
21·03·41 Renals, John, Fm.
10·04·41 Renwick, George W., Fm.
21·12·40 Reynolds, James, Fm.
11·03·41 Richards, Charles H., Fm.
06·12·40 Richards, John G., Fm.
13·03·41 Richardson, Walter S., Fm.
01·11·40 Ridd, Joan M., Fwm.
12·03·41 Ritching, Ernest, Fm.
13·03·41 Roberts, Herbert, Fm.
26·07·40 Roberts, James W., Fm.
04·05·41 Roberts, Robert, Driver
13·03·41 Roberts, Thomas H., Fm.
21·04·41 Roberts, Wilfred A., Fm.
13·10·40 Robertson, Archibald, Fm.
13·03·41 Robertson, William A., Fm.
17·04·45 Robins, Albert C., Fm.
25·03·41 Robins, John S., Fm.
11·05·41 Robinson, Ernest F., Fm.
01·01·44 Roe, John W.
22·12·40 Rogers, Albert E., Pat.O.
17·09·40 Rogers, Arthur H., Fm.
09·04·41 Rogers, Robert C., Fm.
18·03·41 Rogerson, William, Fm.
20·04·41 Roots, Leonard, LFm.
02·01·41 Roots, William R., Fm.
11·12·43 Rose, Maurice S., Col.O.
24·08·44 Rosebridge, Edward A., Fm.
13·07·44 Roseman, Hyman, Fm.
11·05·43 Ross, Alistair M., Pat.O.
28·09·40 Roullier, Richard C., Fm.

17·02·44 Rowe, Charles, Fm.
10·01·41 Rowe, Maurice G., Fm.
31·05·41 Rowe, William A., Fm.
28·08·42 Roy, John, Fm.
16·06·44 Russell, Charles R., Fm.
20·12·39 Rutherford, Charles, Fm.
09·04·41 Ryder, Frederick, Fm.

28·09·40 Sackie, Edward, Fm.
05·06·41 Sales, Stanley J. S., Sec.O.
17·10·40 Salkeld, Frederick C., Sec.O.
03·07·44 Sambrook, Charles W., Fm.
02·10·40 Sander, Laurence W., Snr.Fm.
28·07·44 Sanderson, Charles E., Fm.
22·04·41 Sandwell, Francis J. H., Fm.
09·08·41 Sandy, Percy H., Fm.
14·11·40 Sargant, Stanley, Fm.
27·11·43 Satchell, Robert D., LFm.
15·08·44 Satchell, Thomas F., Fm.
15·11·40 Satchwell, Victor A., Fm.
29·12·40 Saunders, Herbert C. J., Fm.
20·04·41 Saville, Albert A., Fm.
04·02·44 Scane, Harry, Fm.
24·09·44 Scarff, Joseph F., Fm.
17·04·41 Scates, Frederick, Fm.
14·10·40 Schneider, Ernest A., Fm.
23·12·40 Schofield, Benjamin, Fm.
08·05·41 Schooler, Alexander, Fm.
28·08·43 Schwartzberg, Israel, Fm.
04·10·44 Scott, William E. H., Fm.
02·04·42 Scott, William H., Fm.
11·05·41 Seaby, Arthur, Fm.
10·03·41 Searly, James H., Fm.
19·11·40 Selvey, George A., Fm.
20·10·43 Seurre, Anthony T., LFm.
18·04·41 Seymour, Reginald A. L., Fm.
23·12·40 Shakeshaft, Henry E., Fm.
01·09·41 Shanks, George, Fm.
23·02·44 Sharp, Harry W. T., Fm.
25·11·44 Shaw, Edwin, Fm.
09·01·44 Shaw, William, Fm.
23·12·40 Shawcross, Harold, Fm.
08·10·42 Sheard, Leo R., Fm.
03·01·43 Sheath, Percy J., Fm.
11·09·40 Sheldon, Benjamin J., Fm.
20·03·41 Short, Stanley, LFm.
02·06·41 Shortman, James H., Fm.
11·12·40 Shotten, Alfred, Fm.
24·07·41 Shreeves, Graham H., Fm.
08·09·40 Shrimpton, Jack A. W., Fm.
26·02·42 Silfleet, Alfred J. B., Fm.
13·03·41 Simeon, Harry T., Fm.
06·10·44 Simms, Charles W., Fm.
14·03·43 Simons, Robert S., Fm.
20·04·41 Simpson, James, Sec.O.
22·12·40 Singleton, Robert, Fm.

20·04·41 Sinstadt, Richard W., Stn.O.
23·12·40 Skelton, Roy, Fm.
17·04·41 Skinner, Harry R., Fm.
26·03·42 Skinner, Robert E., Fm.
12·12·40 Slack, Stanley, Fm.
06·01·40 Sluman (KM), George, Pilot
22·05·40 Smith, Albert, Fm.
08·03·41 Smith, Alexander, Fm.
19·03·44 Smith, Arthur J., Fm.
23·12·40 Smith, Charles H., Fm.
11·05·41 Smith, Edward H., Fm.
16·12·42 Smith, Frank J., Fm.
11·05·41 Smith, Frederick C., Fm.
08·03·41 Smith, Frederick J., Fm.
23·12·40 Smith, Hubert W., Fm.
11·05·44 Smith, John F., Fm.
26·04·42 Smith, Leonard H., Fm.
29·09·44 Smith, William, Fm.
06·06·40 Smith, William H., Fm.
03·05·41 Smith, William H., Fm.
07·06·40 Smy, Arthur G., Fm.
10·09·40 Snowdon, Thomas J., Fm.
22·09·40 Sorrenti, Romeo C., Fm.
23·12·40 Spalding, James D., Fm.
15·04·41 Spence, George, Fm.
08·03·41 Spence, Walter J., Fm.
12·12·40 Spencer, Frederick P., Fm.
16·08·41 Spice, Percy C. R., Pat.O.
11·05·41 Spiller, A. H., LFm.
17·02·43 Squibb, George W., Fm.
12·12·40 Stacey, Tom, Fm.
30·10·41 Standring, Arthur, Fm.
26·09·40 Stangroom, Harry J., Fm.
23·04·41 Stanlake, John, Fm.
06·11·40 Steele, Oliver J., Fm.
28·09·40 Steers, George R., Fm.
06·11·40 Stevens, Stanley R., Fm.
06·11·43 Stevenson, John, Fm.
23·10·40 Stidorthy, Stanley, Fm.
31·10·42 Strand, Walter, LFm.
01·01·41 Strange, Albert H., Fm.
16·02·44 Strickland, Francis, LFm.
28·09·40 Stringer, Eric C., Fm.
08·09·40 Strutton, Charles, Fm.
11·05·41 Sturk, Alfred C., Fm.
21·09·41 Sunderland, Robert, Fm.
30·12·42 Sunderland, Walter, Fm.
14·11·40 Sutherland, Frederick, Sub.O.
12·12·40 Swaby, John W., Fm.
15·10·42 Swan, Reginald B., Fm.
10·10·42 Swanson, George M., Fm.

11·05·41 Tanner, Robert, Fm.
03·01·41 Taylor, F., Fm.
01·10·44 Taylor, George, Fm.
02·11·40 Taylor, John J., LFm.

17·04·41 Taylor, Mervin J. B., Fm.
23·12·40 Taylor, Walter H., Fm.
10·01·41 Taylor, William H., Fm.
11·05·41 Teague, John, Fm.
10·04·41 Thoburn, Ralph C., Fm.
21·08·40 Thomas, John F., Fm.
03·05·41 Thompson, James, Fm.
02·08·42 Thompson, Sidney, Fm.
26·09·40 Thorpe, Alec K., Fm.
31·12·39 Thurgood, Stanley D., Stn.O.
23·04·41 Tibbs, Leslie G., Fm.
12·09·40 Tidy, Sidney S., Fm.
07·09·40 Tierney, Frederick, Sec.O.
24·12·40 Tipton, William L., Fm.
17·09·40 Tobias, Joseph L., Dist.O.
22·07·42 Tombling, Arthur L., Fm.
14·08·44 Tomlin, Fred, Fm.
03·01·41 Tomlin, Hubert H., Fm.
12·09·40 Tonkin, George H., Fm.
08·10·40 Tooke, Ernest A., Stn.O.
17·06·44 Toomey, Frederick W.,
25·06·40 Trainer, Horace H., Pat.O.
09·01·43 Trimblett, Raymond E., Fm.
28·07·42 Tropman, Sidney C., Fm.
04·11·40 Trotter, Max F., LFm.
03·01·41 Tucker, Charles, Fm.
31·05·41 Tulip, J. S., Fm.
07·09·40 Turley, Walter, Fm.
13·03·41 Turnbull, John B., Fm.
16·11·40 Turner, Albert A., Fm.
04·11·41 Tyers, John, Fm.

09·09·40 Umney, Albert D., Fm.

04·09·40 Van Hulst, Mathys, Fm.
23·12·40 Varah, William H., Fm.
28·09·40 Vernon, James, Fm.
28·09·40 Vesey, Harry C., Fm.
20·04·41 Vick, Edgar W., LFm.
24·11·40 Vincent, Gilbert J., Fm.
23·04·41 Vineer, Arthur S., Fm.

10·03·45 Waddington, Victor J., Fm.
17·04·41 Waghorne, Ronald V., Fm.
03·01·41 Wainwright, John, Fm.
17·04·41 Wakeman, Reginald B., Fm.
13·03·41 Walker, Robert, Fm.
08·05·41 Waller, George W., Fm.
10·09·40 Wallis, Walter W., Fm.
17·09·40 Wand, Myer, Fm.
01·09·41 Wandless, Jack, Fm.
31·05·41 Wanless, George, Fm.
01·06·42 Ward, William E., Fm.
27·04·41 Wareham, John W., Fm.

15·06·41 Waring, Joseph, Sub.O.
14·07·44 Warnes, Lacey V., LFm.
31·12·40 Waterman, George A., Fm.
11·04·41 Watkin, Thomas E., LFm.
14·10·40 Watkins, Frederick J., Fm.
23·06·45 Watson, Edward J., Fm.
17·10·40 Wayte, Henry H., Fm.
27·11·43 Wear, Stanley W., Fm.
17·09·40 Weaver, William E., LFm.
30·10·40 Webb, Percy E., Fm.
07·05·40 Webster, Colin, Fm.
05·05·42 Weekes, Colin H., Fm.
08·09·40 Weightman, Harold, Fm.
24·08·40 Wells, Herbert F., Fm.
09·11·40 Wenbourne, Arthur H., Fm.
08·09·40 Westwood, William, Fm.
10·04·41 Wharton, John, Fm.
04·10·41 Wheeler, Ronald F., Fm.
11·05·41 Whipps, Charles W., Fm.
02·04·42 White, Charles E., LFm.
16·08·41 White, Walter, Fm.
10·01·41 Whiteman, Harry J., Fm.
23·04·41 Whiting, Frederick R., Fm.
29·11·40 Widger, Robert W., Fm.
12·01·41 Williams, Frederick N., Fm.
30·09·40 Williams, John, LFm.
09·04·41 Willn, Ernest, Fm.
12·10·40 Willoughby, Herbert F., Fm.
31·10·41 Wilmore, Leonard, Fm.
06·05·41 Wilson, David, Fm.
01·11·42 Wilson, Henry, Fm.
08·09·40 Wilson, Ronald, Fm.
07·10·40 Wilson (BEM), Leslie, Stn.O.
24·11·40 Wiltshire, Herbert C., Pat.O.
02·11·40 Wingfield, Francis J., Fm.
08·07·44 Wingham, Charles G. W., Fm.
28·09·40 Wolff, Herbert T., Fm.
17·09·40 Wood, Charles, Fm.
24·11·40 Wood, Stephen H., Fm.
17·09·40 Wooder, Walter H., Fm.
13·03·41 Woodhead, David, Mesngr
13·03·41 Woodhead, Robert D. F., LFm.
14·10·40 Woodier, Albert E., Fm.
20·04·41 Woodland, Walter J., LFm.
13·03·44 Woodward, Arthur J., Fm.
13·04·41 Worrod, Eric, Fm.
20·04·41 Wotton, Herbert C., Fm.
03·12·40 Would, Henry, Fm.
16·04·41 Wratten, Victor G., Fm.
01·01·44 Wright, George F., Fm.
23·12·40 Wright, Joseph H., Fm.
21·12·40 Wright, William, Fm.
17·01·45 Wynn, Alfred

08·03·41 Yelland, Charles S., Fm.
09·02·43 Young, Sybil L., Fwm.